Photoshop® Elements 9
Top 100

Simplified®

TIPS & TRICKS

by Rob Sheppard

Visual

WILEY

Photoshop® Elements 9: Top 100 Simplified® Tips & Tricks

Published by
Wiley Publishing, Inc.
10475 Crosspoint Boulevard
Indianapolis, IN 46256
www.wiley.com

Published simultaneously in Canada

Copyright © 2011 by Wiley Publishing, Inc., Indianapolis, Indiana

Library of Congress Control Number: 2010938834

ISBN: 978-0-470-91960-6

Manufactured in the United States of America

10 9 8 7 6 5 4 3 2 1

Trademark Acknowledgments

Contact Us

For general information on our other products and services contact our Customer Care Department within the U.S. at 877-762-2974, outside the U.S. at 317-572-3993, or fax 317-572-4002.

For technical support please visit www.wiley.com/techsupport.

WILEY

Wiley Publishing, Inc.

U.S. Sales

Contact Wiley at
(800) 762-2974 or
fax (317) 572-4002.

CREDITS

ABOUT THE AUTHOR

Rob Sheppard is the author/photographer of over 30 photography books, a well-known speaker and workshop leader, and is editor-at-large for the prestigious *Outdoor Photographer* magazine. As author/photographer, Sheppard has written hundreds of articles about digital photography, plus books ranging from guides to photography such as *Digital Photography: Top 100 Simplified Tips & Tricks* and *Digital Photography Simplified* to books about Photoshop Elements and Lightroom including *Adobe Photoshop Lightroom 2 for Digital Photographers Only* and *Photoshop Elements 8: Top 100 Simplified Tips & Tricks*. His Web site is at www.robsheppardphoto.com and his blog is at www.photodigitary.com.

ACKNOWLEDGMENTS

I have enjoyed doing the Photoshop Elements *Top 100 Simplified Tips & Tricks* books. Photographers are shortchanged when they are simply pushed into Photoshop when what would really work best for them is Photoshop Elements. So first, I have to thank all of the photographers who have been in my workshops and classes because it is their questions and their responses to classwork that helps me better understand what photographers really need to know about digital photography. To do this book right for photographers requires a lot of folks doing work along the way. The folks at Wiley are great both for their work in creating books like this and their work in helping make the book the best it can be. I really appreciate all the work that editor Sarah Hellert did along with her associates in helping keep this book clear and understandable for the reader. I also thank my terrific wife of 30 years who keeps me grounded and focused while I work on my books. I thank the people at Werner Publications, my old home, where I was editor of *Outdoor Photographer* for 12 years and helped start *PCPhoto* magazine — I thank them for their continued support so I can stay on top of changes in the industry. And I thank Rick Sammon for his support and inspiration in doing photography books.

HOW TO USE THIS BOOK

Who This Book Is For

This book is for readers who know the basics and want to expand their knowledge of this particular technology or software application.

The Conventions in This Book

❶ Steps

This book uses a step-by-step format to guide you easily through each task. Numbered steps are actions you must do; bulleted steps clarify a point, step, or optional feature; and indented steps give you the result.

❷ Notes

Notes give additional information — special conditions that may occur during an operation, a situation that you want to avoid, or a cross reference to a related area of the book.

❸ Icons and Buttons

Icons and buttons show you exactly what you need to click to perform a step.

❹ Tips

Tips offer additional information, including warnings and shortcuts.

❺ Bold

Bold type shows text or numbers you must type.

❻ Italics

Italic type introduces and defines a new term.

❼ Difficulty Levels

For quick reference, these symbols mark the difficulty level of each task.

DIFFICULTY LEVEL	Demonstrates a new spin on a common task
DIFFICULTY LEVEL	Introduces a new skill or a new task
DIFFICULTY LEVEL	Combines multiple skills requiring in-depth knowledge
DIFFICULTY LEVEL	Requires extensive skill and may involve other technologies

---

FIX PROBLEM EXPOSURES
with layer blending modes

At times your picture may be simply too dark or too light. The camera makes a mistake in exposure, or the photographer sets the camera wrong. You end up with a picture that needs immediate correction, either to make it brighter or make it darker.

Photoshop Elements gives you a way to do this in its layer blending modes. You need to add an adjustment layer to your photograph. It really does not matter which adjustment you choose because you will not be using the adjustment layer for its original adjustment purpose. You are simply using this layer so that Photoshop Elements has something to work with

when communicating between layers, which is what layer blending modes do. When you first open the blending modes, you see a long list of choices — ignore them and concentrate on two key modes for photographers: Multiply and Screen.

These photos were shot in the chaparral of the Santa Monica Mountains Recreation Area. These mountains are near Los Angeles, yet most Los Angeles photographers overlook this area and miss great shots. Often photographers overlook nearby places, but with an attitude of discovery you can find amazing areas for photography anywhere.

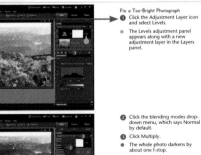

Fix a Too-Bright Photograph
❶ Click the Adjustment Layer icon and select Levels.
● The Levels adjustment panel appears along with a new adjustment layer in the Layers panel.

❷ Click the blending modes drop-down menu, which says Normal by default.
❸ Click Multiply.
● The whole photo darkens by about one f-stop.

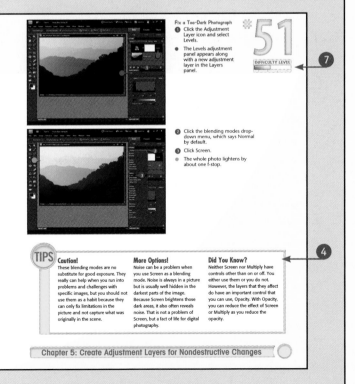

Fix a Too-Dark Photograph
❶ Click the Adjustment Layer icon and select Levels.
● The Levels adjustment panel appears along with a new adjustment layer in the Layers panel.

DIFFICULTY LEVEL ◀ ❼

❷ Click the blending modes drop-down menu, which says Normal by default.
❸ Click Screen.
● The whole photo lightens by about one f-stop.

TIPS

Caution!
These blending modes are no substitute for good exposure. They really can help when you run into problems and challenges with specific images, but you should not use them as a habit because they can only fix limitations in the picture and not capture what was originally in the scene.

More Options!
Noise can be a problem when you use Screen as a blending mode. Noise is always in a picture but is usually well hidden in the darkest parts of the image. Because Screen brightens those dark areas, it also often reveals noise. That is not a problem of Screen, but a fact of life for digital photography.

Did You Know?
Neither Screen nor Multiply have controls other than on or off. You either use them or you do not. However, the layers that they affect do have an important control that you can use, Opacity. With Opacity, you can reduce the effect of Screen or Multiply as you reduce the opacity.

◀ ❹

Table of Contents

1 Organize and Prepare Photos for Processing

#1	Set Up a Workflow	4
#2	Import Your Images	6
#3	View Photos with Full-Screen Mode	10
#4	Sort the Good Pictures from the Bad	12
#5	Stack Your Images	14
#6	Create Albums to Group Your Pictures	16
#7	Use Keywords to Tag Your Images	18
#8	Tag Photos with Face Recognition	22
#9	Change the Organizer Interface As Needed	24
#10	Back Up Your Pictures to Protect Them	26

2 Start Adjusting Your Images in Photoshop Elements

#11	Open Pictures and Use Save As	30
#12	Make the Editor Interface Your Own	32
#13	Set Preferences to Make Editor Work for You	34
#14	You Cannot Hurt Your Pictures	36
#15	Crop Your Photos for Tighter Shots	38
#16	Fix and Rotate Crooked Pictures	40
#17	Use Guided Edit to Help You Learn the Program	42
#18	Use Guided Edit for Special Effects	44
#19	Set Blacks and Whites with Levels	46
#20	Adjust Your Midtones with Levels	48
#21	Adjust Your Midtones with Color Curves	50
#22	Quickly Adjust Dark Shadows and Bright Highlights	52
#23	Correct Color to Remove Color Casts	54
#24	Enhance Color with Hue/Saturation	56
#25	Use Quick Edit to Work Fast	58

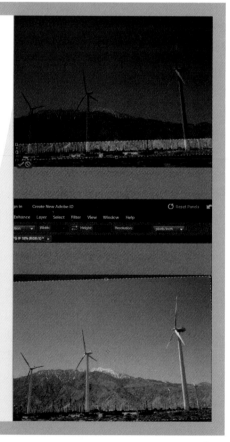

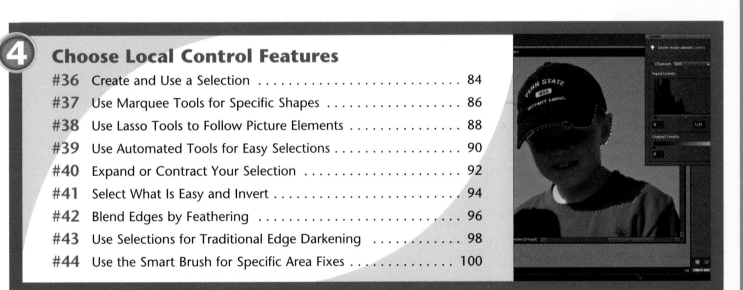

③ Work with RAW Photos in Photoshop Elements

#26 Change Images Nondestructively 62

#27 Crop Your Photos to Start Your Processing 64

#28 Adjust Blacks and Whites to Give a Photo Strength 66

#29 Adjust Midtones to Make Tonalities Light or Dark 68

#30 Correct Color to Clean Up Color Casts 70

#31 Use Vibrance and Clarity to Intensify Images 72

#32 Sharpen Photos with Precision 74

#33 Control Noise in Your Photo 76

#34 Apply Adjustments to Multiple Photos 78

#35 Move Your Picture to Photoshop Elements 80

④ Choose Local Control Features

#36 Create and Use a Selection 84

#37 Use Marquee Tools for Specific Shapes 86

#38 Use Lasso Tools to Follow Picture Elements 88

#39 Use Automated Tools for Easy Selections 90

#40 Expand or Contract Your Selection 92

#41 Select What Is Easy and Invert 94

#42 Blend Edges by Feathering 96

#43 Use Selections for Traditional Edge Darkening 98

#44 Use the Smart Brush for Specific Area Fixes 100

Table of Contents

5 Create Adjustment Layers for Nondestructive Changes

#45 Understand How Layers Work 104

#46 Understand How Adjustment Layers Work 106

#47 Work Blacks and Whites with a Levels Adjustment Layer 110

#48 Work Midtones with a Levels Adjustment Layer 112

#49 Correct Color with an Adjustment Layer 114

#50 Enhance Color with an Adjustment Layer 116

#51 Fix Problem Exposures with Layer Blending Modes 118

#52 Understand How Layer Masks Work 120

#53 Combine Two Photos with Layer Masks 122

#54 Remove Adjustments with Black 126

#55 Add Adjustments Using Black and then White 128

#56 Combine Layer Masks with Selections 132

#57 Balance Colors and Tones in a Picture 134

#58 Bring Out Shadow Detail in Specific Areas 136

#59 Darken Highlight Detail in Specific Areas 138

#60 Flatten Layers When Done 140

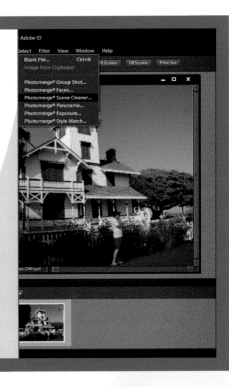

6 Solve Photo Problems

#61   Clone Out Problems 144

#62   Remove People from a Scene with Photomerge
Scene Cleaner 148

#63   Remove Unwanted Objects with Content-Aware
Spot Healing 150

#64   Fix Problems due to Lens Distortion 152

#65   Fix Perspective Problems with Building Photographs 154

#66   Remove Dead Space with Recompose 156

#67   Make an Out-of-Focus Background 158

#68   Remove Distracting Colors 160

#69   Improve Blank Skies 162

#70   Create the Focus with Gaussian Blur 166

#71   Add a New Background for Your Subject 168

7 Size and Sharpen Photos

#72   Basic Workflow for Image Sizing 174

#73   Size Photos for Printing 176

#74   Size Photos for E-mail 178

#75   Sharpen Photos with Unsharp Mask 180

#76   Sharpen Photos with Adjust Sharpness 182

#77   Sharpen Photos When You Have Layers 184

#78   Selectively Sharpen Parts of Your Photo 186

Table of Contents

8 **Go Beyond the Basics**

#79 Convert Color Photos to Black-and-White 190

#80 Adjust Your Photos in Black-and-White 192

#81 Create Toned Images 194

#82 Use the Smart Brush for Creative Effects 196

#83 Create a Hand-Colored Look 198

#84 Photograph a Scene to Get More Exposure Detail 202

#85 Merge Photos for More Photo Detail 204

#86 Photograph a Scene for a Panoramic Image 206

#87 Merge Photos for a Panoramic Image 208

#88 Group Images on a Page 212

#89 Transfer Styles between Photos 216

9 **Software Plug-ins Make Work Easier**

#90 Use Viveza for Quick Creative Adjustments 220

#91 Use Color Efex for Efficient Photo Work 222

#92 Remove Noise with Dfine 224

#93 Get Dramatic Black-and-White with Silver Efex Pro 226

#94 Use Bokeh for Easy Depth-of-Field Effects 228

#95 Try PhotoTune for Fast Color and Tonal Adjustments 230

#96 Use Snap Art for Creative Effects 232

10 Get Photos out of Photoshop Elements

#97 Protect Your Photos with Online Backup 236

#98 Access Your Photos Anywhere Internet Service is Available . . . 238

#99 Create Online Photo Albums 240

#100 Share Your Photos Online 242

#101 Print Your Photos 244

#102 Print a Group of Photos 248

#103 Add a Border Effect to Your Pictures. 250

Chapter 1

Organize and Prepare Photos for Processing

Adobe keeps improving Photoshop Elements and now has reached version 9. This new edition offers both new controls and a revision of how the program processes photos for optimum results. Photoshop Elements has become one of the best image-processing programs on the market, and is certainly one of the best values for the money. It may be Photoshop's smaller sibling, but it is no second-rate program. Photoshop Elements uses the exact same processing algorithms that Photoshop has, but it is simpler and directly geared to photographers. In addition, the Windows and Mac versions of Photoshop Elements Editor are essentially the same, and the tips in this book work the same with either platform except for occasional keyboard commands.

Photoshop Elements is a complete program that enables you to import images, organize them, and sort the good from the bad as well as make changes to optimize individual photos. The order of this book follows a workflow that you can use to work efficiently in Photoshop Elements.

In this chapter, you learn what it means to develop a workflow right from the start. You can quickly import, sort, and organize your pictures so that you can find them more easily in the future. You can customize your workspace to fit your needs and interests and help you work more efficiently. One important thing to remember: To get the most from Photoshop Elements, you must use it, practice with it, even make mistakes, so that you really know the program.

 # 1   Set Up a Workflow 4   DIFFICULTY LEVEL

 # 2   Import Your Images 6   DIFFICULTY LEVEL

 # 3   View Photos with Full-Screen Mode 10   DIFFICULTY LEVEL

 # 4   Sort the Good Pictures from the Bad. 12   DIFFICULTY LEVEL

 # 5   Stack Your Images 14   DIFFICULTY LEVEL

 # 6   Create Albums to Group Your Pictures 16   DIFFICULTY LEVEL

 # 7   Use Keywords to Tag Your Images 18   DIFFICULTY LEVEL

 # 8   Tag Photos with Face Recognition 22   DIFFICULTY LEVEL

 # 9   Change the Organizer Interface As Needed 24   DIFFICULTY LEVEL

#10   Back Up Your Pictures to Protect Them. 26   DIFFICULTY LEVEL

Set up a
WORKFLOW

Digital photography workflow is a term that flows freely with photographers. It simply describes the process of how you work with images from start to finish. By developing a consistent way of working on your images, you will find you gain more reliable results.

This book is structured around a Photoshop Elements workflow that can make your photography work on the computer both easier and more reliable. Although you can skip around in the book to find specific tips, the book is ordered to follow this workflow. As you become familiar with the program, you might find that you have to adapt some of these ideas to your specific needs. Do whatever makes your workflow better. The only guideline you need to follow is to be sure any workflow you choose gets the results you expect from your images.

The photos you see on these two pages with the screenshots of Photoshop Elements 9 are from Joshua Tree National Park and were shot after sunset. Digital cameras can capture amazing images well after sunset, but do use a tripod. Notes on the photography appear throughout the book, but not for every page, nor for every photograph due to space restrictions.

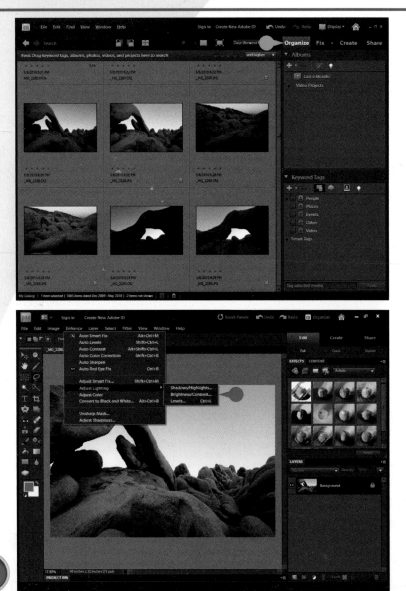

- Start the process by getting your photos into Photoshop Elements in order to sort, keep, delete, and organize them. You can process individual photos without going into the Photoshop Elements Organizer module of the program, but the Photoshop Elements Organizer helps you manage your digital photos.

- Set the tonalities of your photos first, including blacks, whites, and midtones, and then adjust color.

● Fix problems in your photos such as wrong colors, defects in an image, sensor dust, and so on.

● Consider how you want to share your photos with others, including prints, photo books, Web galleries, slide shows, and much more.

TIPS

Did You Know?

Photoshop Elements used to be heavily oriented toward Windows. With Photoshop Elements 8, the Windows and Mac versions came out at the same time. With Photoshop Elements 9, Adobe has worked to make the program largely the same on both platforms.

Did You Know?

Keyboard commands are one of the few places where differences arise between Windows and the Mac when using Photoshop Elements, usually involving the modifier keys. The Windows Control key (Ctrl) has essentially the same functions in Photoshop Elements as the Mac Command key (⌘). The Windows Alt key is basically the same as the Mac Option key. The Windows Control key is not the same as the Mac Control key.

Did You Know?

Editing photos used to mean picking the good from the bad. When Photoshop was developed, the computer folks decided to call the changes to the images *editing*, so there is confusion about what editing really is for the photographer. This book avoids both usages and specifically describes the process being used.

IMPORT
your images

Digital photography is a lot of fun and you probably are taking a lot of pictures. In order to work on them in Photoshop Elements, you must get those photos into your computer and recognized by the program. Organizer in Photoshop Elements helps you sort, delete, and organize your photos. Organizer does not actually hold onto your photographs, your hard drive does. However, Organizer does need to know where those photographs are. It needs, in a sense, a map to where your photos are located. Photoshop Elements can help you import your photos from memory card to hard drive, including copying them from the card

into a specific folder and renaming the files, as well as having Organizer recognize them.

When you first open Photoshop Elements, click the Organizer button to go into the Organizer mode. All importing is done through this mode.

This is a simplified way of getting all of your images from the memory card onto your hard drive and recognized by Photoshop Elements. For more control over your importing, including importing only part of your memory card at a time, see the completion of this task on the next pages.

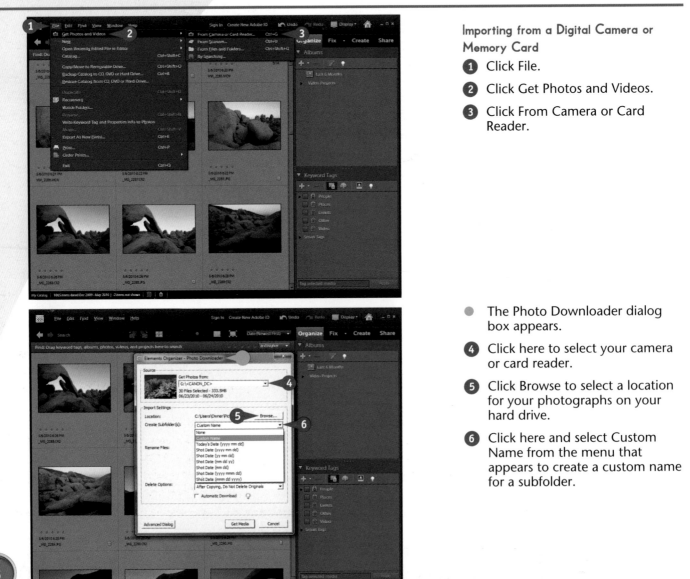

Importing from a Digital Camera or Memory Card

1 Click File.

2 Click Get Photos and Videos.

3 Click From Camera or Card Reader.

● The Photo Downloader dialog box appears.

4 Click here to select your camera or card reader.

5 Click Browse to select a location for your photographs on your hard drive.

6 Click here and select Custom Name from the menu that appears to create a custom name for a subfolder.

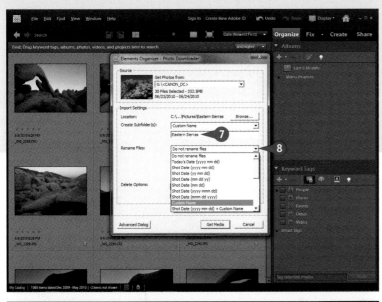

⑦ Type a name for your subfolder specific to the images you want to import.

⑧ Click here to give your photos a custom name, name them by date, or keep the original filenames.

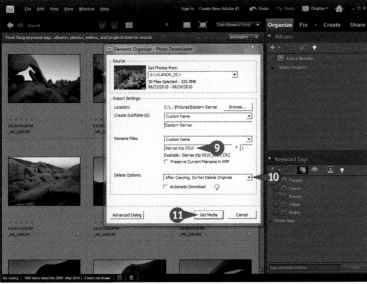

⑨ Type a new name for your photos if needed.

⑩ Click here to leave photos on the memory card so that your camera can reformat the card properly.

⑪ Click Get Media.

The photos will now be imported into your computer.

⑫ When the Files Successfully Copied dialog box opens, click Yes to include them in the Organizer.

TIPS

Did You Know?
A quality memory card reader is the fastest and most dependable way to download images. A card reader needs no power, can be left connected to your computer, and will not be damaged if accidentally knocked to the floor.

Did You Know?
The Automatic Download check box in the Photo Downloader dialog box sets up your computer to automatically download photos based on criteria set in Preferences, found in the Edit menu in Windows and the Photoshop Elements menu on a Mac. This can be a problem because it does not enable you to put photos into specific folders for each download, nor does it enable you to rename photos.

Did You Know?
Most photographers prefer to put images into distinct file folders on their hard drives instead of lumping them together into the Pictures folder. Photo Downloader enables you set up specific folders. You can put photos in a folder based on date and location, for example, inside a larger folder called Digital Photos on your desktop to make them easier to find if the Organizer in Photoshop Elements ever fails.

IMPORT
your images

Sometimes you will have groups of photos on your memory card that you do not want to mix together into a single folder. It can be very helpful to keep your photos separated by folders so that you can always find images on your hard drive, even without Photoshop Elements. The program gives you the option to import only the pictures that you want from a memory card in an advanced dialog box. This dialog box is very similar to the Photo Downloader dialog box, but it includes some additional choices you should know about.

The photos being imported in this chapter are from the Sierra Nevada Mountains in California. They were shot with a wide-angle lens up close to the foreground flowers to give a dramatic perspective to the images. The flowers are the native buck brush or California lilac. Some images also include ladybugs or ladybird beetles.

Photoshop Elements also enables you to import images already on your hard drive. The process is very similar, but does use a slightly different dialog box. This can be useful when you have transferred pictures directly from one computer to another, for example.

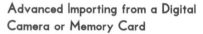

Advanced Importing from a Digital Camera or Memory Card

1. Repeat steps 1 to 4 from the "Importing from a Digital Camera or Memory Card" section to open the Photo Downloader dialog box.

2. Click Advanced Dialog.

● The advanced Photo Downloader dialog box appears.

3. Click Check All to import all photos.

4. Click UnCheck All to deselect all photos to select specific images for import.

5. Click the first photo of your group to import.

6. Create and name a subfolder specific to your images.

7. Rename your photos with a custom name.

⑧ Scroll down to the last photo in the group.

⑨ Shift+click that last photo to select all photos from the first one to this one, but no others.

Ctrl/⌘+click isolated photos to add or remove them from the group.

⑩ Click the check box under any image to check all that are selected (☐ changes to ☑).

2 CONTINUED

⑪ Click here to open the Advanced Options section if it is not already open.

⑫ A good option to select is Import into Album, if you have albums set up (☐ changes to ☑).

⑬ Click here to open the Apply Metadata section if it is not already open.

⑭ Click here to select Basic Metadata.

⑮ Type your name for the Creator and Copyright text boxes.

⑯ Click Get Media.

The photos will now be imported into your computer.

⑰ When the Files Successfully Copied dialog box opens, click Yes to include them in the Organizer.

TIPS

Did You Know?

When the Organizer recognizes photos, Photoshop Elements does not move or change them unless you tell it to. Photoshop Elements is simply creating a map to these image files on your hard drive so that it can find and organize the photos as needed.

Try This!

Use the Light Bulb icons. Photoshop Elements scatters tips throughout the program to help you when you do not understand a particular control or option. Click the icon and a tip appears, providing information on how to use the control or option.

Did You Know?

Having your name and copyright information on a photo helps people keep track of your photos. Even if you are not a pro, having your name in the metadata means that if you give your photo files to someone, such as for an organization's brochure, everyone can know whose photos they are.

Chapter 1: Organize and Prepare Photos for Processing   9

VIEW PHOTOS
with full-screen mode

The Organizer in Photoshop Elements is great for seeing a whole lot of photos at once. When multiple images are shown on your screen, you can quickly make comparisons between them. This can help you check out your latest photo shoot as well as visually find important images. It can also be a great learning experience as you look to see what you did over time as you took pictures. You will discover what you saw or did not see while you were with the subject.

Of course, you should look at single images at a larger size. Seeing larger images enables you to find

the best photos, whether it means checking sharpness, focus, a person's expression, and so on.

Photoshop Elements includes a full-featured full-screen mode that makes it very easy to do those things with a single image. This mode removes all distractions from your monitor so you can focus just on your image. This truly makes the image the star and puts the software in the background. This can make it easier to evaluate your photos after importing them because you can easily move through your images one photo at a time.

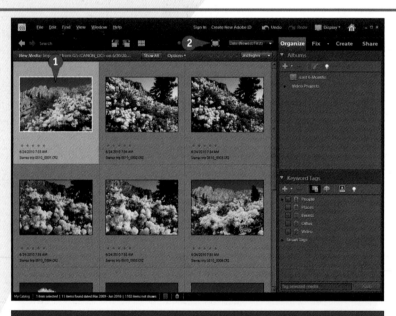

① Click a photo that you want to see full screen.

② Click the Full-Screen icon, the monitor with brackets around it.

A full-screen image appears.

● The playback toolbar also appears at the bottom of the screen.

③ Click the arrows to move the display of photos forward or backward from the whole group in Organizer.

A new photo appears.

4 Move your cursor to the left side to open the Quick Organize panel.

Use the Quick Organize panel for quickly adding keywords or putting a photo into an album.

5 Click the Filmstrip icon on the bottom toolbar.

A filmstrip appears.

● The active photo is highlighted in blue and light gray in the filmstrip and also appears enlarged in the main work area.

6 Click any image in the filmstrip to display it large.

7 Press the Escape key to go back to Organizer.

TIPS

Did You Know?

The full-screen view can be used as a slide show. Click the center arrow of the bottom toolbar to start playing images or pause the slide show. You can change how long each image is on the screen as well as play music with the photos by clicking the Wrench icon, which gives you settings to try. You can play this slide show only when the Photoshop Elements program is open.

Try This!

The full-screen playback can be very helpful, but sometimes you want to go back and forth between the Organizer multi-image view and the full-screen view. You can do this quickly and easily with the function key, F11. Press F11 to go from Organizer to Full Screen, and then press the Escape key to go back to Organizer. If you are using a laptop, you may have to press a special FN or function key, too.

Did You Know?

The Quick Edit panel in the full-screen view can be a useful way to quickly make adjustments to your photos. Position your cursor over the Quick Edit bar to expand the panel. Then choose controls that will enable you to adjust your photo.

SORT
the good pictures from the bad

Traditionally, going through your pictures, finding the good ones and getting rid of the bad has been called photo editing. However, when computer engineers developed programs like Photoshop, they decided to call changing pictures in those programs photo editing, too, so the term can be confusing.

Still, one of the most important things you can do with your photographs after importing them into Photoshop Elements is to go through them and edit them based on the original definition of the word. This is a great opportunity for you to learn from both your successes and your mistakes. It also allows you to get rid of photographs that you will never use and will just clog your folders with junk you do not need.

Photoshop Elements gives you some excellent tools to do just that. You can compare pictures, look at pictures in different sizes, and discover which pictures work well for you and which do not. To save hard drive space and eliminate clutter there, delete images that really do not satisfy you, thus reducing the number of pictures you have to go through to find the really good ones.

Set Up Your View of the Photos

1 Click and drag the thumbnail slider to change the sizes of your photo thumbnails.

2 Ctrl/⌘+click photos to select images that you want to rotate.

3 Click the appropriate Rotate icon to rotate the selected photos.

4 Click the View menu and then Details to show or hide Details.

● Details show up under the photograph and show ratings stars, date and time, and filename.

5 Click the stars to rate your photos.

You can use a system such as one star for those photos you reject, five stars for the best ones, and various numbers of stars in between to define how much you like or dislike particular photos.

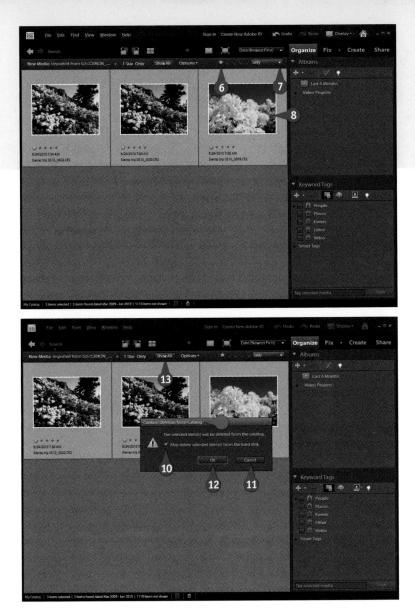

Delete Photos You Do Not Want

6 Click one rating star in the upper right of the thumbnail display.

7 To limit displayed photos to only those with one star, click the box to the right of the stars and select Only.

8 Select all photos with Ctrl/⌘+A.

9 Press Delete.

● The Confirm Deletion from Catalog dialog box appears.

10 Select the Also Delete Selected Item(s) from the Hard Disk check box to throw out your rejects (■ changes to ☑).

Make sure the Also Delete Selected Item(s) from the Hard Disk check box is deselected to remove photos only from Photoshop Elements view (☑ changes to ■).

11 If you feel that you made a mistake, you can click Cancel and change the ratings.

12 Click OK to finish the process.

13 Click Show All to get your photos on-screen again.

DIFFICULTY LEVEL

TIPS

Remember!
You can delete images from Photoshop Elements and/or off your computer altogether. Simply select the image you want to remove and press Delete. This opens a dialog box that enables you to decide if you simply want to remove the photo from Photoshop Elements' view or remove it from the hard drive completely. Generally, if you really do not like an image, get rid of it completely.

Try This!
To quickly see any image at a large size and stay within the overall Organizer, double-click it. This shows you the photo filling the thumbnail area without any other photos. This helps you better see details in your photos, such as sharpness or exposure problems. Double-click the image again to go back to the thumbnail view.

Did You Know?
You can turn off the view of filenames using the View menu. Click View and then select or deselect filenames. Clicking Show Details on or off turns on or off everything under the photo, including filenames.

STACK
your images

Once you own a digital camera and a large memory card or multiple cards, there is no cost for taking pictures. This means you can freely photograph a subject, trying different angles or varied techniques. However, as you do this, you accumulate a lot of similar photos in your digital files. That can make working with a particular group of photos more challenging because you have to look at a lot of similar images before you come to the new ones.

Stacking is a great feature of Photoshop Elements Organizer. It enables you to place special subgroups of your photos into stacks that then display as if they were one image. This can simplify the view of your photos in Organizer. You can also use stacks to keep a particular small group of photos together.

In the group of images that were imported on these pages are a number of images that show close shots of the flowers and include ladybugs or ladybird beetles. The photos are similar enough that they are worth grouping as a stack. Stacks are a tool to help you better organize your photos as you go through them.

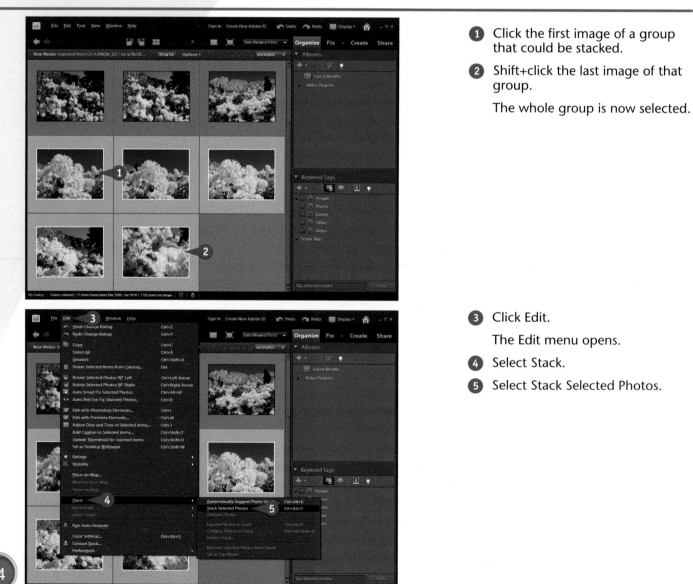

1 Click the first image of a group that could be stacked.

2 Shift+click the last image of that group.

The whole group is now selected.

3 Click Edit.

The Edit menu opens.

4 Select Stack.

5 Select Stack Selected Photos.

The images are visually stacked so you see only one.

- The Stack icon appears in the upper right corner of the stack to inform you it is a stack.

6 Click the small arrow at the middle of the right side of the photo thumbnail.

DIFFICULTY LEVEL

- The stack opens and is highlighted as a group.

7 Click the small arrow at the middle of the right side of the last photo to collapse the stack again.

TIPS

Compare!

Many times you will find that two photos look similar and you simply want to find and keep the best. You do not necessarily want or need a stack. Photoshop Elements has a great tool that enables you to compare photos two at a time. Select two photos, and then click the Display button at the top right of the interface and select Compare Photos Side by Side. The two photos are then displayed full screen next to each other.

Try This!

You can also use stacking to simplify and organize your thumbnail view. For example, you could stack photos of each child at a birthday party so that the entire group of party photos is organized into stacks based on individuals. A Ctrl/⌘+click isolates photos to select them.

Did You Know?

Stacking is simply another way to group photos so they are useful to you. It is based on an old technique slide shooters used when sorting photos. They would pile similar slides on top of each other, making stacks that kept their light tables better organized.

CREATE ALBUMS
to group your pictures

Albums are groupings of pictures based on your needs. You can create albums based on events such as birthdays, people you know such as family members, and much more. Albums are not specific to any folder of images that you have imported. For example, in the photos shown in this chapter from the Sierra Nevadas, you could create an album on the Sierra Nevada if you wanted to include the images just imported in addition to ones taken at other times you had been there, or as another example, you could create an album related to the ladybugs.

Albums enable you to group pictures together even if they were not taken at the same time. For example, you could set up an album based on a child's name and then put images of that child into that album. If you did this over time, you would have a collection of images of that child from many different times and places.

Albums do not duplicate photographs. They only create references to where the pictures are on your hard drive. For that reason, individual pictures could be in many albums, which can help you find them faster in different ways.

① Ctrl/⌘+click photos to select individual images, or click a photo and then Shift+click the last image in a group to select photos in order.

You can also press Ctrl/⌘+A to select all photos.

② Click the large green plus sign under Albums and select New Album to add an album.

● You can open the Albums section of the task panel by clicking the arrow next to the word Albums.

● The Album Details panel appears.

③ You can group albums by using the Album Category function, but start with None (Top Level).

④ Type a name for your album.

⑤ Deselect the Backup/Sync check box until you have a Photoshop.com account (☑ changes to ■) and you really have an album you want to back up.

● Your selected photos appear in the Content box.

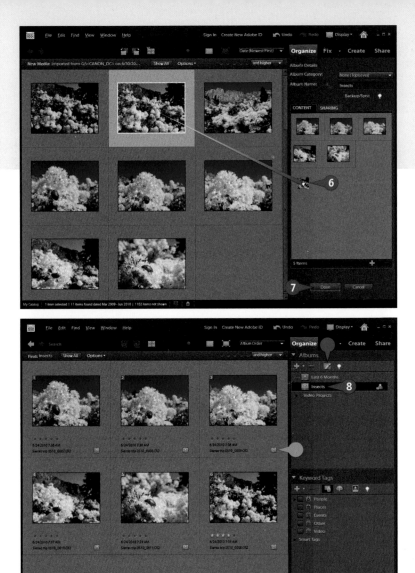

#6

DIFFICULTY LEVEL

⑥ Click an image and drag it into the Content box to add it to an album.

Note: *Neither adding nor deleting photos from an album affects their position on the hard drive.*

⑦ Click Done.

The new album now appears in the Albums panel.

⑧ Click the album to select it.

● The photos you put in the album have a small icon below them to indicate they are in albums when you select Show Details in the View menu.

● You can edit your album by clicking the Edit icon.

TIPS

Did You Know?

You can add photos to an album at any time. Whenever you see a photo that belongs in an album, click it and then drag it to the album. It is automatically placed in the album and appears there whenever that album is opened. Remember you are only creating references to photos and not actually moving any.

Try This!

You can immediately put any new photos just imported into Photoshop Elements into an album. Select all images in that new group of photos, add an album with a name appropriate to that group, and the photos should appear in the Contents box. If not, select and drag the new pictures into that Item box.

Smart Albums!

You can create a smart album that automatically adds photos to the album. You set up criteria, such as filenames, keywords, and camera type, in the New Smart Album dialog box, which you access by clicking the Albums plus sign. Any photo with those criteria appearing in Photoshop Elements is automatically included in the smart album.

USE KEYWORDS
to tag your images

Keywords are words that you connect to your photo in Organizer. They can be a useful way for you to organize and find your pictures because keywords are searchable. Albums are great for creating large groupings of pictures that you can readily access in a very visual type of search. Keywords offer a very different search when you use the search function in Organizer — you can go to specific images depending on the keywords you have used.

The challenge, however, is that you have to spend the time attaching keywords to your photographs in order to use them. You may know that you have a

photograph of a bear somewhere in your collection, but if the keyword "bear" is not associated with that image, it will be very hard to find.

Keywords can be as detailed as you want. You can simply add words to large groups of selected pictures, which makes this process easier. Or, if you want to be able to really find specific images, you can add a lot of very specific keywords to individual pictures.

Regardless of how you use keywords, they are an important part of Photoshop Elements to understand and use as needed.

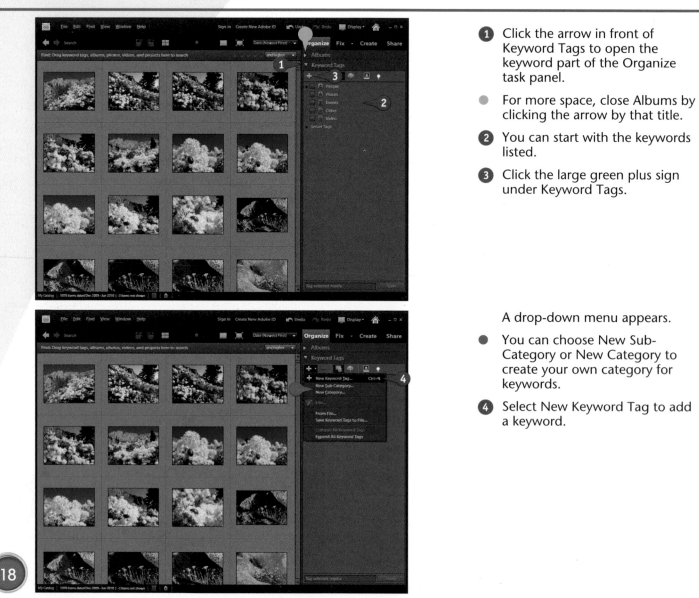

1 Click the arrow in front of Keyword Tags to open the keyword part of the Organize task panel.

● For more space, close Albums by clicking the arrow by that title.

2 You can start with the keywords listed.

3 Click the large green plus sign under Keyword Tags.

A drop-down menu appears.

● You can choose New Sub-Category or New Category to create your own category for keywords.

4 Select New Keyword Tag to add a keyword.

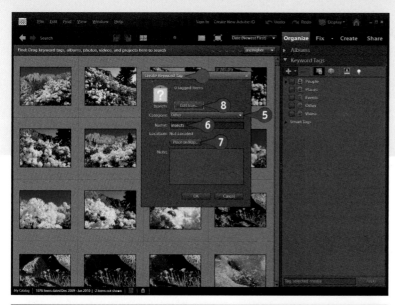

- The Create Keyword Tag dialog box appears.

⑤ Choose a category.

⑥ Type a name for your keyword tag.

⑦ Choose a location if you want to add a specific location for your photos, including locating them on a map.

⑧ Choose an icon if desired by clicking Edit Icon.

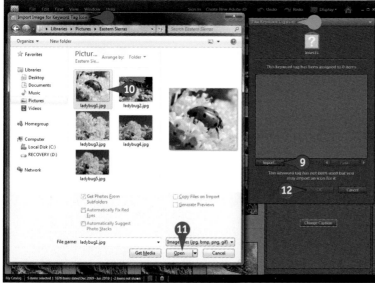

- The Edit Keyword Tag Icon dialog box appears.

⑨ Click Import to look for something to use as an icon.

- The Import Image for Keyword Tag Icon dialog box appears.

⑩ Find a photo that looks interesting, perhaps from the same group of images.

⑪ Click Open to select this photo for your icon.

⑫ Click OK to use this new icon for your keywords.

Note: It is not required to have an icon for every keyword tag.

⑬ Click OK again to accept the changes to the Create Keyword Tag dialog box.

TIPS

Try This!

When all the task panel controls are open, your interface can get cluttered and confusing. Click the arrows at the left of the panel category titles to open and close a category of control, such as Albums. Simplify the workspace by closing panel categories you are not using.

Important!

Pick keywords that help you find your photos. Your keywords will be unique to your type of photography. Adding keywords that others use but do not fit your images will make your searches confusing. Ask yourself, "What do I need to find?" in order to create keywords that work for you and your needs.

Customize It!

You can add as much or as little information as you want to keyword tags. The Create Keyword Tag dialog box includes the option to add notes or a specific address for a location. These are not requirements, only options that some photographers use frequently, and others not at all. Use what you need and what works for you.

USE KEYWORDS
to tag your images

Keywords are one of those things that many photographers put off creating. The best time to add keywords is when you first import pictures into Photoshop Elements. At that time, you remember the most about your pictures. Adding keywords at this time is also easier because all your pictures are right in front of you.

It is important to understand that you can add keyword tags to one picture and only one picture, to a few, or to hundreds. Keywords enable you to be very specific, down to putting a specific name on something that appears only in one picture. They also enable you to be broader in your approach and put a single word across a whole group of pictures so that you can find that group again. Keywords work across all pictures within Organizer so that you can find pictures throughout Organizer by simply searching for keywords.

Once you add a keyword to Photoshop Elements, it stays there until you remove it. You do not have to add the same keywords to the program every time you import photographs. After you have keywords in the program, you can use them with any new or old photographs at any time.

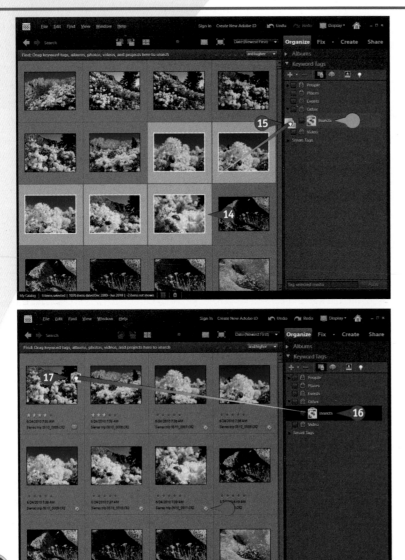

- A new keyword tag appears in the category you chose in step 5.

14 Select the photos that need this keyword.

The selected photos have a white frame around them.

15 Click and drag the selected photos onto the tag and they gain that tag.

You can click and drag multiple times, with different groups of photos, to add more keyword tags to photos.

- A small keyword tag icon appears below your photos when Show Details is selected in View.

16 To put a keyword on specific photos, click the tag.

17 Drag the tag and drop it on the photo.

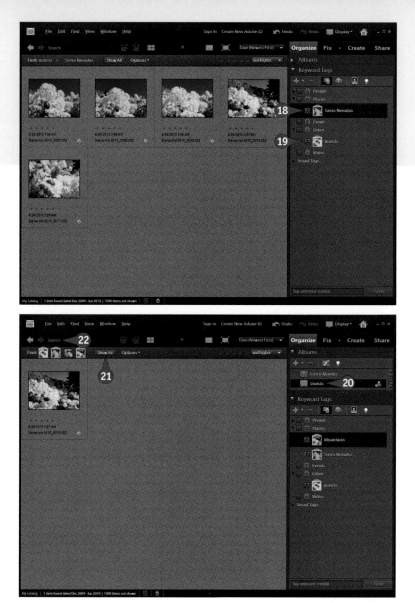

18 Find specific images based on your keyword by selecting the box in front of a specific keyword tag.

19 Click additional tags to narrow your search.

20 To show specific items in an album, click the album before selecting Keyword Tags.

21 To search for images throughout your image files, click Show All first.

22 Type a name in the search box to show photos related to that name quickly.

TIPS

Customize It!

Take any existing keyword tag and customize it for your needs. Right-click any keyword tag to get a context-sensitive menu. This enables you to edit your keyword or keyword category, add a new keyword to the category, add a new subcategory, or remove keywords or categories as needed.

Did You Know?

Professional photographers frequently use extensive keywords to help them find photographs in their files. When a client wants something specific, such as young people at a Fourth of July parade, keywords help find photos with those criteria. Keywords would include young people, Fourth of July, parade, and so on.

Try This!

You can type a list of keywords based on common descriptions of things in your photos. You can then import this list into Photoshop Elements by clicking the large green plus sign under Keyword Tags and selecting From File. This file must be an XML (Extensible Markup Language) file. You can save a Word file as an XML file for this purpose.

TAG PHOTOS
with face recognition

Keywords are a great tool to help you find specific subjects or types of photos. They do require you to set the keyword and find the appropriate photos for them. Many photographers like to identify people in their photos so they can find them later based on specific individuals in the images. Photoshop Elements helps you connect people with keywords through face recognition and people tags in the Keyword Tags panel.

Photoshop Elements works to "recognize" people in your photos for you. Face recognition can help you quickly go through photos to find specific instances of a person and add keywords for them. This can be

important even for family photos where you know everyone in the pictures. The challenge is usually not knowing who the people are, but finding the photographs of people in your collection of digital photos. By keywording people, you can find specific instances of those people and groupings by searching for keywords.

The program does a pretty good job of finding faces in everything, including portraits, group photos, and small people in larger scenes. You can even have Photoshop Elements highlight all the faces it can see as faces so you can give keywords for the individuals.

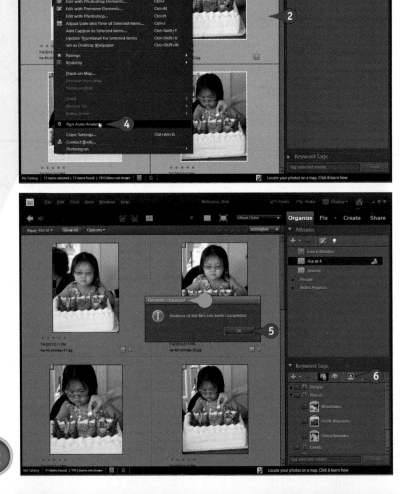

1 Open a group of photos to analyze for faces.

This can be in recently imported photos, albums, folders, and so on.

2 Select all images by pressing Ctrl/ ⌘+A.

3 Click the Edit menu.

4 Select Run Auto-Analyzer.

Photoshop Elements analyzes your group of photos for faces and other similarities.

● The Elements Organizer confirmation dialog box appears.

5 Click OK.

6 Click the Face Recognition icon in the Keyword Tags panel.

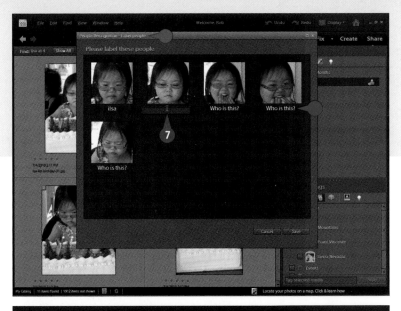

- The People Recognition window opens.

- Faces appear with the message, "Who is this?"

⑦ Click "Who is this?" and type the person's name in the blank area that appears.

DIFFICULTY LEVEL

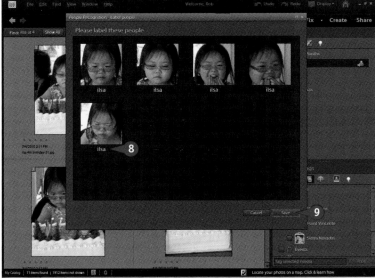

⑧ Do this for all faces highlighted in this window.

Photoshop Elements will start to recognize the person when you do this again in a different album and click the Face Recognition icon.

⑨ Click Save when you have assigned all the names.

TIPS

Did You Know?

Software companies have been trying to develop advanced facial recognition for many years. A big demand for it exists in security markets. The ability to quickly scan security videos, for example, to watch for terrorists or other threatening travelers would be a huge benefit for security agencies.

Try This!

Right-clicking a mouse is standard procedure for Windows users. It is an efficient and quick way to access important contextual menus in Photoshop Elements. However, until recently, Apple did not use a right-click mouse, even though programs supported it. Today, all Mac users, whether they program an Apple mouse for right-click functionality or buy another brand, need to have and use a right-click mouse.

Did You Know?

All the organizing tools shown in this chapter are simply that — tools. You have to supply the organization; Photoshop Elements does not. Organize your photos using Albums and Keyword Tags to mimic how you file anything. Following a plan that is true to your own organizational methods is more likely to create a versatile and efficient system for you.

CHANGE THE ORGANIZER
interface as needed

Photoshop Elements has been designed for photographers and its interface reflects that. However, every photographer has unique needs and ways of working. You can change the way the interface for Organizer looks, and consequently acts, to customize it for your needs. You will also likely change the interface as you work. For example, you may find that you need to look at the thumbnails small and as a large group, or large so you can see individual images better, depending on your project.

The controls that affect the look of the interface are buttons in the top option bars, such as Thumbnail Size

icons, and in the View and Window menus. Do not be afraid to try different looks for your interface — you can always change back to the original look by clicking the button or menu item a second time.

However you set up your interface, it should be something that helps you work more efficiently. Do not simply use something because it is available or someone else uses it. Be sure that it really helps your work in the program. Working in Photoshop Elements should be a fun way of interacting with your pictures.

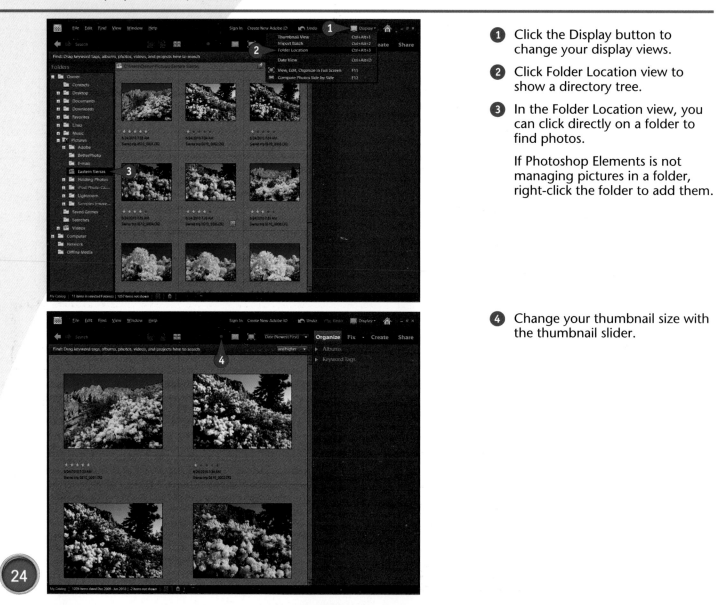

1 Click the Display button to change your display views.

2 Click Folder Location view to show a directory tree.

3 In the Folder Location view, you can click directly on a folder to find photos.

If Photoshop Elements is not managing pictures in a folder, right-click the folder to add them.

4 Change your thumbnail size with the thumbnail slider.

5 Click here to expand or collapse the panel section.

6 Click and drag along an interface edge to make it larger or smaller.

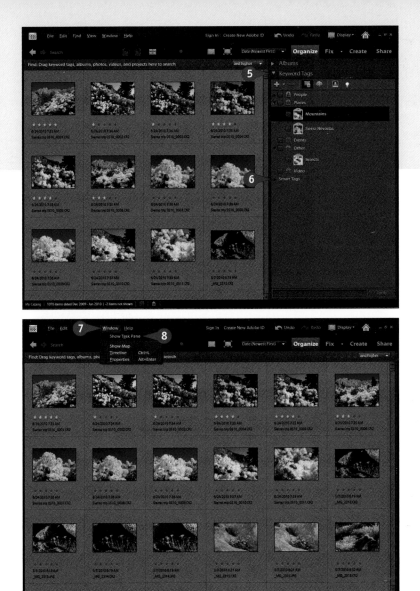

7 Click Window to change what appears in the interface.

8 Click Hide Task Pane for a large image-viewing area; click Show Task Pane for the normal view.

TIPS

Did You Know?
You can control many features of Photoshop Elements with keyboard commands. These enable you to quickly access controls with just a couple of keystrokes. These keystrokes are listed next to the controls in the menus. For example, you can turn on and off the detail display for thumbnails by pressing Ctrl/⌘+D.

Try This!
The Timeline in Photoshop Elements can help you find photos by date. You can turn it on in the Window menu. It works for the entire database, so click the Show All button at the top left of the thumbnails first and then select a specific time; photos appear below from that time. You can also drag the left and right sliders to limit the dates to show images.

Did You Know?
Photoshop Elements 9 has had some significant changes for the readability and usability of the interface. In Photoshop Elements 8, some things such as menu buttons were very hard to see. Text sizes have been changed to be more readable, and menu buttons have been accentuated so you can see them well.

BACK UP YOUR PICTURES
to protect them

Whenever you read about fires and other disasters destroying people's property, you always read about people wanting to save their photo albums. Photos are important to us in so many ways, whether they are memories of children growing up or artistic visions of a great natural setting.

Digital photos are vulnerable to loss from a hard drive failure — and hard drives do fail. Plus, without a hard copy, you have no other record of the images. By backing them up, you can add more security to your

pictures than is possible with traditional film. It is very easy to back up your photos onto accessory hard drives that plug in to your computer. These have come down so much in price that many photographers back up their pictures on more than one.

Backup is so important that Adobe added special backup features to Photoshop Elements 9, which are covered in task #97. You should have some backup system of your own that you can control and access easily, which is covered here.

An external hard drive is one of the best ways to back up the images on your computer's hard drive.

Back Up to an External Hard Drive

1. Click the Display button in the top menu bar.

2. Select Folder Location.

3. Find a folder you want to duplicate for backup in the folder tree.

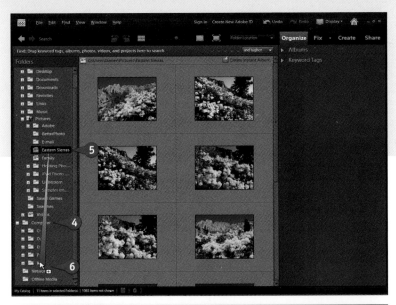

4 If necessary, reveal the external hard drive using the right scroll bar and clicking the Computer icon.

5 Click the folder you want to duplicate.

6 Drag the folder to the external hard drive.

The folder is saved on the external hard drive.

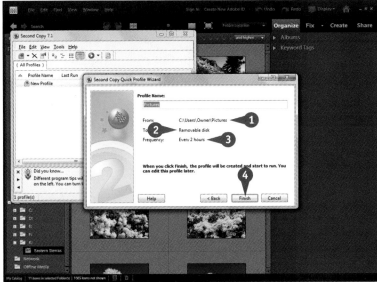

Use Backup Software

Note: *You can obtain special backup software to help you with backing up your photos. All of these programs work slightly differently, though the steps are similar.*

1 With your backup software open, choose the folder or folders you want to back up.

2 Select the location for backup.

3 Select when to make the backup.

4 Click Finish to start the backup.

The backup software saves the folder or new images in the folder to the designated location at the time you specify.

TIPS

Did You Know?
Backup software can make your backups easier. Once you set up backup software for specific folders and a specific accessory drive, the software remembers those locations. The next time that you ask it to back up, it simply compares what is in those two locations and adds only what is new. Check out Second Copy for PCs at www.centered.com and Déjà Vu for Macs at www.propagandaprod.com.

Try This!
Small portable hard drives designed for laptops are more expensive than other accessory hard drives. However, they can be handy for accessing your photographs from your laptop or other computer. In addition, you can easily store such a hard drive in a location separate from your main computer, giving you added protection. You can also use large USB flash drives for this purpose.

Try This!
You can create a duplicate file structure on your backup drive that matches your main computer in order to make your backups simpler. Simply create folders and levels of folders that include the files you want to back up that are the same on both. For example, if your photos are structured by year and then by specific event, then use the same year and event structure. Then you can simply copy a folder from one drive to another in the same filing setup.

Start Adjusting Your Images in Photoshop Elements

One of the great challenges that photographers have always had is that the camera does not see the world exactly the way a person does. The camera is limited by the capabilities of its sensor, how the camera engineers have designed its internal processing, and its lens. Although the digital camera does a great job of capturing an image from the world, this image is not necessarily a correct interpretation of that world. Cameras have image-capture capabilities that meet the needs of a wide range of users, so the camera is rarely perfect for any one photographer.

That is where Photoshop Elements comes in. With most images, you need to spend a short time tweaking them so they accurately reflect what you originally saw. In this chapter you learn some basic steps to get your photos looking more the way you expect a photograph to look. This chapter also reflects a workflow from start to finish that you can use as you work on your pictures. A few of the steps, such as setting blacks and whites, adjusting midtones, and color correction, are important steps for any photograph, and are also important steps when you are processing RAW files or using layers.

Top 100

#11 Open Pictures and Use Save As . . . . 30 DIFFICULTY LEVEL

#12 Make the Editor Interface Your Own . . . . 32 DIFFICULTY LEVEL

#13 Set Preferences to Make Editor Work for You . . . . 34 DIFFICULTY LEVEL

#14 You Cannot Hurt Your Pictures . . . . 36 DIFFICULTY LEVEL

#15 Crop Your Photos for Tighter Shots . . . . 38 DIFFICULTY LEVEL

#16 Fix and Rotate Crooked Pictures . . . . 40 DIFFICULTY LEVEL

#17 Use Guided Edit to Help You Learn the Program . . . . 42 DIFFICULTY LEVEL

#18 Use Guided Edit for Special Effects . . . . 44 DIFFICULTY LEVEL

#19 Set Blacks and Whites with Levels . . . . 46 DIFFICULTY LEVEL

#20 Adjust Your Midtones with Levels . . . . 48 DIFFICULTY LEVEL

#21 Adjust Your Midtones with Color Curves . . . . 50 DIFFICULTY LEVEL

#22 Quickly Adjust Dark Shadows and Bright Highlights . . . . . . 52 DIFFICULTY LEVEL

#23 Correct Color to Remove Color Casts . . . . 54 DIFFICULTY LEVEL

#24 Enhance Color with Hue/Saturation . . . . 56 DIFFICULTY LEVEL

#25 Use Quick Edit to Work Fast . . . . 58 DIFFICULTY LEVEL

Open pictures and
USE SAVE AS

To start working on photos in Photoshop Elements, you need to get a picture into the Editor workspace of Photoshop Elements. You can work with Organizer to do this or you can get images directly into Editor from the Editor's File menu. The advantage of working with Organizer is that you have access to lots of pictures at once. If you are working with a specific picture and you know exactly where it is on your hard drive, opening the picture directly in Editor can be easier.

Many photographers worry about adversely affecting an image and, therefore, are cautious when working

on it. If you immediately save any picture as a new file when it is opened into Photoshop Elements, you are protecting your original image file. This frees you to work on your image without worrying about permanently damaging it. You cannot damage your original because you are not working on it at this point.

This task and all of the other tasks in this chapter are directly related to JPEG or TIFF files. If you shoot RAW files, then you will be working with Adobe Camera Raw, which comes with Photoshop Elements and is covered in the next chapter.

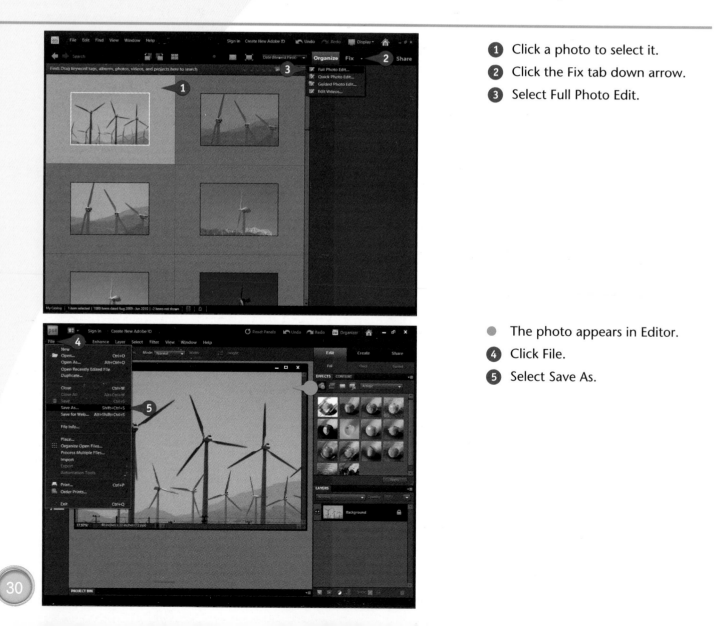

1 Click a photo to select it.

2 Click the Fix tab down arrow.

3 Select Full Photo Edit.

● The photo appears in Editor.

4 Click File.

5 Select Save As.

● The Save As dialog box appears.

6 Choose a location to save your photos.

7 Give your photo a name that makes sense to you.

8 Choose either Photoshop (.psd) or TIFF (.tif) for the format.

9 Uncheck Save in Version Set with Original (☑ changes to ☐) unless you have good reasons to keep all of your versions with the original file.

10 Click Save.

If you chose Photoshop in step 8, your photo is saved without any additional steps.

If you chose TIFF in step 8, you see Save Options choices.

11 Click Save and the TIFF Options dialog box appears.

12 Select None (◉ changes to ◉) for image compression, although LZW can be used if your photos will be opened only in a limited number of programs, including Photoshop Elements.

13 Leave the radio buttons in the Pixel Order and Byte Order sections at the default settings.

14 Click OK.

Photoshop Elements saves the photo.

TIPS

Try This!
You can open photos directly from Editor. Click File and then choose Open. This takes you to the Open dialog box. Navigate to where your digital photos are kept, and then find the folder and the image. When you click a photo once to select it, a preview appears. Click Open to open it in Editor.

Did You Know?
Photographers should save images in Photoshop, TIFF, and JPEG formats. You should not use JPEG as a working file format; that is, a format that you use to work on images while you are in Editor. JPEG is a compressed file format and should be used only for archiving images when you need to keep file sizes small or for e-mail and Web purposes. Both Photoshop and TIFF enable you to open, adjust, and save an image as much as you want without any loss of quality.

Did You Know?
JPEG is a common photo format digital cameras use. It stands for Joint Photographic Experts Group and represents a very sophisticated form of file compression for images. It allows the saved file size to be quite a bit smaller than the actual megapixels of a camera would indicate.

MAKE THE EDITOR INTERFACE
your own

The Editor interface of Photoshop Elements is very adaptable. Most photographers find it helpful to make some adjustments to the interface so that the program works better for them. One adjustment you might perform right away is how Effects and Undo History are displayed. Adobe put Effects in the right-side panel bin as a default rather than Undo History. Although many photographers use Effects, almost all use Undo History.

In this task, you learn to create an efficient workspace suitable for most photographers. You also learn how to add or subtract panels from the interface so you can do your own customization.

You can always turn on or off parts of the interface by selecting items in the Window menu. Do not be afraid to deselect parts of the interface that you do not use or select something that seems useful for your purposes even if it is not included here. You can also reset the interface in the Window menu by clicking Reset Panels.

The photo seen here is of wind turbines for electricity generation outside of Palm Springs, California. A telephoto lens was used to create a tight composition of the windmills.

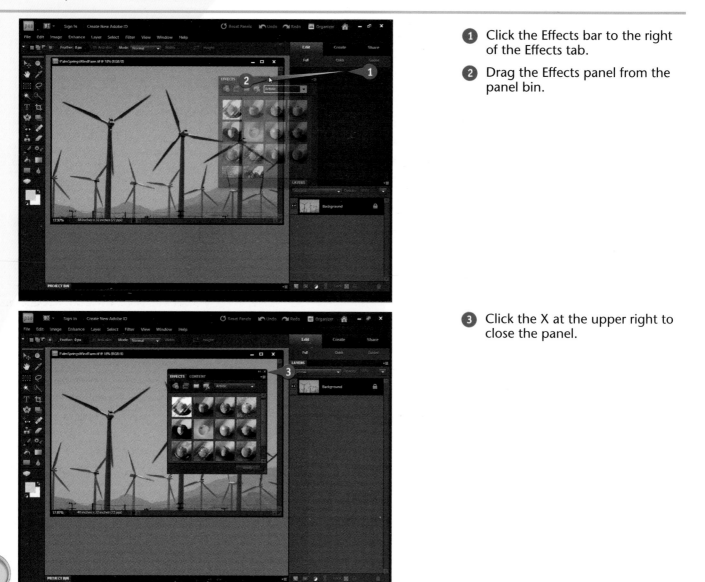

1 Click the Effects bar to the right of the Effects tab.

2 Drag the Effects panel from the panel bin.

3 Click the X at the upper right to close the panel.

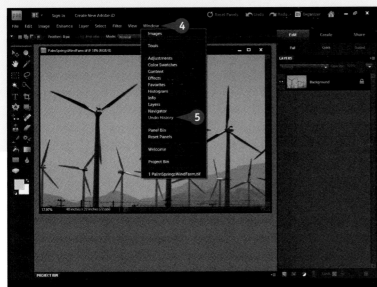

④ Click Window.

⑤ Select Undo History in the menu.

● The Undo History panel appears in the panel bin.

TIPS

Try This!

The Project Bin at the bottom of the interface shows the active images in Photoshop Elements, whether there is one or more. If you want more working space, you can always hide this panel. Simply double-click anywhere along the bar that includes the Project Bin tab. To bring the bin back, double-click again.

Try This!

You can make the Undo History panel larger or smaller in the panel bin. Click and drag the separating line between it and the Layers panel; the cursor changes to a small double arrow when you are over the right spot. You can also make your panel bin larger or smaller by clicking and dragging the left edge.

Did You Know?

Adobe deliberately chose the dark gray interface of Photoshop Elements. This color sets pictures off well and makes them the stars of the interface. In addition, the neutral color does not compete with or affect people's perception of colors in a photograph.

SET PREFERENCES
to make Editor work for you

Just as in the Organizer (see task #9), Editor has preferences you can set to make the program run more efficiently on your computer. They are in the same place in the menu as they are in Organizer: under the Edit menu, at the bottom of the menu for Windows and in the Photoshop Elements menu for the Mac. You can use all the defaults in the preferences and still have good results. Adobe put a lot of thought into the defaults, so they do work. However, a lot of them are based on what most people might choose, but not necessarily what you would choose.

In Preferences, you can choose to affect all sorts of things, including how files are saved, the performance of Photoshop Elements with your computer, plug-ins, and more. Most of the options are fairly self-explanatory, and if you are not sure what they do, you can always try them and then reset everything later if needed.

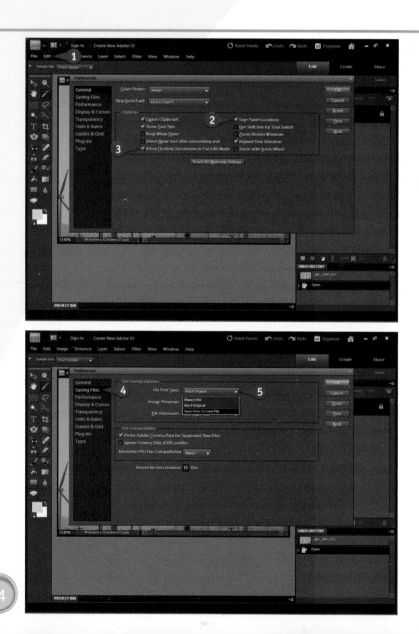

① Click Edit, select Preferences, and then click General to open the Preferences dialog box.

On a Mac, click the Photoshop Elements menu first.

You can leave most of the General settings at the default selections.

② Select Save Panel Locations to save your interface configuration (■ changes to ☑).

③ Select Allow Floating Documents in Full Edit Mode (■ changes to ☑) to allow your images to float within the interface.

④ Click Saving Files.

⑤ From the On First Save drop-down menu, select Save Over Current File for efficient work or Always Ask if you want to be extra safe.

The defaults work well for the remaining options.

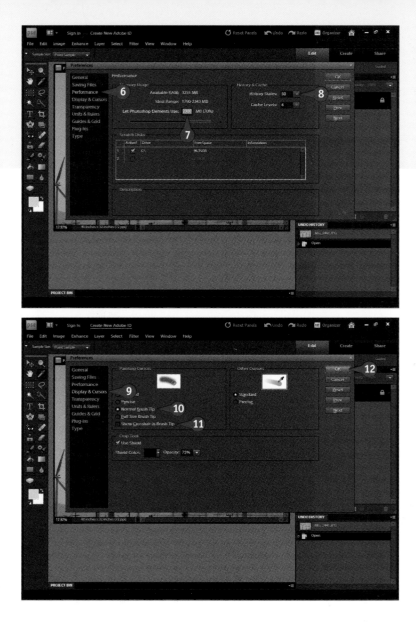

#13

⑥ Click Performance.

⑦ Under Memory Usage, set the usage in the Let Photoshop Elements Use field to close to the highest number shown in the Ideal Range unless you have less than 1GB of RAM.

This setting is not completed until Photoshop Elements is closed and opened again.

⑧ Choose History States of at least 50 so you have room to back up in the Undo History panel.

⑨ Click Display & Cursors.

⑩ Select how your brush will appear with painting cursors (● changes to ◉).

You can keep the defaults to start, but change this later if you prefer, for example, a precise cursor.

⑪ Select Show Crosshair in Brush Tip to show the center of a working brush (■ changes to ✓).

⑫ Click OK to close the Preferences dialog box.

Photoshop Elements saves your preferences.

TIPS

Did You Know?

When Photoshop Elements runs out of RAM or "thinking space," it needs someplace to work, and uses space on a hard drive. This is called *scratch space*, and the drive being used is the *scratch drive*. It can be helpful to have more than one drive designated for scratch space so that Photoshop Elements never runs out of room to think.

More Options!

Color Settings are a group of preferences that have their own separate settings. They are accessed in the Edit menu in both Windows and on a Mac. You will do okay when they are set at the defaults, but you get more capabilities and options for how color can be adjusted if you select Always Optimize for Printing. This gives you what is called the AdobeRGB color space.

Did You Know?

A color space is something a computer uses to describe how colors are rendered. A common color space for JPEG files is sRGB, which works fine for many images but is a smaller color space than AdobeRGB. AdobeRGB gives you more flexibility and options when you are adjusting color and tonality.

YOU CANNOT HURT
your pictures

Another reason many photographers are cautious when working on pictures in Photoshop Elements is that they are afraid of hurting their images. You cannot really hurt your pictures. This is important to remember because it frees you to work more confidently with your pictures. It also lets you experiment without worry. Experimenting with controls in Photoshop Elements is one of the best ways of learning this program. If you are not sure how something works, just try it and see what it does.

As long as you have done a Save As for your original image (see task #11), you cannot hurt the original image because you are now working on a copy. And as you work, you can always undo everything that you have already done. As long as you do not save what you have done, no change is made to the file you are working on except what you see within Photoshop Elements. The Undo History panel gives you even more options for undoing your adjustments. Knowing this can help you try things without restraint and discover the possibilities for your image.

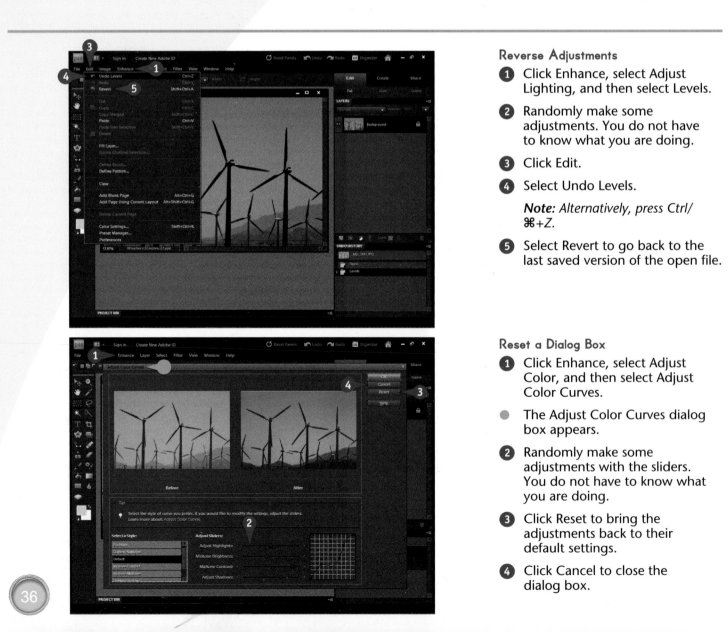

Reverse Adjustments

1. Click Enhance, select Adjust Lighting, and then select Levels.

2. Randomly make some adjustments. You do not have to know what you are doing.

3. Click Edit.

4. Select Undo Levels.

   Note: Alternatively, press Ctrl/⌘+Z.

5. Select Revert to go back to the last saved version of the open file.

Reset a Dialog Box

1. Click Enhance, select Adjust Color, and then select Adjust Color Curves.

● The Adjust Color Curves dialog box appears.

2. Randomly make some adjustments with the sliders. You do not have to know what you are doing.

3. Click Reset to bring the adjustments back to their default settings.

4. Click Cancel to close the dialog box.

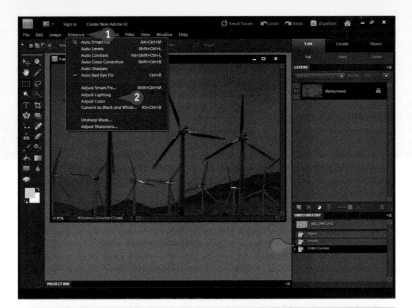

Use Undo History

1 Click Enhance.

2 Randomly make some adjustments from Adjust Lighting and Adjust Color. You do not have to know what you are doing.

● All adjustments appear in the Undo History panel.

3 Click any adjustment in the Undo History panel to go back to an earlier adjustment.

Note: You can also keep pressing Ctrl/⌘+Z to back up in this panel.

TIPS

Try This!

Set your Undo History panel for more or fewer adjustment steps or states by clicking Edit in Windows or Photoshop Elements on a Mac, selecting Preferences, and then selecting Performance (see task #13). History states are simply the specific lines of things you have done in the Undo History panel. Too many states can slow your computer down, but too few can be frustrating to work with.

Important!

You will see keyboard commands throughout the book. This is one place where Windows and Mac differ with Photoshop Elements. Ctrl (Control) in Windows is the same as ⌘ (or Command) on a Mac. Alt in Windows is the same as Option on a Mac.

Caution!

There is one way you can lose your ability to back up from adjustments. If you make a lot of adjustments to a picture and then save and close it, you lock those adjustments to the picture. Save your photo as you go, but only when you are sure that your adjustments are okay. Later in this book (see task #26), you learn how to make nondestructive adjustments that enable you to close and save an image with those changes intact and still adjustable.

CROP YOUR PHOTOS
for tighter shots

A common problem for photographers is getting too much in a picture. Sometimes this comes from not being able to get close enough to the subject. Regardless of the reason, many photos look better when they are tightened up by cropping out extraneous space.

Another challenge for photographers is when unwanted details start creeping into the edges of a picture. That can make the photograph less than its best and even unappealing.

Luckily, Photoshop Elements makes this easy to fix. You can crop your picture down to the essential elements of that image. *Cropping* is simply cutting off parts of the picture to reveal the image previously obscured by extra details. Cropping to strengthen an image and get rid of junk is best done early on in the process. Cropping to a specific size should be done after you have adjusted your photograph optimally.

The image here is from a child's birthday party. So often photographers wait for the blowing out of the candles. That can be a cliché sort of picture; everybody snaps that shot. Be ready for great expressions and great moments before and after the blowing out of the candles.

① Click the Crop tool in the toolbox at the left.

② Delete any numbers in the Width, Height, or Resolution boxes.

③ Click a corner of the area you want to keep.

④ Drag your cursor to the opposite corner of the area and release.

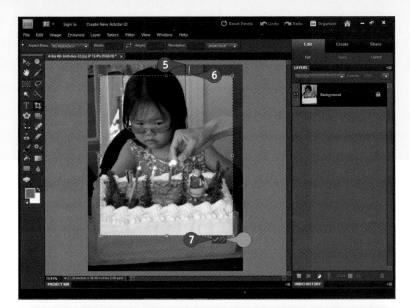

DIFFICULTY LEVEL

5 Click any edge of the crop box.

6 Drag that edge left or right, or up or down, to change the size of the crop box.

7 Click the green check mark to complete the crop.

● The red circle with the diagonal slash removes the crop box.

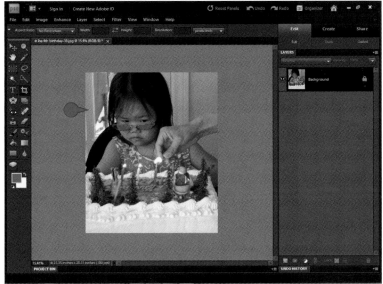

● The cropped image now appears in the work area at the same pixel size, but less of the original image appears because of the crop.

Note: *You can resize a cropped image to fill the work area by pressing Ctrl/⌘+0.*

TIPS

Try This!
If the Crop tool is not cooperating, you can reset it easily. This is true for all tools. Just above the work area and the toolbox is the Options bar for the tool that you are working with. At the far left is a small down-facing arrow. Click it to see options for resetting this tool or all tools. Click Reset Tool.

Try This!
You do not have to use the green check mark to finish your crop. Sometimes searching for it is not efficient. You can use the keyboard and simply press Enter, or you can use your mouse and double-click inside the crop box to complete the crop.

Did You Know?
Cropping out the junk early on in the photograph helps as you process the image in Photoshop Elements. Whenever you make any adjustment, Photoshop Elements looks at the entire picture. Details in the picture that really do not belong can throw off your adjustment.

FIX AND ROTATE
crooked pictures

Getting crooked pictures is easy. Even the pros get them. If you become so excited by the scene or the action within that scene, you might not pay strict attention to the horizon. Landscapes are probably the most common photographs that end up crooked. Viewers notice when a photograph has a slanted horizon.

You might miss a crooked horizon on the LCD of your camera when you are out taking the picture. However, when you view that photo on the computer, you will see that the horizon is not oriented correctly. This is not something people viewing the photo

typically overlook. If they do, however, the photographer will not miss it and will be disappointed. Pictures can have crooked verticals, too, but the steps you take to correct them are the same as those for crooked horizontals.

Photoshop Elements makes it easy to straighten a horizon. You can do it a couple of ways. The method you choose depends a lot on the photograph, the degree of crookedness, and your workflow needs. The photo being corrected here is of wind turbines for electricity generation in the Palm Springs, California area.

Use the Straighten Tool

1. Click the Straighten tool.
2. Click the Canvas Options box for its drop-down menu.
3. Select Crop to Remove Background.
4. Click one side of the crooked horizon.
5. Drag and release the mouse button when you have created a line across the crooked horizon.

● Photoshop Elements straightens the horizon and crops the image appropriately to make a complete photograph.

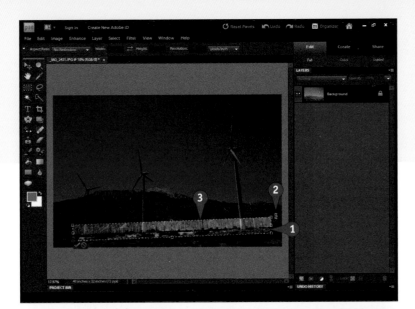

Straighten with the Crop Tool

① Make a narrow crop selection near the horizon using the Crop tool.

② Position your cursor outside the bounding box until it turns into a curved, two-headed arrow.

③ Click and drag to rotate the bounding box so an edge is parallel to the horizon.

④ Expand the crop box until it covers the correct parts of the photo.

⑤ Click the green check mark to finish.

Photoshop Elements crops the image and straightens the horizon.

Note: Using the Crop tool for straightening the image allows you to both crop and straighten at the same time.

DIFFICULTY LEVEL

TIPS

Try This!

Extreme angles can be fun. Try rotating the crop box to odd and unusual angles and see what happens to the photo. Sometimes you find interesting, stimulating results, but other times you get nothing. Keep trying!

Did You Know?

There is a Photoshop joke that applies to Photoshop Elements, too. How many Photoshop Elements experts does it take to screw in a light bulb? One hundred and one — one person to screw in the bulb and a hundred to describe another way to do it. Photoshop and Photoshop Elements are powerful, flexible programs. Use the tools that work for you and ignore people who tell you that you are doing it all wrong. You have to find your own way through Photoshop Elements. It can take some work and time, but it is well worth it when you can work more efficiently.

USE GUIDED EDIT
to help you learn the program

A quick and easy way of working on your images in Photoshop Elements is to use the Guided Edit feature. Guided Edit not only guides you through working on an image, but also gives you a good idea about how Photoshop Elements works.

The Guided Edit feature gives you a lot of different options for adjusting the picture, while keeping distracting controls hidden. This enables you to focus on just what you need to do to a photograph. Guided Edit does not cover everything in Photoshop Elements, but it does provide a good overview of the program. When you click any option in Guided Edit,

you go to the control you need as well as instructions on how to use it. Guided Edit contains 26 controls within 7 groups, plus a special Automated Actions category. Each control has specific guidance on how to use it.

The steps that follow show two controls working on a photograph of a chuckwalla lizard in the Joshua Tree National Park in California. Chuckwallas are common lizards in parts of the park, but they are shy enough that you need a telephoto lens in order to photograph them.

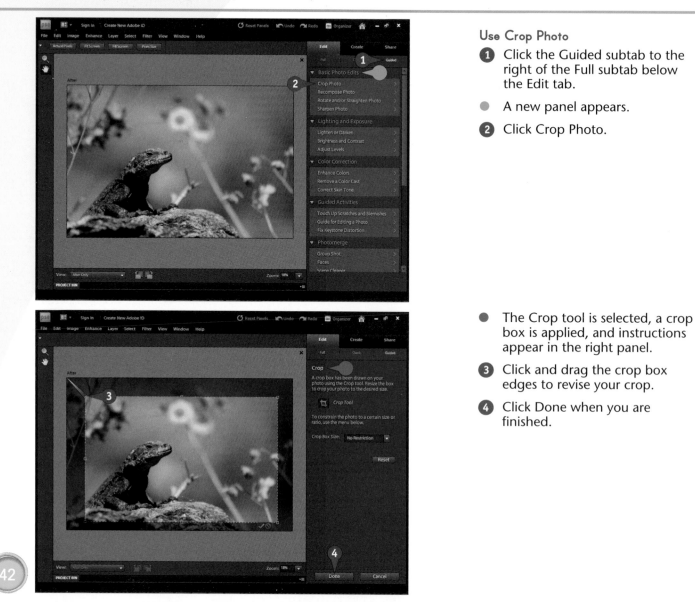

Use Crop Photo

① Click the Guided subtab to the right of the Full subtab below the Edit tab.

● A new panel appears.

② Click Crop Photo.

● The Crop tool is selected, a crop box is applied, and instructions appear in the right panel.

③ Click and drag the crop box edges to revise your crop.

④ Click Done when you are finished.

Use Enhance Colors

1 Click Enhance Colors.

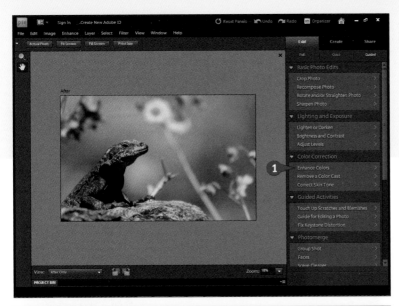

2 Click Auto if your colors seem off.

Photoshop Elements adjusts the colors.

3 Drag the Hue slider to change the colors in your photo.

4 Drag the Saturation slider to change the intensity of the colors.

5 Drag the Lightness slider to change the brightness of colors.

6 Click Done when you are finished.

TIPS

Caution!

It is easy to overdo several controls in the Guided Edit panel, creating problems when you want to print your photo or use it in other ways. Be very careful with how strongly you use the brightness and contrast, sharpening, and saturation slider controls so they are not too extreme. No warnings about this appear in the panel.

Try This!

When using the Guided Edit panel, you may find that you inadvertently get adjustments you thought you canceled. That is not a problem. No harm is done, but do not try to correct the adjustment while still in the Guided Edit panel. Go to Edit Full and use your Undo History panel.

Remember This!

Almost all the panels in Guided Edit have a Reset button. This can be a real help. On some of the panels, it is easy to go quickly and overadjust certain controls. It can be hard and confusing to try to readjust them back to zero. Instead, click the Reset button.

USE GUIDED EDIT
for special effects

All sorts of special effects reside inside Photoshop Elements. One of the challenges with using special effects has always been how to apply them. Usually they require more than one step, and how do you know which steps to use?

Photoshop Elements 9 has a number of special effects which Adobe calls Photographic Effects and Fun Edits. These are at the bottom of the Guided Edit panel. If you like special effects, it can be worth experimenting with all of these just to see what happens. Remember

that you cannot hurt your image unless you save over it. You can apply any of these effects then go back to Full Edit and undo them in the Undo History panel.

These effects typically have a series of steps as shown in the example here. As you go through these steps, instructions tell you what they do and what your options are. You can take the steps as laid out in the Guided Edit or you can skip steps that do not seem to do what you want. There is no right or wrong to how you work with special effects.

① Click the Guided subtab to the right of the Full subtab below the Edit tab.

● A new panel appears.

② Scroll down to the bottom of the panel.

③ Click Line Drawing in Photographic Effects.

● A new panel appears.

④ Click Pencil Sketch.

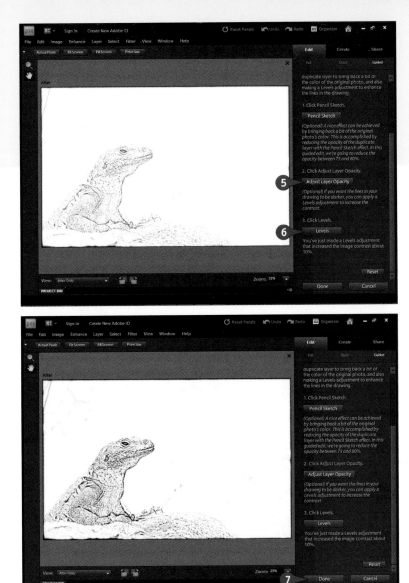

The image changes and starts to look like a pencil sketch.

⑤ Click Adjust Layer Opacity if you want some of the original color of the photograph to reappear.

⑥ Click Levels if you want the lines in the "sketch" to be darker.

⑦ Click Done when you are finished.

TIPS

Try This!

Action Player is a unique part of Photoshop Elements 9. Actions are ways of playing back adjustments and changes you are making to a photograph so that you can duplicate those same adjustments and changes on another image, and they have long been part of Photoshop. Photoshop Elements has simplified actions and gives you seven different actions to start with that include such things as adding neutral borders around your photographs and adding captions. You can create your own actions, but to do that, you need to go to Photoshop Elements' very fine Help file and look up creating and adding your own action sets.

Have Fun!

Special effects can be a fun way to play with images. Sometimes they can create fascinating and dramatic photographs from what started out as rather average images. Do not have any expectations when you are first trying special effects. Just try them and have fun with them.

Did You Know?

Photoshop Elements uses layers for special effects. Layers are explained in Chapter 5. Layers give you more flexibility in how you apply special effects because the original image sits underneath the special effect.

SET BLACKS AND WHITES
with Levels

A very important part of any photograph is how the pure black and pure white elements of the image are adjusted. Many cameras do not give a pure black in the image files. Camera designers recognize that black needs vary depending on the type of photography, so they keep this adjustment minimal with the expectation that the photographer should adjust it.

For most pictures, you want a pure black and a pure white somewhere in the picture. Without a proper black and white, the picture will not have the best color, the best contrast, or the best overall look.

Photographers are often amazed at how much only adjusting the blacks and whites affects the look of the picture. This is a good starting point for any photograph.

The photograph here is of a young girl during a quiet moment at her birthday party. Moments like these can add a lot of depth to your photography. Stay alert and take pictures beyond the expected times. The background here is outdoors and in the sun. It will be overexposed if the girl is exposed properly, so that area will be pure white when adjusting for blacks and whites.

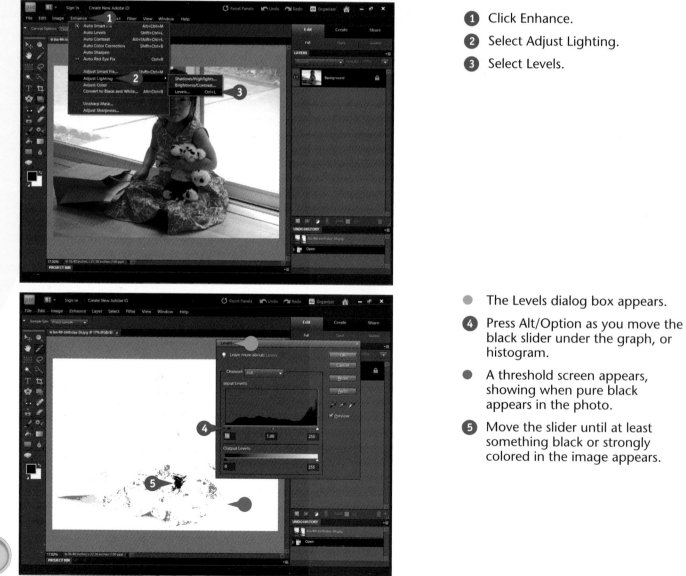

1 Click Enhance.

2 Select Adjust Lighting.

3 Select Levels.

● The Levels dialog box appears.

4 Press Alt/Option as you move the black slider under the graph, or histogram.

● A threshold screen appears, showing when pure black appears in the photo.

5 Move the slider until at least something black or strongly colored in the image appears.

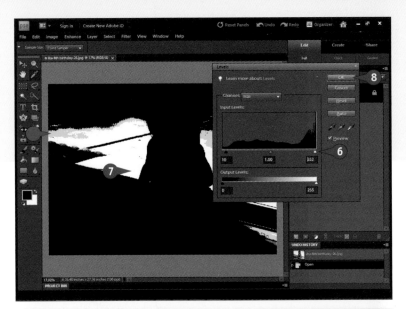

6 Press Alt/Option as you move the white slider under the graph or histogram.

● A threshold screen appears showing when pure white appears in the photo.

7 Move the slider until at least something shows.

White is very sensitive, so you can stop when colors appear on or near your subject. Do not worry about very bright areas that are not part of your subject.

8 Click OK when you are done.

The image in the work area now has better color and contrast.

9 Click between Open and Levels in Undo History to see the differences.

19

DIFFICULTY LEVEL

ADJUST YOUR MIDTONES
with Levels

When you set blacks properly, you often find your photo is too dark. Actually it is not the whole photo that is too dark, but the *midtones*, the tonalities between black and white. In addition, you may find that digital photos have their dark tones too dark, making the photos muddy or murky with ill-defined and dark colors that do not reveal themselves well.

In fact, these middle tonalities are extremely important to your photograph. They affect the overall brightness of the image, the colors of the photo, and the ability of a viewer to see detail within the picture,

including the dark tones. Some photographers refer to brightening the midtones as "opening up" certain tonalities. This is a good way to look at it. You are trying to open up certain parts of the picture so that the viewer can better see them.

This adjustment is subjective. There is no right or wrong. You have to look at your picture and decide what is the right interpretation for the subject and for how you saw it. It is important, however, to calibrate your monitor so that your adjustments are predictable and consistent.

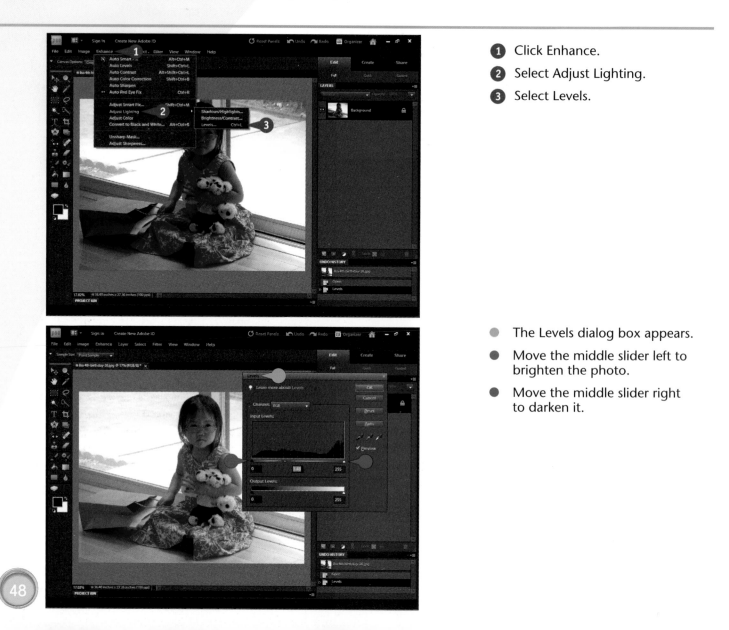

1 Click Enhance.

2 Select Adjust Lighting.

3 Select Levels.

● The Levels dialog box appears.

● Move the middle slider left to brighten the photo.

● Move the middle slider right to darken it.

④ Select and deselect the Preview check box (☐ changes to ☑ and vice versa) to turn the view of the adjustment on and off.

This enables you to better see what is happening in the photo.

⑤ Click OK when you are done.

The image in your work area now has more open midtones and color.

⑥ Click between Open, Levels, and Levels in Undo History to see the differences.

The two Levels make it easy to see the different adjustments.

TIPS

Did You Know?

By separating the adjustments into two instances or uses of Levels, you can more easily see the adjustments and make corrections to them. This step-by-step approach also keeps the steps separate in the Undo History panel. That makes it easier for you to find exactly where a particular adjustment is affecting your picture.

Did You Know?

The graph in the Levels dialog box is called a *histogram*, which is a chart of the brightness values of the pixels in your photograph. As you adjust Levels, you see small gaps, or white lines, appear in the histogram. Gaps are not a problem. Whether this *combing* of the histogram (as it is called) is a problem depends on what you see happening to the photo. Pay attention to your photo, not arbitrary computer rules.

Important!

The middle slider in the Levels dialog box is a midtones slider, but it affects more than just the very middle tones. As you work in Photoshop Elements, you will start noticing differences between the dark tones with details, middle tones, and bright tones with details.

ADJUST YOUR MIDTONES
with Color Curves

Another way of adjusting midtones is to use Color Curves. Do not be misled by this name. Although the Color Curves adjustment affects color to a degree, it really is a way of affecting tonalities.

The midtones slider in the Levels dialog box affects midtones separately from blacks and whites, with most of the adjustment near the middle tones. You cannot adjust darker tones separately from lighter tones, for example.

Color Curves enables you to separate these adjustments by using what are called parametric sliders. The sliders in Color Curves are called *parametric* sliders because

they affect very specific parameters. They include making highlights brighter or darker, changing the brightness or darkness as well as the contrast of middle tones, and making shadows brighter or darker.

This gives you more control over the whole range of tones in your picture between the blacks and the whites. This can enable you to open up dark areas, while keeping bright areas at their original darkness, for example. This is important because the camera often captures tonalities in a scene far differently from the way you see them. Color Curves gives you one way of adjusting for that.

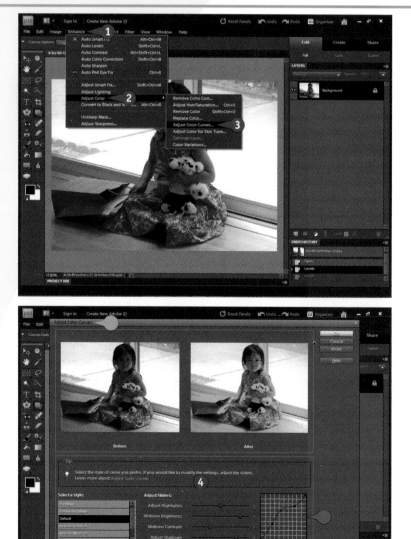

① Click Enhance.

② Select Adjust Color.

③ Select Adjust Color Curves.

● The Adjust Color Curves dialog box appears.

④ Move the parametric sliders to adjust specific tones in your photo.

Moving the sliders to the right makes tones brighter or contrast higher.

Moving the sliders to the left makes tones darker or contrast less.

● The graph, which shows curves for the adjustments, changes as you move the sliders, but you do not have to know anything about it to use this tool.

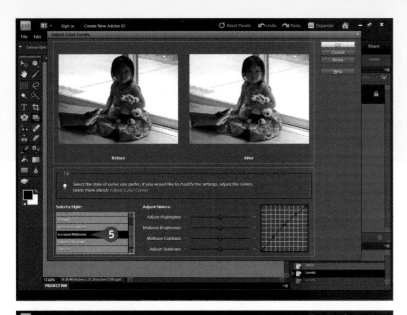

5 Select a style at the left side to create adjustments semiautomatically based on the short descriptions that appear in the tip section.

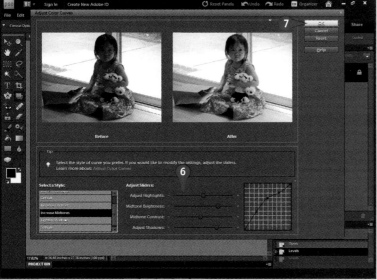

6 Click and adjust the parametric sliders as needed to tweak the style.

The image in your work area now has adjusted midtones.

7 Click OK when you are done.

TIPS

Did You Know?
Right in the middle of the Adjust Color Curves dialog box you will see a tip. Photoshop Elements provides tips throughout the program. If you are unsure about some adjustment, for example, you can often click the blue highlighted part of the tip in order to learn more about the adjustment.

Did You Know?
Color Curves is named after an important adjustment in Photoshop called Curves. As you adjust individual tonalities within a picture, such as highlights separately from shadows, the graph creates curves in its main line; thus the name Curves. The graph represents black at the bottom left and white at the top right.

Try This!
Quick adjustments are better than slow adjustments. Many photographers try to make small adjustments when working in Photoshop Elements. Seeing the difference between a good and a bad adjustment is easier if you make the adjustments quickly.

QUICKLY ADJUST
dark shadows and bright highlights

One challenge that consistently faces photographers is a scene that has very bright highlights, or bright areas, and very dark shadows, or dark areas, all within the photo you want to take. The camera then has trouble balancing the brightness throughout the picture. You can see the shadows and highlights just fine, but the camera cannot see them the way you do.

Photoshop Elements can help with this with an adjustment control called Shadows/Highlights. This control searches out the darkest parts of the picture and then adjusts them while limiting the adjustment

to those tones. It also finds the brightest parts of the picture and then limits any adjustments to them. Shadows/Highlights is a very handy control to know about, but you should use it after you adjust blacks and whites as well as midtones.

The photo here is of cholla cactus in Joshua Tree National Park. Shooting into the sun is a dramatic way to use light, but it also creates a high-contrast image. If you brighten the overall picture, the sun pattern in the sky becomes weaker. Being able to selectively affect dark areas is very helpful.

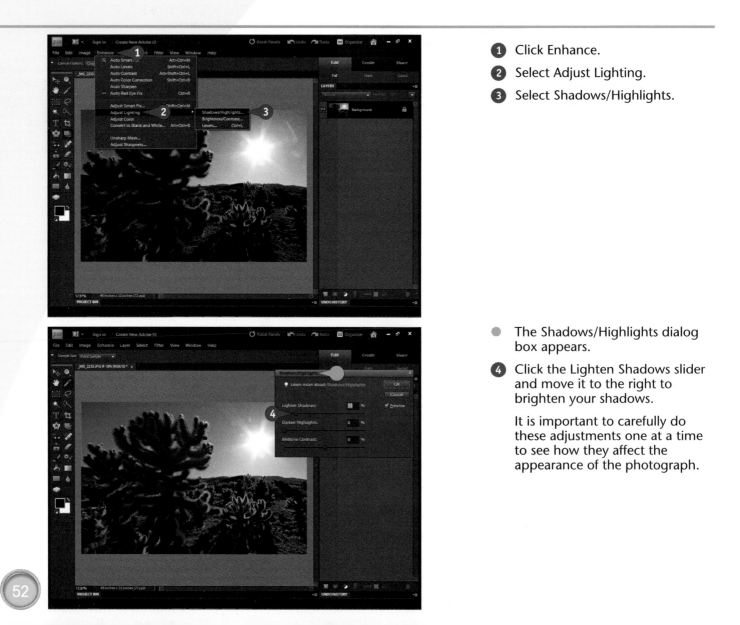

① Click Enhance.

② Select Adjust Lighting.

③ Select Shadows/Highlights.

● The Shadows/Highlights dialog box appears.

④ Click the Lighten Shadows slider and move it to the right to brighten your shadows.

It is important to carefully do these adjustments one at a time to see how they affect the appearance of the photograph.

#22

DIFFICULTY LEVEL

⑤ Click the Darken Highlights slider and move it to the right to make your highlights have more color and detail.

⑥ Click the Midtone Contrast slider and move it to the right or left to make the picture look more natural.

⑦ Click OK to finish.

The adjusted photo now appears in the central work area of Photoshop Elements.

⑧ Click different lines, called states, of Undo History to see if the adjustments are doing what you want done to your image.

Note: *Double-click the bar to the right of the Undo History tab to open or close this panel.*

TIPS

Important!

Shadows/Highlights is no magic bullet — it cannot cure all contrast problems in a photograph. Your picture must have detail to work with in the dark and light areas. Shadows/Highlights cannot add detail that the camera did not originally capture, so it helps to be aware of what your camera can and cannot do with contrasty scenes.

Did You Know?

Noise creates a sandlike pattern in a picture and can be very annoying. Noise is rarely noticeable in bright areas with normal exposures. However, it lurks, hidden in the dark areas of the picture. When you brighten dark areas with Shadows/Highlights, noise often becomes more obvious. See task #33 for more on noise.

Caution!

The Shadows/Highlights control is easy to overdo. Watch your picture. Do not simply adjust it so you can see lots of detail in shadows or more detailed highlights. That can result in unnatural-looking images. Make your adjustments so that your picture looks like it was taken on this planet!

CORRECT COLOR
to remove color casts

Color casts are those slight overall colors that seem to permeate the picture. They make neutral colors no longer neutral, and can hurt the appearance of colors so the colors are no longer accurate to the way you saw them. Color casts can cause problems for your subject and your rendition of the scene.

Many outdoor scenes have natural color casts, especially at sunrise or sunset. Auto white balance in digital cameras can sometimes remove important color casts, so you need to adjust your picture to return to the actual color of the scene. In this photograph at Kelso Dunes in the Mojave Desert

National Reserve in California, auto white balance has removed some of the color from the low sun.

Color casts come from all sorts of things, such as fluorescent lights, blue skies, and improper white balance, which fill a scene with colors, compromising the look of an image. They used to be a big problem with film, but they are less of one with digital because of the *white balance control*. White balance reduces color casts due to the color of light. This helps, but you can still get a picture with color casts that need to be corrected.

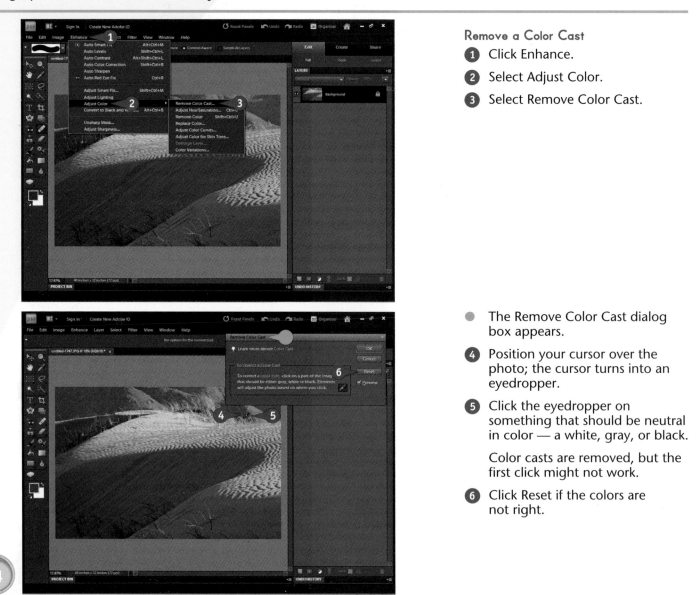

Remove a Color Cast

1 Click Enhance.

2 Select Adjust Color.

3 Select Remove Color Cast.

- The Remove Color Cast dialog box appears.

4 Position your cursor over the photo; the cursor turns into an eyedropper.

5 Click the eyedropper on something that should be neutral in color — a white, gray, or black.

Color casts are removed, but the first click might not work.

6 Click Reset if the colors are not right.

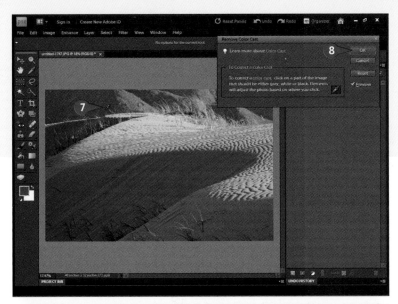

7 Keep clicking different tones that should be neutral, clicking Reset if the colors are bad, until you get a good color balance.

8 Click OK to finish.

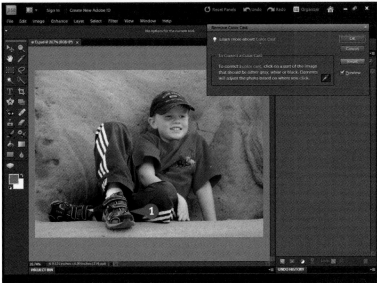

Remove Another Color Cast

This technique works great for people photographs.

1 With the Remove Color Cast dialog box open, click different tones in the photo that should be neutral until the color is corrected.

TIPS

Did You Know?
The Levels dialog box has three eyedroppers on the right side. The black and white eyedroppers affect blacks and whites, but they are heavy-handed and not as effective as using the Levels sliders. The middle eyedropper is, in fact, essentially the same eyedropper as the one used in the Remove Color Cast dialog box.

Did You Know?
You can further adjust the color of skin tones by clicking Adjust Color in the Enhance menu and then clicking Adjust Color for Skin Tone. In this control, you click the skin of a person and Photoshop Elements adjusts the color of the whole picture to make the skin look better. You can further tweak this with some sliders.

Try This!
As you click around in your photograph, you will often find the picture changes to some rather odd colors. That is not a problem because you can click the Reset button. However, you may sometimes find these colors interesting. You can even try clicking any color in the picture just to see what happens.

ENHANCE COLOR
with Hue/Saturation

When photographers discover that they can increase *saturation*, or the color intensity, of the picture with Hue/Saturation, they sometimes take the option too far. The saturation control in Hue/Saturation can very quickly go from enhancing colors to making them look garish.

Although you can adjust the overall colors with Saturation, be careful that you do not overdo it. An adjustment of 10 points or so is usually plenty. The best way to adjust the saturation in a picture is to adjust individual colors. Your camera does not capture colors equally, so adjusting individual colors is a way of getting better color with any photograph.

In this desert scene from the Mojave Desert National Preserve, brightly colored cactus flowers are in the foreground. This image was shot with a wide-angle lens close to the ground and the cactus. The background sky is somewhat weak in color, but if the overall color were adjusted to affect it, the flowers would be too intense.

Hue/Saturation also enables you to adjust the color of the color, or its *hue*. Using the techniques described here, you can, for example, correct the hue of a flower or change the color of someone's jacket by changing the Hue slider.

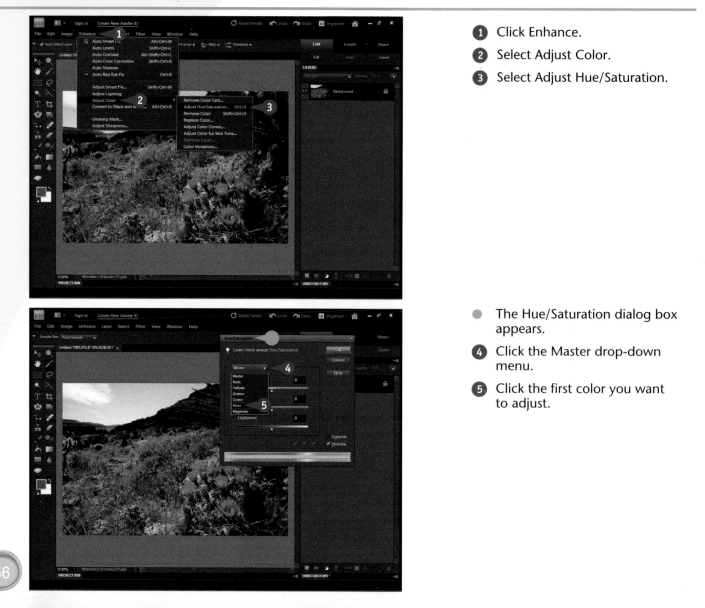

① Click Enhance.

② Select Adjust Color.

③ Select Adjust Hue/Saturation.

● The Hue/Saturation dialog box appears.

④ Click the Master drop-down menu.

⑤ Click the first color you want to adjust.

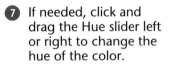

- The Master menu now changes to the color you have selected and Photoshop Elements restricts adjustments to that color.

6 Click and drag the Saturation slider to the right to increase saturation.

7 If needed, click and drag the Hue slider left or right to change the hue of the color.

8 Click in the Master drop-down menu again to pick a new color.

9 Click and drag the Saturation slider to the right to increase this color's saturation.

10 Click and drag the Hue slider if needed.

11 Click OK to finish.

TIPS

Try This!

Use your cursor to click in the photo to define color for Hue/Saturation. Once you have selected a color in the Master menu, simply position your cursor over the picture and it turns into an eyedropper. Click the color in the photo and Hue/Saturation identifies that color more precisely.

Did You Know?

Lightness looks like it should be a good control in Hue/Saturation. Unfortunately it is not. It tends to dull colors instead of making them lighter or darker. Using it in small amounts is okay, but you will find that your colors do not look their best if you try to use it more than that.

Caution!

Be wary of oversaturating your pictures. This control quickly blocks up your colors and makes them look garish if you are not careful. Make your adjustments quickly so that you can see how different the colors are changing and so that your eye does not get used to the gradual color changes.

USE QUICK EDIT
to work fast

Sometimes you have pictures that you want to work on quickly. You may have promised some prints to a friend, or maybe you need to get them ready for presentation. Although all the controls that you have seen in this chapter work well, one challenge is that you have to open up each control individually. That takes time.

The photo seen here is a simple portrait of a mother and her son. This was shot with soft light coming from a bright sky in front of the people. This is the kind of shot that people want quickly and do not

necessarily want to wait until you get around to seriously processing the image.

In Photoshop Elements Quick Edit, you gain a number of adjustments all in one place that do not need to be opened separately. You cannot control these adjustments as much as the main controls, and they are not as flexible. However, they do work quickly. Quick Edit also includes some auto controls. These can be helpful for fast adjustments, but they can take you in the wrong directions for your picture because they are based on formulas instead of what your picture actually looks like.

① Click the Quick subtab below and to the right of the Edit tab.

● The Quick Edit panel opens with a variety of adjustments.

② Try clicking Auto in Smart Fix, though Smart Fix may or may not help your photo.

③ Tweak Smart Fix if the photo looks almost good enough using the Fix slider.

If you do not like any adjustment, you can move the Amount slider back to zero or press Ctrl/⌘+Z to undo the change.

④ Select the check mark to accept the adjustments or the X to cancel them.

Note: After each of the trial auto fixes mentioned below, select the check mark to accept the adjustments or the X to cancel them.

⑤ Click the small triangle to close any panel when you no longer need it.

⑥ Click the Levels and Contrast Auto buttons to see if they help your photo.

If you do not like what these auto functions do, use Ctrl/⌘+Z to remove their adjustments.

⑦ Adjust the Lighting sliders to make your photo gain the right tonalities.

8 Click the Color Auto button to see if it helps the photo.

9 Adjust the overall color saturation as needed.

10 Adjust Temperature and Tint to affect color casts and the warmth of a photo.

11 Click the Magnifier tool in the toolbox at the left to start working with Sharpness.

12 Click the photo to magnify important details.

13 Click the Hand tool in the toolbox at the left to move the position of your magnified image.

14 Adjust the Sharpen slider to give an attractive amount of sharpening to your photo.

TIPS

Try This!

Try the auto controls, but if they do not work, immediately press Ctrl/⌘+Z. Auto controls are based on formulas developed by the Photoshop Elements designers. They can work, but they are also somewhat arbitrary because a designer cannot know every person's photos. If things get mixed up, go back to Full Edit and use the Undo History panel.

Did You Know?

Smart Fix is a useful adjustment when the photo looks a bit off right from the start. For many photos, however, you will find that using Levels and Contrast Auto buttons gives better results. You can use Levels alone or add Contrast — this gives you more options and control.

Try This!

You can also use Quick Fix as a starting point for other adjustments. You do not have to make this an either/or question; that is, use Edit Full or Quick Edit. Use Quick Edit to start the process and then refine your adjustments in Edit Full. If you do this, do not use the Sharpen panel area.

Work with RAW Photos in Photoshop Elements

The RAW format available in all digital single lens reflex (dSLR) cameras is a distinct choice from JPEG shooting. Some advanced compact digital cameras also have the RAW format. You can get outstanding results from digital photos whether they are shot in JPEG or RAW.

However, RAW maximizes the information that comes from your sensor and includes a great deal more tone and color steps than are possible with JPEG. This gives you a lot more flexibility when processing an image. RAW files enable you to dig more detail out of bright areas in a picture, unearth more tones in dark areas, and ensure better gradations when adjusting smooth gradients like skies and out-of-focus sections of a photo. You can do a lot of things with a JPEG image in Photoshop Elements, but you can do more with a RAW file.

One problem is that RAW is a proprietary camera file. Every time a new camera comes out, there is also a new version of that RAW file. You have to update the Camera Raw part of Photoshop Elements to access the new version, and you have to wait until Adobe has unraveled the new version as well.

Top 100

#26 Change Images Nondestructively . . . . 62 DIFFICULTY LEVEL

#27 Crop Your Photos to Start Your Processing . . . . 64 DIFFICULTY LEVEL

#28 Adjust Blacks and Whites to Give a Photo Strength . . . . 66 DIFFICULTY LEVEL

#29 Adjust Midtones to Make Tonalities Light or Dark . . . . 68 DIFFICULTY LEVEL

#30 Correct Color to Clean Up Color Casts . . . . 70 DIFFICULTY LEVEL

#31 Use Vibrance and Clarity to Intensify Images . . . . 72 DIFFICULTY LEVEL

#32 Sharpen Photos with Precision . . . . 74 DIFFICULTY LEVEL

#33 Control Noise in Your Photo . . . . 76 DIFFICULTY LEVEL

#34 Apply Adjustments to Multiple Photos . . . . 78 DIFFICULTY LEVEL

#35 Move Your Picture to Photoshop Elements . . . . 80 DIFFICULTY LEVEL

Change images
NONDESTRUCTIVELY

A RAW file is an incomplete photograph. You cannot display such an image file or even print from it without some sort of processing. You can always display a JPEG image in all sorts of programs on your computer, plus you can take a JPEG file straight from the camera and have a print made. That is an advantage of JPEG files. However, RAW files include a great deal of tonal and color information that you can use while processing such files in Camera Raw, Photoshop Elements' RAW software.

A RAW file must be interpreted by software for it to become a photograph. No changes are ever made to the original RAW file. All adjustments are instructions the computer uses to interpret and process the RAW file. This is called *nondestructive processing* because no pixels from the original file are ever changed. This can be very freeing to you as a photographer because it means you can try almost anything and never damage the original file.

The photo here is of an alligator in Florida. It was photographed from a boardwalk through a wetland in the Alligator Farm in St. Augustine. A 400mm telephoto lens was used to get the close shot.

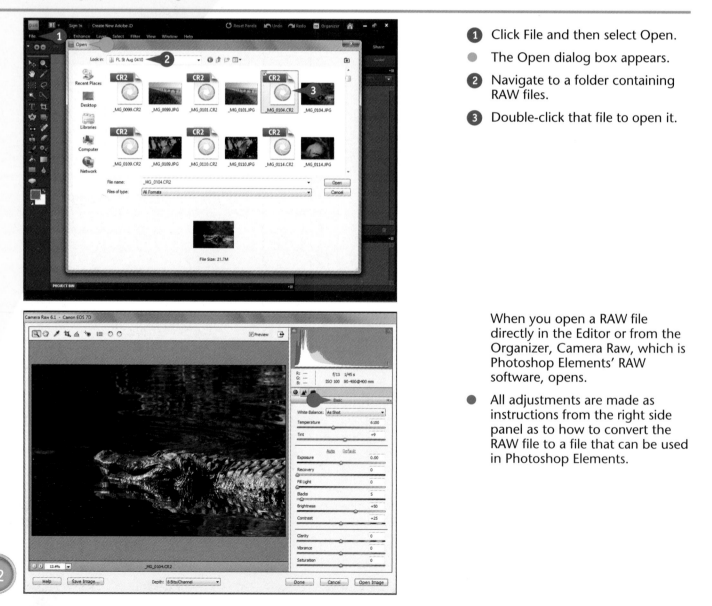

1 Click File and then select Open.

● The Open dialog box appears.

2 Navigate to a folder containing RAW files.

3 Double-click that file to open it.

When you open a RAW file directly in the Editor or from the Organizer, Camera Raw, which is Photoshop Elements' RAW software, opens.

● All adjustments are made as instructions from the right side panel as to how to convert the RAW file to a file that can be used in Photoshop Elements.

- The Camera Raw interface offers a lot of adjustments that do not require you to go to a menu.

- The interface also includes a simple toolbox of frequently used tools for photographs.

TIPS

Did You Know?

Whenever you work directly on a photograph in Photoshop Elements, you are working directly on pixels. Those pixels are then changed, which is called *destructive editing*, because the original pixel data is "destroyed" as changes are applied. Camera Raw allows you to make nondestructive changes.

Try This!

You can change the magnification of the displayed photo in Camera Raw by using the magnifier in the toolbox and clicking or dragging the photograph. You can also click the magnification number at the lower left of the photograph to get a drop-down menu of specific magnification sizes.

Did You Know?

JPEG is a processed RAW file. The camera takes the image data coming from the sensor and processes it quickly. The JPEG is a locked-down, camera-processed RAW file. It is good that this file is processed optimally for the particular camera being used, and the file size is much reduced, but it also means the flexibility of the original RAW file is lost.

CROP YOUR PHOTOS
to start your processing

The world does not always cooperate and give you the opportunity to make perfect pictures every time. Sometimes the world does not fit the frame defined by your camera. At other times, stuff creeps in along the edges of your picture that really does not belong with your subject. Or you may find that you simply need to tighten up the composition of your photo so that the subject shows up more clearly to the viewer.

You should remove extraneous things from your photograph as soon as you start working on an image. This allows you to really focus on the important part of the picture and not let unimportant things distract you. It also allows you to adjust the picture optimally for what needs to be adjusted and not be influenced by other parts of the original picture; the controls in the Camera Raw software affect everything in the picture, so they can be influenced by parts of the photograph you really do not want.

Cropping is what enables you to keep the details that detract from your image, or the "junk," out of your picture and refine it to the key elements of your subject and scene.

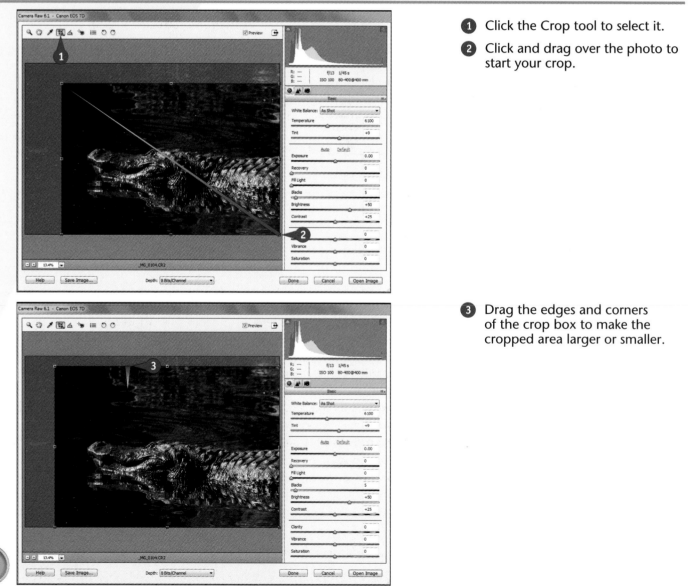

1 Click the Crop tool to select it.

2 Click and drag over the photo to start your crop.

3 Drag the edges and corners of the crop box to make the cropped area larger or smaller.

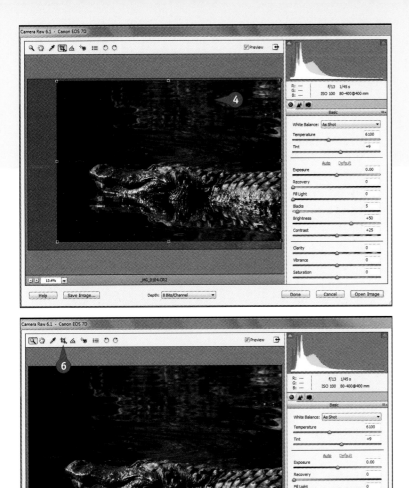

4 Click inside the photo and drag the crop box to reposition it.

5 Press Enter to see the photo as cropped in the work area.

6 Click the Crop tool at any time to go back and recrop the image.

No crop is permanent; a crop can be changed at any time.

TIPS

Did You Know?

You can recrop at any time. This is part of the whole idea of the nondestructive processing of an image. Camera Raw remembers how you cropped a particular RAW file, and lets you change that at any time, even after closing the file (Done or Open Image) and reopening it.

More Options!

You can rotate your crop box by simply positioning your cursor outside the box so that the cursor changes to a curved double-arrow cursor; then you click and drag to rotate. You can remove or clear your crop by right-clicking the photo to get a menu that includes Clear Crop.

More Options!

You can crop to specific proportions within Camera Raw; however, they are not specific to inches. You can get the specific proportions by either right-clicking the photograph when using the Crop tool to get a context-sensitive menu, or by clicking and holding the Crop tool to get the same menu.

ADJUST BLACKS AND WHITES
to give a photo strength

Chapter 2 describes the importance of adjusting blacks and whites in a photograph. This is a very important adjustment to make in Camera Raw because it sets the tonalities for everything else. You have even more flexibility and control when doing this in Camera Raw. You can not only adjust the blacks and whites, but you can also adjust the brightness of the very dark areas and the very bright areas separately. In addition, you can bring out added detail in the darkest and brightest areas that might otherwise be lost.

Blacks can be especially important in giving a photograph and its colors strength. Adjusting blacks is very subjective, but also important. You will find that some photographs need minimal black areas, whereas others need quite large areas of black throughout them. Photoshop Elements helps you out, in a way, by calling this adjustment Blacks. Whites are adjusted, on the other hand, by Exposure. However, Exposure is misnamed and you should not use Exposure for adjusting the overall brightness or darkness of the picture. You will be doing that with midtones as described in the next task.

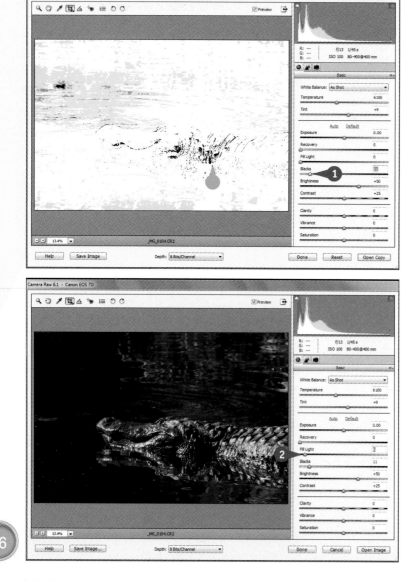

1 Press Alt/Option and click and drag the Blacks slider.

The blacks threshold screen appears.

● Watch where the pure blacks and maxed-out color channels appear.

Note: *Where anything shows as pure black, it will be a pure black in the photo. Where anything shows as a color, you will be maxing out a certain color in that area.*

2 Adjust the Fill Light slider to give a boost to the darkest areas.

Beware of overadjusting Fill Light so that the photo looks unnatural.

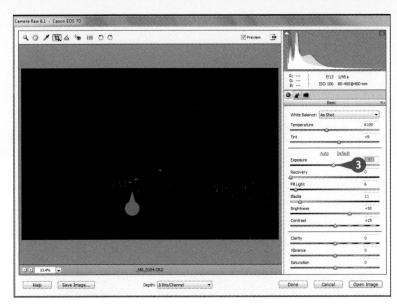

#28

DIFFICULTY LEVEL

③ Press Alt/Option and click and drag the Exposure (whites) slider.

The whites threshold screen appears.

● Watch where the pure whites and maxed-out color channels appear.

Whites are very sensitive and should be adjusted cautiously. You can adjust exposure both + and – to get better results.

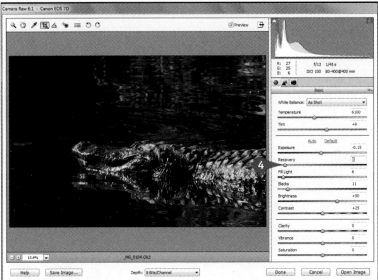

④ Adjust the Recovery slider when highlights look weak and washed out.

Often the Recovery slider is not needed and just makes your photo look dull. Never feel you have to use either the Recovery or Fill Light sliders.

TIPS

Did You Know?

Photographers often refer to the black areas of a photograph as the *blacks* but not because black comes in different brightnesses — it obviously does not. This use of the term *blacks* refers to all the small areas of black scattered throughout the photograph.

Did You Know?

Some people wonder why you need to adjust both the Blacks and Fill Light sliders. They seem to counteract each other. However, such an adjustment gives a different, better look to the dark areas of the picture than occurs if you adjust either one alone or neither one at all.

Important!

Always adjust your blacks first, before using the Fill Light, Exposure, and Recovery sliders. Setting your blacks right away enables you to better see your adjustments for tonality and color. If you adjust Fill Light first, you often find the picture starts to look very gray.

ADJUST MIDTONES
to make tonalities light or dark

In Chapter 2, you also learned about adjusting midtones in a photograph. Once again, this is a very important adjustment to make in Camera Raw. It makes the overall picture lighter or darker. This is where you work to deal with exposures that are a little too dark or a little too bright, not with the Exposure slider. If your photograph is very much underexposed, then you use Exposure to brighten the picture in the adjustment step before that because you need to get your whites bright so they look like whites.

Midtone adjustment makes the picture look right — neither dark and muddy nor bright and washed out.

Adjusting your overall tonalities in Camera Raw enables you to get the optimum results from these tones as well.

You adjust midtones using two sliders in Camera Raw in Photoshop Elements: Brightness and Contrast. Sometimes you will change only the Brightness slider, but just as often you will adjust both. You rarely adjust only the Contrast slider for most general types of photography, though it can be interesting for certain effects. Brightness and Contrast go well together for adjusting the midtones of your photograph.

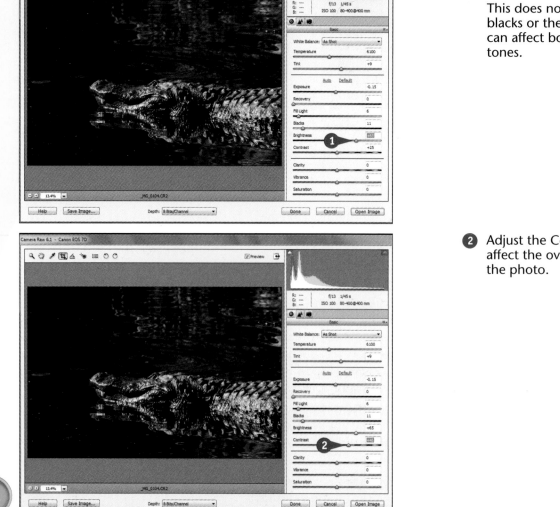

① Click and drag the Brightness slider to make the overall photo brighter or darker.

This does not affect either the blacks or the whites, although it can affect both bright and dark tones.

② Adjust the Contrast slider to affect the overall contrast of the photo.

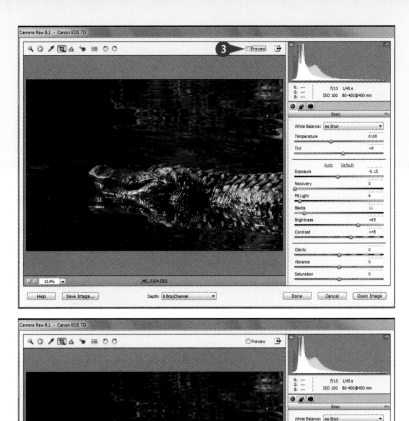

③ Select and deselect the Preview check box (☐ changes to ☑ and vice versa) to compare before-and-after adjustments.

④ Readjust the Brightness and Contrast sliders as needed to adapt to the interaction of these controls' changes.

TIPS

Important!
Adjust your blacks and whites first. Adjusting these tones truly does affect everything else in the photograph. Without a good black in most pictures, colors never look as good and images never print as well. Remember, though, that blacks are subjective and not all photos have them.

Did You Know?
Color is strongly affected by the blacks, whites, and midtones in the picture. Color is not simply a part of your subject; it is subjective and strongly affected by tones all around it. This is why adjusting your blacks, whites, and midtones before trying to control color is so important.

Important!
RAW is no magic bullet that can correct a bad exposure. You need to be especially sure that your bright areas are exposed properly in your image. RAW files have a lot more flexibility in how you can adjust an image, but they cannot bring in detail or tones that the camera and sensor did not originally capture.

CORRECT COLOR
to clean up color casts

Color casts are slight tints of color that appear over the entire photograph. They can be desirable and undesirable. If you are photographing at sunrise or sunset, you want a warm color cast for the photograph. But often, color casts are a problem. They keep you from clearly seeing the colors in a photograph and can put unwanted colors into neutral tones.

One problem that occurs with digital cameras is that auto white balance is inconsistent and often gives a bluish color cast to outdoor photos. You should therefore shoot a specific white balance instead of using auto white balance. Choose a white balance that matches the conditions or a white balance that warms up the scene.

However, you can correct unwanted color casts easily in Camera Raw by quickly making a correction and then undoing or redoing it as needed if you do not like it. Because everything in Camera Raw is nondestructive, this is never a problem. By repeatedly making corrections to color to clean up color casts in a photograph, you can learn about color casts and how to better see them.

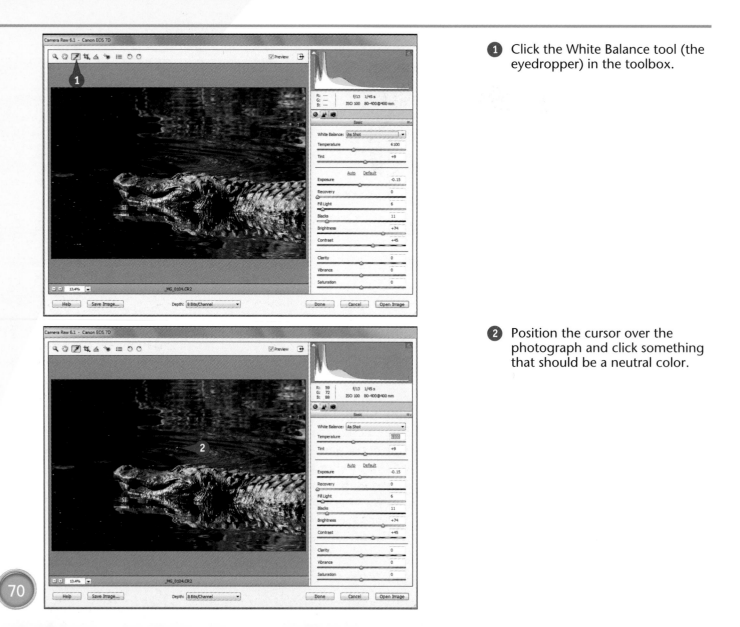

1 Click the White Balance tool (the eyedropper) in the toolbox.

2 Position the cursor over the photograph and click something that should be a neutral color.

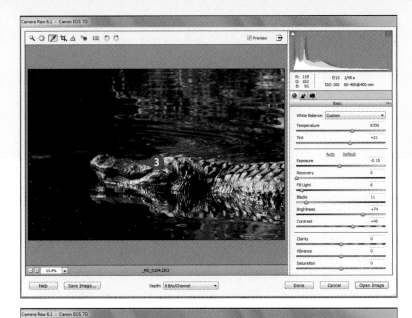

Camera Raw makes that neutral color neutral and removes a color cast. Note that it can also create a different color cast that may or may not be appropriate to the photo.

③ Try clicking another location to see if you get a better color.

When the color looks good, you are done.

If the color looks really bad, press Ctrl/⌘+Z to undo the last adjustment.

④ Change the Temperature and Tint sliders to further adjust the color.

TIPS

Try This!

You can use Camera Raw's white balance settings to affect your photograph. Click the White Balance down arrow and you get a drop-down menu of white balance settings. Click any one to see what it does to a photo and what the image looks like. These are not the same as settings on your camera, but are Adobe interpretations of white balance settings.

Caution!

Because the white balance settings in Camera Raw look like the settings on a camera, you might think they are the same settings, and that you could use them the same way even if you did not set a specific white balance while shooting. Although they are similar, these settings represent Adobe colors based on how Adobe engineers deal with colors for the settings. They are not the same as you get from setting a white balance during shooting.

Important!

RAW is sort of a magic bullet when it comes to white balance. You can change your white balance settings as much as you want without any harm to the picture, plus you can adjust a picture that is way out of balance quite easily. Still, selecting a white balance setting in your camera is best because this makes your colors more consistent and makes for less work in the computer.

USE VIBRANCE AND CLARITY
to intensify images

Vibrance and Clarity are two distinct adjustments in Camera Raw in Photoshop Elements. Vibrance affects color. This control can increase or decrease the intensity of a color. It is like Saturation, an older, much more heavy-handed tool, but Vibrance does not oversaturate colors as easily. Vibrance also affects less-saturated colors more than Saturation does and has a strong effect on skies.

Clarity adjusts the contrast of midtones, and it is a visual effect that is hard to explain. A way to see how it affects an image is to drag the slider all the way to the right, look at the effects on the picture, and then drag the slider all the way to the left and view those effects. Then move the slider in the direction that seems best for your picture, though generally not to one of the extremes.

These controls affect something that has been called *presence* in a photograph. Presence refers to how an image grabs your attention and makes it more "present" for you. It comes from the theater where an actor is said to have presence when he or she really comes alive for the audience.

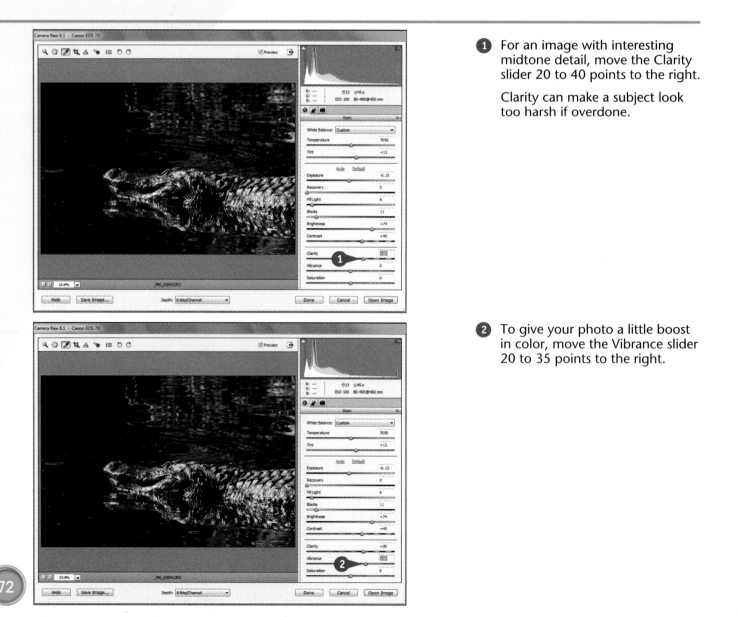

① For an image with interesting midtone detail, move the Clarity slider 20 to 40 points to the right.

Clarity can make a subject look too harsh if overdone.

② To give your photo a little boost in color, move the Vibrance slider 20 to 35 points to the right.

③ If the color looks good but seems to pick up a color cast, try adjusting the Temperature and Tint sliders.

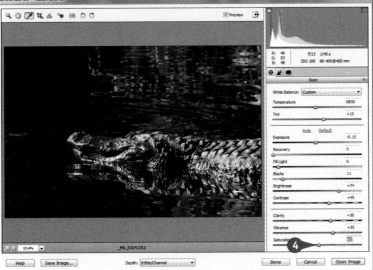

④ If you feel the photo still needs more lively colors, try moving the Saturation slider up to about 12 points.

Be wary of using the Saturation slider because its effects are easily overdone.

TIPS

Try This!

Whenever you want to reset a slider in Camera Raw, double-click the slider adjustment "knob." This immediately resets any slider to its default. It can be a good way of seeing exactly what your adjustment is doing to a picture. Just remember what your setting is before you double-click.

Did You Know?

Some people confuse Clarity with sharpness. Clarity is not sharpness, but a way of affecting a very specific contrast within your picture — the contrast of midtones. This can make a picture look like it is being sharpened, but Clarity is not as refined an adjustment as sharpening.

Attention!

Portraits and increased Clarity do not always go well together. Clarity intensifies pores, wrinkles, and defects in a person's skin, which is not always very flattering. In fact, portraits sometimes look better if Clarity is decreased so that skin texture is not as pronounced.

SHARPEN PHOTOS
with precision

Traditionally, the standard recommendation for sharpening has been to sharpen your image at the very end of your processing. This is because some of the strong adjustments to a photograph can affect sharpening. If you are doing all of your adjustments in Photoshop Elements, that would be true. Sharpen after you have done your adjustments.

However, the sharpening tools in Photoshop Elements Camera Raw offer newer algorithms than those in the main program and they work quite well. In addition, you are doing most of your strong adjustments in Camera Raw, so sharpening here is appropriate.

Finally, Camera Raw smartly applies sharpening at the right time during processing when you are done, no matter when you apply that sharpening while working on your photo.

With experience, you might find certain photographs require much more adjustment in Photoshop Elements itself. When that happens, you may decide to do sharpening at the end of all your adjustments. Photoshop Elements has good sharpening tools, so doing sharpening there instead of in Camera Raw is okay. But if Camera Raw becomes an important part of your workflow, you will do most of your sharpening in it.

① Click the Detail tab in the adjustment panel on the right.

● This opens the Sharpening and Noise Reduction adjustments.

② Click 100% in the magnification menu at the lower left so that you can better see the sharpening effects.

③ Move the Amount slider to the right until the image starts to look sharp, but no more.

DIFFICULTY LEVEL

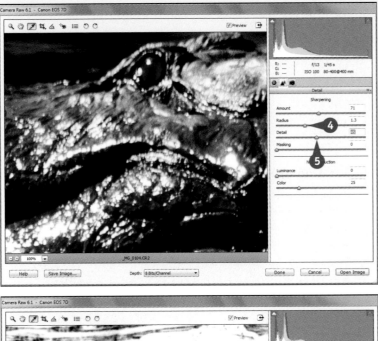

④ Try moving the Radius slider a little to the right to see if it helps your photo.

⑤ Use the Detail slider to help bring out small detail in the photograph.

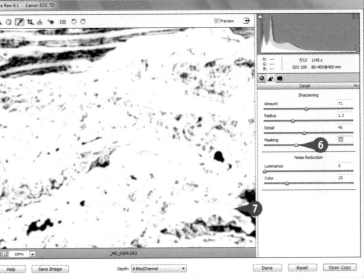

⑥ Use the Masking slider to limit your sharpening to the strongest edges.

⑦ Press Alt/Option to see the mask where white allows the sharpening and black blocks it.

Masking can be very important when your subject is sharp and the background is out of focus.

TIPS

Did You Know?

Amount controls the intensity of the sharpening. Radius affects how far sharpening is applied around pixel-sized detail. Detail modifies how strongly Radius interacts with Amount on details. Masking changes where sharpening is applied by blocking it from less-detailed areas.

Try This!

Press and hold Alt/Option as you adjust any of the Sharpening controls when the image is at 100% and the image changes to a black-and-white rendition of how that control is affecting the picture. Some photographers find it easier to see the sharpening effects this way because color can be distracting.

Did You Know?

High megapixels can be confusing when sharpening. The 100% setting is larger than you normally look at a photograph unless it is a really big print. This can make the detail look less sharp than it really will appear in the final print. Simply use the 100% setting as a guide to using the sharpening sliders.

CONTROL NOISE
in your photo

Noise is inherently a part of digital photography. The latest cameras control noise extremely well, especially with proper exposure. However, every camera has its own noise characteristics for an image file. Cameras with smaller image sensors have more noise — smaller sensors include the APS-C and Four Thirds sizes as well as all compact or point-and-shoot cameras. Higher ISO settings increase noise, and underexposure of a scene also increases noise in the final picture. All this makes noise more apparent as you sharpen the photo.

This is why Camera Raw includes Noise Reduction in the Detail tab along with Sharpening. Noise reduction

controls have been changed significantly in Camera Raw for Photoshop Elements 9. In the past, noise reduction in any Adobe product was only of limited value because it really did not affect strong noise. Now you can use the Noise Reduction sliders to good effect.

You can affect two types of noise — the sandlike pattern of luminance noise and the color pattern of color noise. Be careful about overusing noise reduction because it can make fine details in your photograph soft. If you find you have severe noise in an image, you need special software designed specifically for noise reduction.

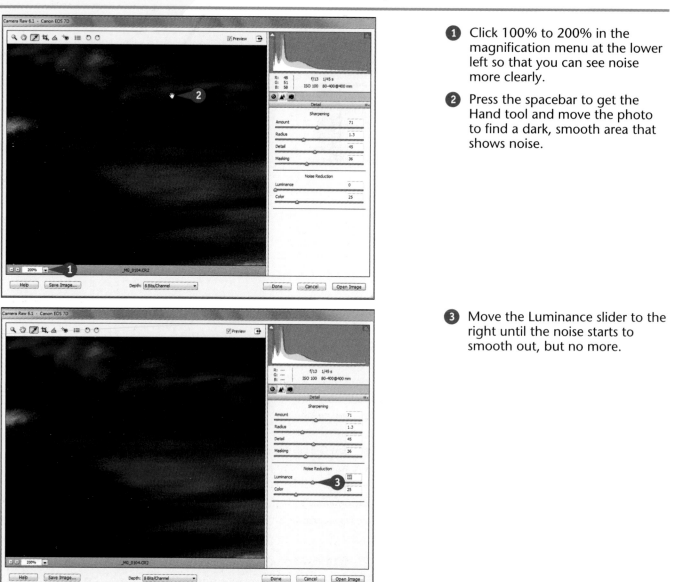

① Click 100% to 200% in the magnification menu at the lower left so that you can see noise more clearly.

② Press the spacebar to get the Hand tool and move the photo to find a dark, smooth area that shows noise.

③ Move the Luminance slider to the right until the noise starts to smooth out, but no more.

You can move the Color slider to the right if you see colored speckles that represent color noise.

④ Move the Color slider to the left from the default setting if, as in this example, no color noise is present.

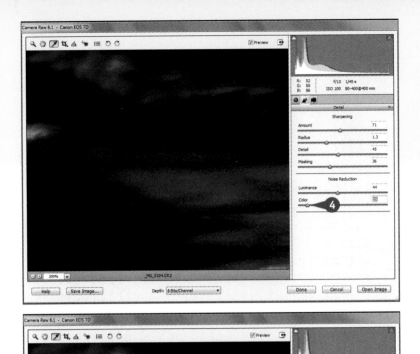

● Avoid high amounts of Luminance or Color noise reduction, as shown here, because it can adversely affect the small detail and color in your photo.

TIPS

Did You Know?

Dark areas show noise more quickly than any other parts of a photograph when they are brightened. This is why you should avoid underexposing your pictures, forcing you to brighten dark areas, thereby increasing noise.

Caution!

Noise is essentially tiny details in your picture. Reducing noise can also reduce other tiny details, so you need to be careful about how strongly you use the Noise Reduction sliders. The Color slider can also affect small but important color detail in your picture.

Check It Out!

When noise starts to become problematic in a photograph, you need to use other methods of noise reduction than what Camera Raw makes available. Dfine from Nik Software (www.nik software.com) and Noiseware from Imagenomic (www.imagenomic.com) are two programs that work well with Photoshop Elements. See task #92 for more about Dfine.

Apply adjustments to
MULTIPLE PHOTOS

Often, you will photograph a subject or scene a variety of ways. Yet the exposure and the light are basically the same among all these shots. The photos you see here are of a blister beetle feeding on brittlebrush in the Mojave Desert of Southern California. The light and exposure do not change much. It would be a nuisance to have to process each one of these individually, one at a time.

It would also take a lot of time to do that, but you do not have to. Camera Raw in Photoshop Elements allows you to apply multiple adjustments to

photographs at the same time. Process one image to your liking and then apply those same adjustments to all the rest. That is a big timesaver.

This is also a benefit for photographers who shoot certain subjects in standardized ways, such as portraits under a specific lighting setup. Portrait photographers, especially, often take a lot of pictures of a single subject or several subjects with few changes in exposure or lighting. Processing all those pictures would really be a pain if you could not do something to adjust all of them very quickly.

1 Ctrl/⌘+click to select several similar RAW images in Organizer that need the same sorts of adjustments.

2 Click the Fix tab down arrow.

3 Select Full Photo Edit to move the images to Camera Raw.

Camera Raw opens, now with a series of photos on the left. Be patient with your computer if this does not happen quickly.

4 Click the photo that can be adjusted most easily first.

That photo appears in the work area.

5 Click Select All to select the whole group of photos.

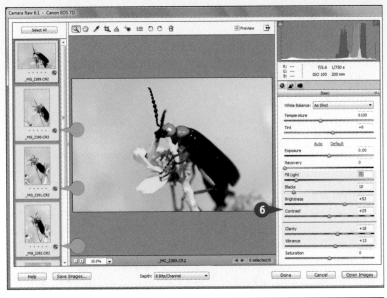

6 Adjust the work area photo as best you can.

● Adjustments are automatically applied to the other photos, as well.

7 Click any individual photo.

8 Refine the adjustments on that photo as needed.

● Adjustments are applied only to this photo.

TIPS

Try This!

You can use this technique when you want to change one or two adjustments for your group of pictures and not have everything changed as you go. First, make only the specific adjustments you want to use across multiple pictures. Then go in and perform the normal adjustments to individual pictures as needed.

Check It Out!

As you make adjustments, an icon (⬚) appears at the lower right-hand corner of your image that tells you adjustments have been made. This helps you keep track of which images have been adjusted if you are adjusting a group of photos one at a time.

Warning!

As you adjust your photographs in Camera Raw, you may notice a small yellow triangle with an exclamation point in it in the upper right-hand corner of the images. This is a warning icon, but not something you have to worry about. It indicates your computer is working on processing these images for display.

MOVE YOUR PICTURE
to Photoshop Elements

Once you are done working on your image in Camera Raw, you need to move your picture to the Photoshop Elements Editor. Camera Raw is a separate program from Photoshop Elements, so you have to get your pictures out of that program and loaded into Editor.

Everything you do in Camera Raw is just instructions on how to process and convert the image from the RAW file to an actual picture file. That offers a great benefit in using RAW and Camera Raw because you can make any adjustments you want to a photograph, yet they have no effect on the original image file. You

get an effect only when that file is converted to an image that can be used outside of Camera Raw. That conversion is based on the instructions that you created as you did processing inside Camera Raw.

These instructions are also saved as a separate, companion file to your RAW file, called an XMP file, so that if you open that RAW file again in Camera Raw, all your adjustments are still there. Because the RAW file cannot be changed, only converted, no adjustments are actually applied to any of the data in that file.

Move Your Picture to Photoshop Elements

1. Click the Depth pop-up menu.
2. Choose 8 Bits/Channel.
3. Click Open Image.

● The photo opens into Photoshop Elements, converted from the RAW file based on the adjustments you made in Camera Raw.

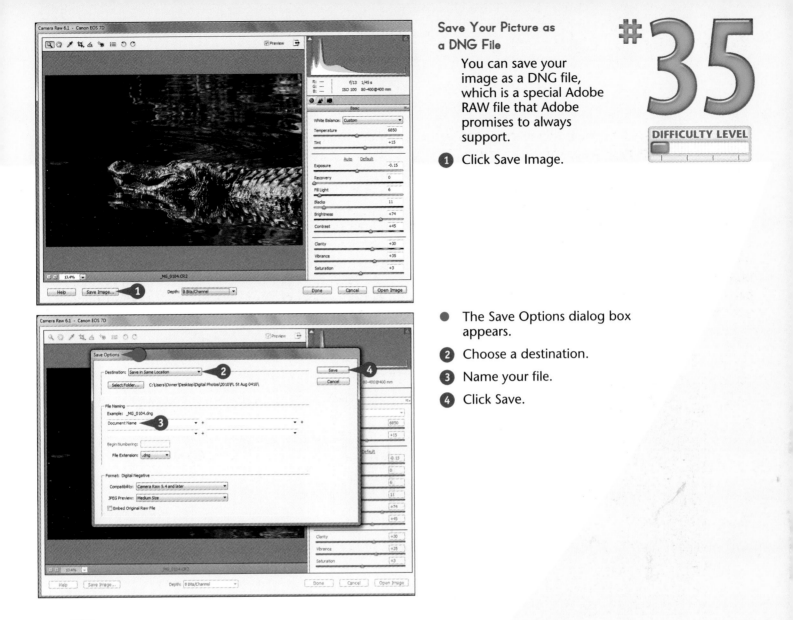

Save Your Picture as a DNG File

You can save your image as a DNG file, which is a special Adobe RAW file that Adobe promises to always support.

1 Click Save Image.

● The Save Options dialog box appears.

2 Choose a destination.

3 Name your file.

4 Click Save.

TIPS

Did You Know?

Bit depth represents how much processing flexibility you have in an image file. You are processing in Camera Raw at the maximum capability of 16-bit regardless of what you choose for export bit depth from the Depth option. Unless you are planning to do a lot of processing in Photoshop Elements, you can easily use the smaller 8-bit file there.

More Options!

The Done option for Camera Raw saves all of your adjustments as a separate XMP file with your image. XMP files are also created when you open a file in Photoshop Elements. You can use Done when working with a group of images that you want to adjust, but you do not need to open them all in Photoshop Elements for final work now.

Did You Know?

A DNG file is Adobe's RAW file — DNG is short for digital negative. It is a generic file that supposedly guarantees you will always be able to use a RAW file even if your camera's proprietary file is no longer supported by the manufacturer. The latter seems unlikely, but if you are the cautious type, you can save your images as DNG files.

Choose Local Control Features

Ansel Adams used to say that when you took the photograph, the photographer's work was only partly done. A problem everyone has, from the top pro to the beginning amateur, is that the camera does not always interpret the world the way that people see it. A photograph of a beautiful natural scene is not the same as that natural scene.

One way to deal with these challenges is to work at seeing the world from your camera's perspective. What can or can it not capture? Check your LCD to see what the camera is truly seeing and decide if you need to try something different to get a better photo.

Another way to correct these problems is to isolate them while processing a photograph so you can adjust them separately from the rest of the image. This is called *local control* as compared to overall or global control over the whole image. With Photoshop Elements, you have the ability to select and isolate very specific parts of the picture and then make corrections to that isolated area so that no other parts of the picture are affected. That can make a big difference in how a photograph interprets a real-world scene.

Top 100

#36 Create and Use a Selection 84   DIFFICULTY LEVEL

#37 Use Marquee Tools for Specific Shapes 86   DIFFICULTY LEVEL

#38 Use Lasso Tools to Follow Picture Elements 88   DIFFICULTY LEVEL

#39 Use Automated Tools for Easy Selections. 90   DIFFICULTY LEVEL

#40 Expand or Contract Your Selection 92   DIFFICULTY LEVEL

#41 Select What Is Easy and Invert. 94   DIFFICULTY LEVEL

#42 Blend Edges by Feathering 96   DIFFICULTY LEVEL

#43 Use Selections for Traditional Edge Darkening 98   DIFFICULTY LEVEL

#44 Use the Smart Brush for Specific Area Fixes. 100   DIFFICULTY LEVEL

CREATE AND USE
a selection

Selections are a key way of isolating a part of the picture for adjustment separately from the rest. A selection is a little bit like building a fence. If you build a fence in the middle of a field and put all the cows in there, they eat the grass there and nowhere else. If you create a selection in the middle of the picture, any adjustments that you make occur inside that selection and nowhere else.

Photoshop Elements offers a number of ways to create selections, and you learn them in this chapter. The reason for the choice of selection tools is to make selections easier, more effective, and more precise for the specific needs of individual pictures. In this task, you learn what a selection can do, how it works, and how it combines with adjustments to control where an adjustment occurs.

Architectural details are always an interesting subject matter for photographs. The stairway shown here is more than simply a stairway photograph. It is about lines and patterns as they come together within the frame of the image.

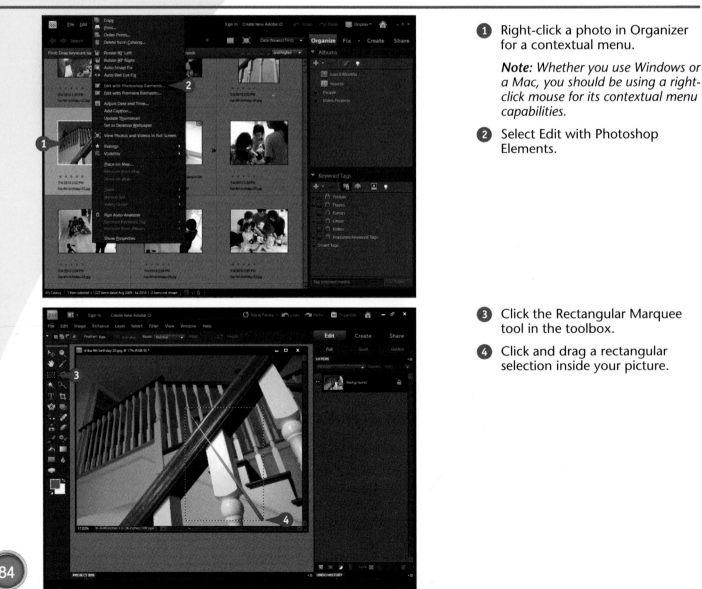

① Right-click a photo in Organizer for a contextual menu.

Note: Whether you use Windows or a Mac, you should be using a right-click mouse for its contextual menu capabilities.

② Select Edit with Photoshop Elements.

③ Click the Rectangular Marquee tool in the toolbox.

④ Click and drag a rectangular selection inside your picture.

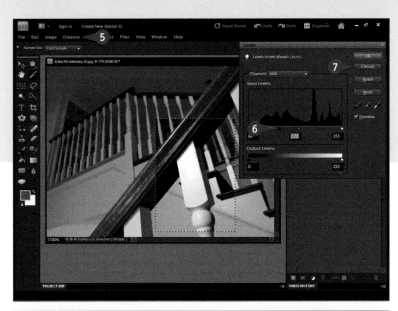

#36

5. Click Enhance, select Adjust Lighting, and then select Levels to open the Levels dialog box.

6. Make an extreme adjustment in the Levels dialog box to see the effect.

7. Click Cancel.

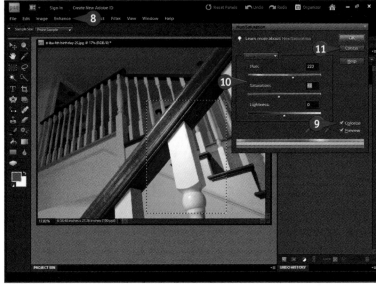

8. Click Enhance, select Adjust Color, and then select Adjust Hue/Saturation to open the Hue/Saturation dialog box.

9. Select the Colorize check box (■ changes to ☑).

10. Make an extreme adjustment with Hue and Saturation so that you can see the effect.

11. Click Cancel.

TIPS

Try This!

As you experiment with new controls in Photoshop Elements, you will typically close one file and open another to see the effects on varied subjects. You can always close and open images from the File menu. You can also close any open photo by clicking the small X in the image area tab that sits above the image.

Change It!

Once you have a selection, you can easily get rid of it and start a new selection at any time. Press Ctrl/⌘+D to deselect your selection. You can also click your cursor outside of a selection to deselect, so long as you are still using a selection tool.

Did You Know?

Colorize is an interesting part of Hue/Saturation because it does not simply change colors in a picture — it adds colors to a picture. When you select that check box, the adjustment adds whatever color is chosen in the Hue area to the photograph. You can then adjust the intensity of this color using the Saturation slider.

USE MARQUEE TOOLS
for specific shapes

The rectangular and elliptical selection tools in the toolbox are called the Marquee selection tools. They both sit in the same place at the upper left side of the toolbox. By default, the Rectangular Marquee tool is visible. The Elliptical Marquee tool is underneath the rectangle. To access the elliptical tool, click and hold the Rectangular Marquee tool until a small menu appears that shows both tools. You then select the one you want.

The rectangular and elliptical tools provide exactly what you expect, rectangle and ellipse shapes. Experimenting with them when you are learning selections is great because they are so obvious. They

tend to work very well with photographs of architecture and other man-made structures because those structures typically have rectangles and ellipses. Their shapes are so specific, however, that most photographers use them infrequently because most photographs do not have these specific shapes. Still, when you do need them, they give you specific, precise shapes in a hurry.

The image seen here is shot with what is called a full-frame fisheye lens. The full-frame refers to how the lens fills up the entire image area as compared to a traditional fisheye lens that gives a circular image.

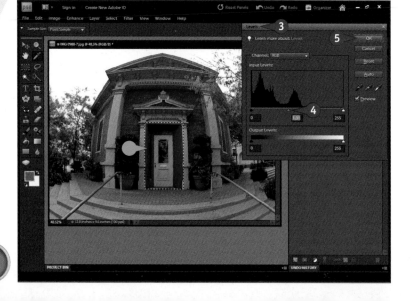

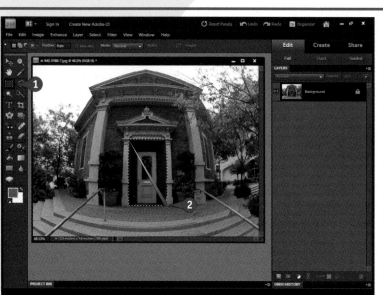

Use the Rectangular Marquee Tool

1 Click the Rectangular Marquee tool in the toolbox.

2 Click and drag a selection around an area that works with the shape.

3 Choose an adjustment appropriate for the selected area inside your photograph.

4 Make the adjustment.

In this example, the midtones are adjusted with the appropriate sliders in Levels.

5 Click OK.

● The adjustment occurs only inside the selected area.

Use the Elliptical Marquee Tool

1 Click the Elliptical Marquee tool in the toolbox.

2 Click and drag a selection around an area that works with the shape.

The elliptical tool takes some practice getting used to.

Experiment with it to see how it might work for you.

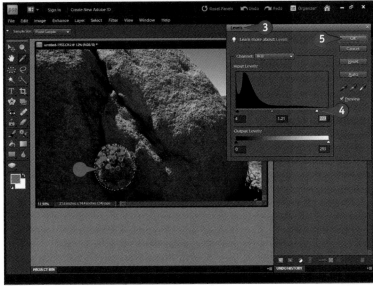

3 Open an adjustment appropriate for the selected area inside your photograph.

4 Make the adjustment.

5 Click OK.

● The adjustment occurs only inside the selected area.

TIPS

More Options!

The Marquee tools also do the square and circle selections. To get a square, choose the Rectangular Marquee tool and press and hold Shift as you make the selection. To create a circular selection, choose the Elliptical Marquee tool and press and hold Shift again as you make the selection.

Try This!

Once you have created a selection, you can move it to a better place in your photograph as needed. While still using your selection tool, simply click in the selection area and hold down the mouse button. Then drag the selection to a new area. You can also move your selection with the arrow keys.

More Options!

If you look closely, you notice that a lot of the tools in the toolbox have a little black triangle to the bottom right of the icon. This indicates that more tools are available than what is showing. Clicking and holding the icon reveals a stack of tools.

USE LASSO TOOLS
to follow picture elements

The Rectangular and Elliptical Marquee tools are pretty restrictive as to what they can do in a photograph. Photoshop Elements gives you freehand tools such as the Lasso, the Polygonal Lasso, and the Magnetic Lasso tools for selecting around any shape.

The Polygonal Lasso is probably the easiest to use. You simply click to start and then move your cursor along a shape, clicking as you go to anchor the selection. You can move the cursor anywhere without effect so you can carefully find exactly the spot to select before you click. Complete the selection by

clicking the beginning point or double-clicking anywhere. The Magnetic Lasso is an automated lasso that finds edges for you if you have a strong edge where your selection needs to be. The Lasso tool itself works totally freehand, but it can be hard to control without a lot of practice.

The photo here shows two brothers playing outside. The challenge is the light. The front brother has light on his face and light reflecting into the shadow under his hat. The other brother is looking down and is heavily shadowed on his face. That needs correction.

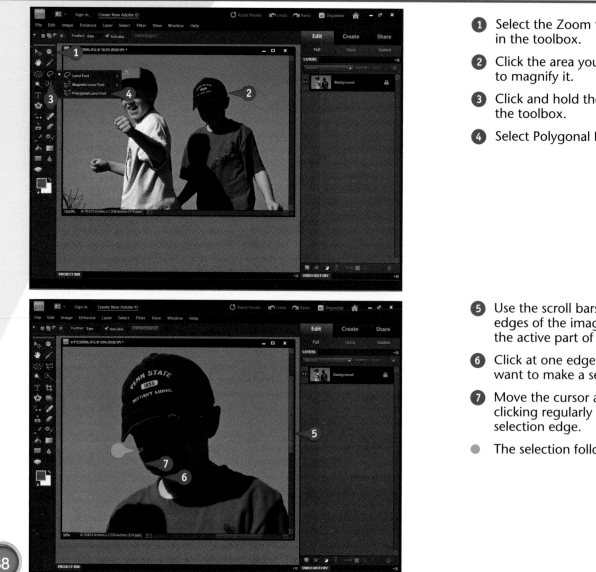

① Select the Zoom tool or magnifier in the toolbox.

② Click the area you need to select to magnify it.

③ Click and hold the Lasso tool in the toolbox.

④ Select Polygonal Lasso Tool.

⑤ Use the scroll bars around the edges of the image to reposition the active part of the photo.

⑥ Click at one edge where you want to make a selection.

⑦ Move the cursor along the edge, clicking regularly to anchor the selection edge.

● The selection follows your cursor.

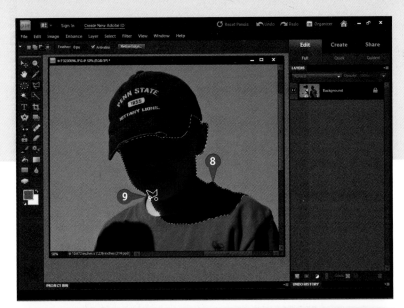

8 Click and move your cursor around the area that you want to select.

9 Finish the selection by clicking where you started.

A small o appears at the cursor's lower right when it is over the starting point.

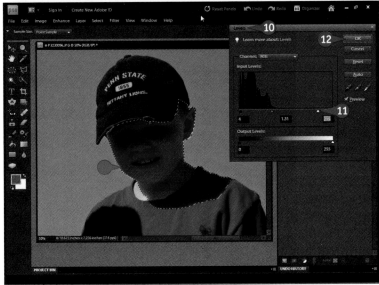

10 Choose an adjustment appropriate for the selected area inside your photograph.

11 Make the adjustment.

In this example, the boy's face has been lightened using Levels.

12 Click OK.

● The adjustment is made only inside the selected area.

TIPS

Important!

Selections definitely take practice. When you first start using selections, you may find it frustrating to make your selections go exactly where you want them. With practice, you get much better. You can also find ideas in the rest of this chapter that can help you create selections easier.

Try This!

The Magnetic Lasso is very useful when you have a picture in which, for example, your subject contrasts strongly against a simple background. The Magnetic Lasso looks for contrasting edges and finds them for you. This makes selection easy as long as you have those edges.

More Options!

Because the Polygonal Lasso goes in a straight line from click to click, you might think it is not useful for curves. In fact, this tool is actually good for curves because it is easy to control: Just move your cursor in short distances as you click around a curve.

USE AUTOMATED TOOLS
for easy selections

Photoshop Elements' diversity of selection tools offers you options for matching a tool with the selection challenge in a photograph. Adobe has even added some automated tools that help you find edges and create selections quickly for certain types of pictures. One of them, the Magnetic Lasso, was described in the previous task.

Three more very useful automated selection tools are the Magic Wand, the Selection Brush, and the Quick Selection tool. The Magic Wand is used for areas that have a consistent tone or color. Click that area and the Magic Wand finds all pixels similar to the color

and tone where you clicked. The Selection Brush enables you literally to paint a selection in the picture by brushing your cursor over an area. The Quick Selection tool is sort of in between. You use it to brush through an area; it finds additional pixels that match that area in tone and color.

In the photo seen here, the dark ground of volcanic rock requires an exposure that makes the sky too bright. By selecting the sky, the sky can be adjusted separately from the ground. This is an old lava flow area in the cinder cones section of the Mojave National Reserve.

① Click the Magic Wand in the toolbox.

② Click in an even-toned, colored area to begin the selection.

● A selection is created based on the color and tone where you click.

③ Change the Tolerance for the tool if the selection goes too far or does not go far enough.

④ Click the tool once in an unselected area or twice if those areas are small; click once to remove the old selection, and click once again to create a new selection.

You may also find that it helps to click in different places.

Press Ctrl/⌘+D to deselect the selection.

⑤ Click and hold the tool next to the Magic Wand.

⑥ Click the Selection Brush tool.

⑦ Paint over an area you want to select using the Selection Brush.

⑧ Change the size if the brush is too big or small for the area.

TIPS

More Options!
The Contiguous check box for the Magic Wand is very useful. When it is selected, the selection captures only contiguous, or connected, areas. When it is deselected, the selection looks for any places in your photograph that have the same colors and tone, connected or not.

More Options!
The Tolerance setting for the Magic Wand is an important option. It tells the tool how to look at tones and colors within the picture to make the selection. Set it lower to restrict your selection, and higher to make it find more parts of the picture.

Save It!
Once you have a good selection, you may want to keep it so that you can go back to the selection later. You can save that selection. Click the Select menu and select Save Selection. Type a name for the selection, keep New Selection selected, and click OK.

EXPAND OR CONTRACT
your selection

You may often find that a selection you create is not quite right, which is normal. Making a perfect selection in one try can be difficult. Luckily, Photoshop Elements has features that enable you to refine a selection and make it do what you want it to. You can easily add to a selection or subtract from a selection as needed.

This is very important because it makes selecting easier. You do not have to worry about making a selection perfect right from the start. In fact, making your first selection very quickly and then refining that

selection to the final area is often easier and faster than trying to do it exactly right as you go. No matter what you do, you will often find little jags, corners, and other odd shapes easier to deal with after you have done your first selection work.

Here you see a young girl talking to a young woman. It is a nice moment, but the young woman is closer to the window and has light jeans that unbalance the image. After the jeans are selected, they can be darkened to improve the photo.

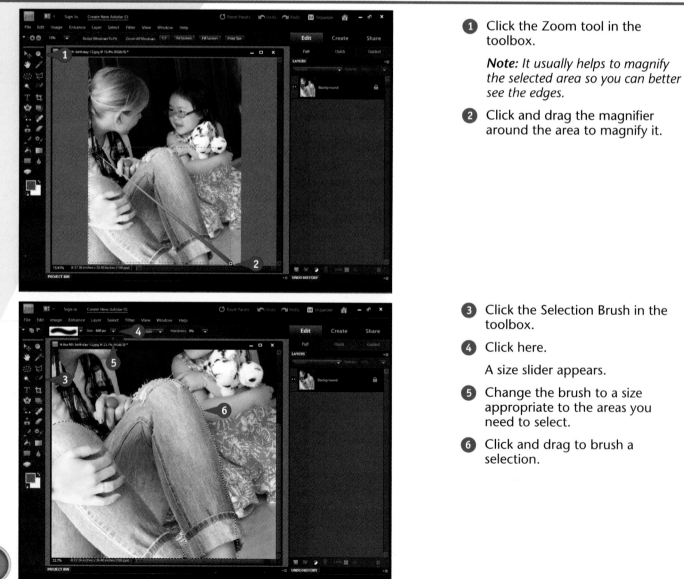

① Click the Zoom tool in the toolbox.

Note: It usually helps to magnify the selected area so you can better see the edges.

② Click and drag the magnifier around the area to magnify it.

③ Click the Selection Brush in the toolbox.

④ Click here.

A size slider appears.

⑤ Change the brush to a size appropriate to the areas you need to select.

⑥ Click and drag to brush a selection.

7 Press and hold Alt/Option and then click and drag the Brush tool to remove part of a selection.

Remove all excess selection areas.

DIFFICULTY LEVEL

8 Resize the brush as needed to add specific areas to a selection.

9 Refine your selection by adding to it or subtracting from it. You can repeatedly go back and forth between the default add function and the subtract function of the brush. Remember that the brush automatically adds to a selection unless you press and hold Alt/Option.

TIPS

Try It!

The Lasso tool is ideal for adding to and subtracting from a selection. It can be hard to use when trying to make a large selection, but for little adjustments and selection refinements, it works well. Press and hold Alt/Option to remove part of a selection, and press and hold Shift to add to a selection when using the Lasso tool.

More Options!

You might have noticed that your cursor changes when it goes over the word Size in the Options bar. Your cursor becomes activated and you can simply click Size and drag left and right to make the brush size smaller or larger respectively without using the Size slider. Many numerical options in Photoshop Elements work this way.

Try This!

You can make your brush size larger or smaller very quickly by using the keyboard. To the right of the letter P are the bracket keys, [and]. Press [and the brush gets smaller. Press] and the brush gets larger. You will find this very handy for sizing your brush to the perfect size.

SELECT WHAT IS EASY
and invert

Photographs can be challenging at times. You want to make an adjustment to a very specific part of the picture, but selecting that area is difficult.

One way to deal with this is to look at your picture carefully before you start making a selection. You may discover that selecting something beside, around, or behind your subject is easier. This would not help you if it were all you could do, because you do not really want to select that area. However, Photoshop Elements enables you to make a selection and then invert it or flip it over so that what was selected is now unselected and what was unselected is now selected. Often when you look at a picture you can find easier ways of making a selection than simply creating an outline around it.

The palm trees at this desert oasis in Joshua Tree National Park are a good example of this. It would be nice to hold the color in the sky by adjusting the landscape with palms separately from that sky. If the sky is selected first, that selection can be inverted to end up with a selection of the palms and desert landscape.

Note: Skies are often very easy to select with the Magic Wand and can be used to start a selection around a complex shape.

1. Click the Magic Wand in the toolbox.

2. Deselect the Contiguous check box (☑ changes to ▇).

   This enables Magic Wand to select similar areas throughout the photo, even when they are not connected.

3. Click the sky to begin the selection.

4. Press and hold Shift and click the sky again to add to the selection.

5. Click Select.

6. Choose Inverse.

Everything except the sky is now selected.

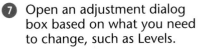

⑦ Open an adjustment dialog box based on what you need to change, such as Levels.

⑧ Make an adjustment.

● The adjustment applies to the area you originally wanted to work on, but not to the sky.

TIPS

More Options!

Remember that you do not have to do a complete selection in one try. You can use this technique to do the best you can, such as selecting the sky and inverting the selection. Then you can add to that selection or subtract from it using other selection tools. Simply press and hold Shift while selecting to add, or Alt/Option to subtract.

Try It!

Sometimes the outline around your selection can be distracting. Pressing Ctrl/⌘+H temporarily hides the selection outline, yet it is still there. Press Ctrl/⌘+H again and the selection outline reappears. Do not forget that you used this command or you will get frustrated that controls are not working right because of a "hidden" selection.

Put It Together!

Use whatever selection tools make it easiest to get your selection started. Then use the Inverse command as well as adding to and subtracting from a selection to refine your selection as needed. Using multiple tools like this helps a lot in getting better selections.

BLEND EDGES
by feathering

Selections create a hard edge between selected and unselected areas, a hard edge that is really not normal in a photograph. Magnify any photograph and you rarely see a razor-sharp edge anywhere. This is because of the way light works as well as how things go in and out of focus in an image. Using an unmodified selection this way can look very unnatural in the picture.

You can see this in the photo used here when you look at the edge of the boulder in amongst other rocks just after sunset. The image you see has been enlarged to

show the boulder's edge. It has an unnatural edge to it when simply selected and adjusted. These rocks are in the Joshua Tree National Park.

Photoshop Elements gives you the opportunity to make this edge blend in. This is called *feathering*. Feathering has to be adjusted for every selection because how much of a blend is needed depends entirely on the subject in the photograph. This is why feathering after you have made a selection is best because if you do not like the effect, you simply undo it and try another amount. The selection remains unchanged.

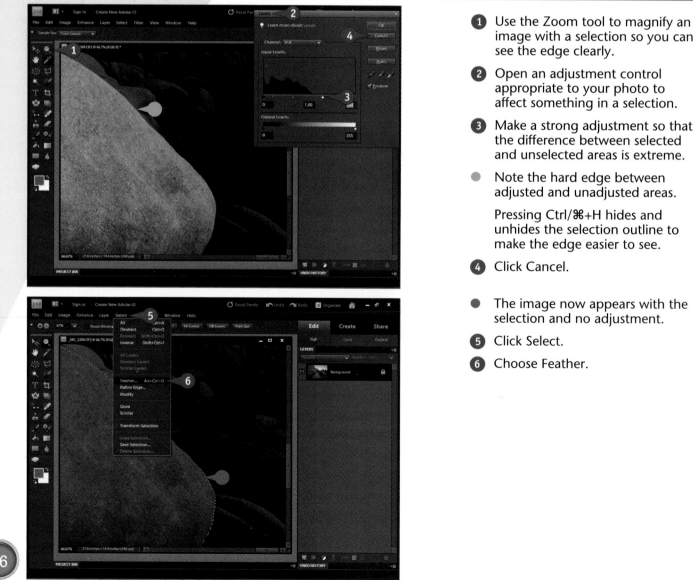

① Use the Zoom tool to magnify an image with a selection so you can see the edge clearly.

② Open an adjustment control appropriate to your photo to affect something in a selection.

③ Make a strong adjustment so that the difference between selected and unselected areas is extreme.

● Note the hard edge between adjusted and unadjusted areas.

   Pressing Ctrl/⌘+H hides and unhides the selection outline to make the edge easier to see.

④ Click Cancel.

● The image now appears with the selection and no adjustment.

⑤ Click Select.

⑥ Choose Feather.

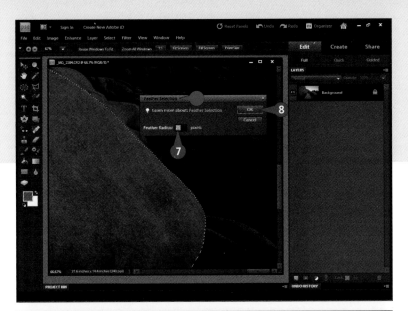

- The Feather Selection dialog box opens.

7 Type a moderate number for Feather Radius such as 15–25.

Note: *The amount of Radius is relative and will be "large," "moderate," or "small" based on the size of the selection and the pixel size of the photo.*

8 Click OK.

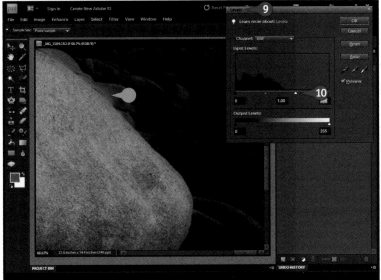

9 Open an adjustment dialog box, the same one you did before that was appropriate to your image.

10 Make a strong adjustment now that really changes the selected area.

- Note how the adjustment now blends nicely in the photo.

TIPS

More Options!
To get the equivalent of a feathered edge on your selection when using the Selection Brush, choose a soft-edge brush. After choosing the Selection Brush, right-click the photograph to get choices for brush sizes. You can see the difference between a soft- and hard-edge brush by the softness or hardness of the little circles.

Did You Know?
When you choose an adjustment control after making a selection, the dialog box that opens shows you what is happening only inside the selection. For example, the Levels dialog box shows something distinctly different for the selection than if you use Levels for the entire picture. The control is affecting only that selected area.

Change It!
Feathering values affect how far a selection blends between the selected and unselected areas. If the photograph has fairly sharp edges as in the example, you typically use a low number, such as one between 5 and 10. If no sharp edge exists or you want the blend to cross a wider part of the picture, use a high number, such as one between 60 and 100.

USE SELECTIONS FOR
traditional edge darkening

In the past, photographers working in the traditional darkroom typically added a little bit of darkness along the edges of their pictures. This is called *burning in* the edges because of the way light is used to darken these edges. Ansel Adams considered this a critical part of working on an image in the darkroom. He felt that the viewer's eye had a tendency to drift off a photograph because of distractions around the photo. Darkening the edge would help keep the viewer's eye focused on the photograph.

You can do this using a selection. How much you darken an edge is subjective and depends on your

photograph. You do not want to make the effect too obvious, and you want to keep a good blend across the edge between the darkening and the rest of the photograph. Once you try this, you will discover that it gives your picture a more dimensional and livelier look.

This really works well with portraits and portrait-like images such as this paperbag bush flower from the Mojave Desert. This plant gets its name from the seed "container" that dries brown and looks like a little paper bag.

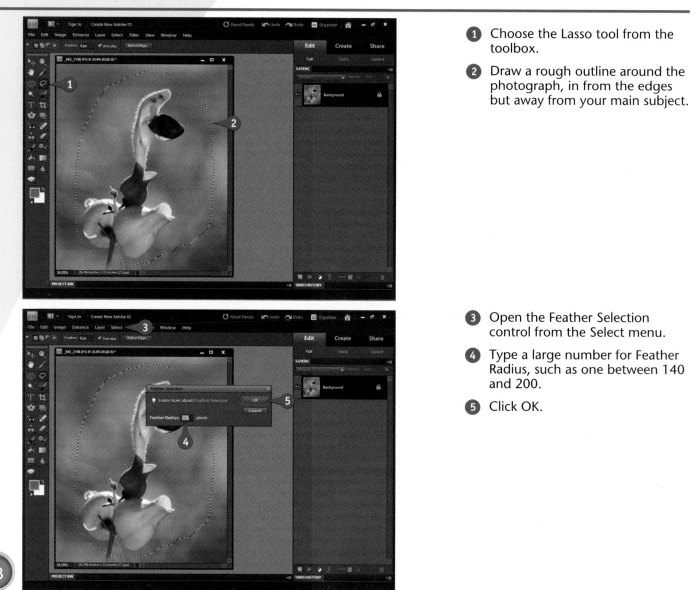

① Choose the Lasso tool from the toolbox.

② Draw a rough outline around the photograph, in from the edges but away from your main subject.

③ Open the Feather Selection control from the Select menu.

④ Type a large number for Feather Radius, such as one between 140 and 200.

⑤ Click OK.

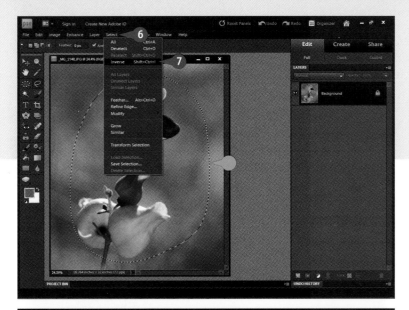

- The selection outline smooths its shape, though you cannot see the actual feathering yet.

6 Click Select.

7 Select Inverse.

The selection is now along the outside edges of the image.

8 Click Enhance, select Adjust Lighting, and then select Brightness/Contrast to open the Brightness/Contrast dialog box.

9 Click and drag the Brightness slider to the left to darken the outside edges of the photograph.

Pressing Ctrl/⌘+H hides the selection outline to make the edge easier to see.

10 Select and deselect the Preview check box to see how the effect works (■ changes to ☑ and vice versa).

11 Click OK.

TIPS

Attention!

Brightness/Contrast seems like it would be a good all-around adjustment for photographers. It is not. Its use should be restricted to special purposes such as darkening the outside edges of a photograph. It is a rather blunt-edged instrument for most adjustments in a photograph. It works for this task because it mimics what happens when edges are "burned in" when in the traditional darkroom.

Test It!

Experiment with feathering. Feathering is not some absolute thing for which you can pick an arbitrary number and be done with it. The same feathering numbers can look perfect on one photograph and awful on another. It is okay to try a number, do the adjustment, undo the effect if you dislike it, and try again.

Did You Know?

Ansel Adams was a master landscape photographer who spent a lot of time in a traditional darkroom. He felt that the original exposure was only an approximation of what he really saw at the scene. He used his time in the darkroom to bring out the best in his images so that the scene was interpreted more closely to the way he actually saw it.

USE THE SMART BRUSH
for specific area fixes

Photoshop Elements includes a special brush that enables you to brush on local adjustments in a photograph. The Smart Brush combines the Selection Brush with a whole range of preset adjustments that you choose and then use on your photograph. These adjustments specifically define how such things as color, contrast, and special effects are applied to your photograph in restricted areas. They are easy to use, and are well worth experimenting with to see what all the presets can do for your photographs. Some photographers find all of the presets very useful, whereas others use only a limited group.

In this photo, the girl needs to be brightened, but not anything else in the photo. By brightening or darkening only certain parts of a photo, you can bring emphasis to parts of your photograph.

Although you do not have to know anything about layers or layer masks to use the Smart Brush, this tool uses layers and layer masks for its effects. You will see a new layer appear in the Layers panel when you use the brush. Layers and layer masks are covered in Chapter 5. As you learn to use layers, you will also gain more control over the Smart Brush.

1 Choose the Smart Brush from the toolbox.

2 Click the Preset selector.

3 Choose the preset appropriate for your photo's needs.

4 Change the size of your brush with the bracket keys ([and]) until it is sized correctly for the space.

5 Brush the preset change onto the photo over the area that needs the adjustment.

● A selection appears, marking the edges of the adjustment.

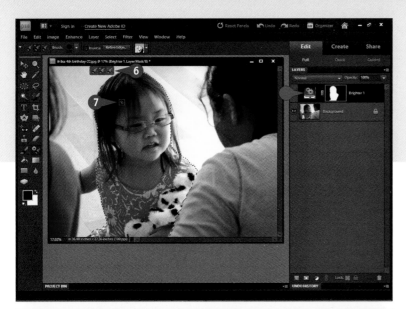

6 Add or subtract from the changed area with the plus and minus brushes.

Examine the change; if it is good, continue working on the photo.

7 Double-click the red Smart Brush icon to refine the adjustment.

● You can also double-click the adjustment layer icon with the gears in the Layers panel.

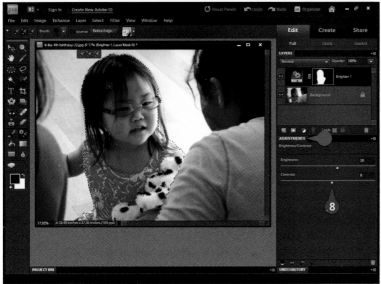

● An Adjustments panel opens that automatically gives you the correct adjustment controls. If it does not open, use the Window menu and select Adjustments.

8 Change the adjustment to refine the work that the Smart Brush started.

This adjustment is up to you and varies depending on the type of brush you choose.

In this image, the contrast was slightly changed.

TIPS

Did You Know?
The Smart Brush is a very handy tool because you can reopen its adjustment and readjust the controls as much as you want. No harm comes to your picture when you do this, which makes it a great tool to experiment with. Just click the appropriate Smart Brush working icon for each adjustment.

Did You Know?
You can start a new Smart Brush adjustment using the same adjustments by clicking the first Smart Brush icon (⬛) again. This enables you to do the same adjustment, but at different locations in the photo and with different amounts. The Smart Brush working icons change color as you add Smart Brush adjustments.

Test It!
To totally remove a Smart Brush adjustment, you need to remove the layer on which the adjustment was made. That is easy to do. Simply go to the Layers panel, click the layer named for the adjustment you want to remove, and then drag it to the Trash Can icon below the layers. This is explained in more detail in the next chapter.

Chapter 5

Create Adjustment Layers for Nondestructive Changes

Photoshop Elements is pixel-editing software, designed to work directly with the pixels of a digital image. This is what you have been doing in the book so far except for your work with the Smart Brush in task #44. One problem with working directly on the pixels of an image is that every time you change them, the potential for the loss of image quality increases. The pixels cannot gain more information, but they can lose it.

You can work on your image without changing any pixels by using adjustment layers and layer masks. Adjustment layers give you a huge range of flexibility and power that you do not

get when working directly on the pixels of an image. If you have seen adjustment layers in earlier versions Photoshop Elements, you may notice a change to adjustment layers in this version. These controls are now opened as a panel in the panel bin.

Adjustment layers are a lot like filters on a camera. If you put a filter on your lens, the scene does not change, but it does look different coming through the lens and onto your sensor. An adjustment layer does something very similar, changing how the pixels of a photograph appear yet not actually changing any pixel in the underlying picture.

Top 100

#45   Understand How Layers Work. 104   DIFFICULTY LEVEL

#46   Understand How Adjustment Layers Work 106   DIFFICULTY LEVEL

#47   Work Blacks and Whites with a Levels Adjustment Layer . . .110   DIFFICULTY LEVEL

#48   Work Midtones with a Levels Adjustment Layer 112   DIFFICULTY LEVEL

#49   Correct Color with an Adjustment Layer 114   DIFFICULTY LEVEL

#50   Enhance Color with an Adjustment Layer 116   DIFFICULTY LEVEL

#51   Fix Problem Exposures with Layer Blending Modes. 118   DIFFICULTY LEVEL

#52   Understand How Layer Masks Work 120   DIFFICULTY LEVEL

#53   Combine Two Photos with Layer Masks 122   DIFFICULTY LEVEL

#54   Remove Adjustments with Black 126   DIFFICULTY LEVEL

#55   Add Adjustments Using Black and then White. 128   DIFFICULTY LEVEL

#56   Combine Layer Masks with Selections. 132   DIFFICULTY LEVEL

#57   Balance Colors and Tones in a Picture. 134   DIFFICULTY LEVEL

#58   Bring Out Shadow Detail in Specific Areas 136   DIFFICULTY LEVEL

#59   Darken Highlight Detail in Specific Areas 138   DIFFICULTY LEVEL

#60   Flatten Layers When Done .140   DIFFICULTY LEVEL

Understand
HOW LAYERS WORK

One reason that many photographers get intimidated by layers is that layers seem very much of the computer and alien to taking pictures. Mentally step away from Photoshop Elements and the computer and you will discover you already know quite a bit about layers. A layer cake is made up of actual layers — you can see them from the side, but you cannot see them from the top. If you have layers of paint on a wall, the last layer is all that shows. However, if you scrape off some of that top layer, you start to see the old layers of paint.

This is important to keep in mind because layers in Photoshop Elements act the same way. They are simply a stack of digital things, from adjustment layers to actual photographs. The stack has a top and a bottom, the top covers up everything underneath it, and you examine a stack from top to bottom. Real-world layers appear to us in exactly this way, too.

The photograph here shows layers of ridges in the Santa Monica Mountains west of Los Angeles, California. It was shot with a telephoto lens from a high ridge in the early morning.

Where did the photo go? All you can see is a light blue rectangle.

- The original photo is at the bottom of the layer stack, but you are not seeing that.

- Pieces of the photo are in the layer stack, but you are not seeing them.

- A solid color layer blocks any view of the original photo, just as if you painted blue on a piece of plastic over a photo.

  Just like the paint on plastic, the original photo is still there, unharmed.

- Move that top layer down just like shuffling paper in a stack of photographs and papers and you now see the photograph.

- Notice something about the layer stack. The blue layer is solid and covering up the original photo.

- The remaining layers above the blue layer have separate picture elements, and they combine visually to look exactly like the original photo.

- Now the blue layer is moved in between the separate picture element photos.

- The photo changes so that it looks like a light blue sky is behind the mountain.

- Because layers affect what is underneath them, the new position of the blue layer keeps the rest of the scene hidden.

  Layers always work so that higher layers affect layers underneath them.

Because layers separate parts of a photo, you can easily change one part without affecting another.

- The blue layer has been moved up again in the layer stack.

- Now the photo looks like just a hill and sky.

- The original photo is still there, untouched.

TIPS

Did You Know?

If for any reason you discover that your panels are not appearing, select the Window menu. It has a list of items to display in the Photoshop Elements interface. You can turn any of them on or off by clicking the name of the panel.

Try This!

You can easily move layers up and down in the Layers panel. Click a layer and drag it to a new position. Look at the line between layers as you move a layer. When it thickens, your layer is ready to be dropped into position. Photoshop Elements automatically opens a space for it and shifts the other layers to make room for it.

Did You Know?

The biggest benefit of layers is the ability to isolate parts of a photo. This enables you to work separately on those parts, and having layers gives you more options for blending separate elements in different layers.

Understand how
ADJUSTMENT LAYERS WORK

Adjustment layers include many of the adjustment controls that you have seen so far in the book. An adjustment layer even shows the same sliders and other parts of the original adjustment's dialog box. For example, the Levels adjustment dialog box for Levels has identical controls to the Levels panel for an adjustment layer.

Yet using an adjustment layer is considerably different from adjusting on the photograph. These special layers are basically instructions. As you make an adjustment, the underlying picture appears to change, yet it really does not. What changes is the

view through the adjustment layer. That means you can adjust and readjust the controls in an adjustment layer because the underlying picture never changes. This also means that the adjustments are nondestructive because pixels are not damaged in any way. In this task you try an adjustment layer to see how these layers work.

Do not put your camera away at a birthday party after the candles on the cake are blown out. There can be lots of great opportunities for fun photos throughout a kids' birthday party, especially when the cake has nearly disappeared.

Use the Menu to Add an Adjustment Layer

① Click Layer.

② Select New Adjustment Layer.

③ Select Hue/Saturation.

● A New Layer dialog box opens.

④ You can change the layer's name by typing it into the Name box or leave it Hue/Saturation 1.

Leave the other options at the default settings.

⑤ Click OK.

● A Hue/Saturation adjustment layer is then created and the Hue/Saturation adjustment panel appears.

Use the Icon to Add an Adjustment Layer

① Click the Adjustment Layer icon at the bottom of the Layers panel.

② Select Hue/Saturation.

● The Hue/Saturation adjustment panel opens; it looks nearly identical to the dialog box that you open by selecting Adjust Color and then Adjust Hue/Saturation in the Enhance menu.

● The difference is that an adjustment layer appears automatically over the original picture, now the background layer.

TIPS

Did You Know?

Opening an adjustment layer with the Adjustment Layer icon on the Layers panel is quick and easy. You simply click the black and white circle (◑) to get a list of adjustments, and then select the one you want. Opening an adjustment layer with the Layer menu gives you the same list but also includes the ability to name the layer immediately and change its blending mode, its opacity, and how it is grouped with other layers.

Try This!

Naming your layers can help you keep track of what they are doing to your picture. You can name or rename a layer at any time by simply double-clicking the name in the layer and typing a new name.

Did You Know?

The extra menu choices that show up when you click the Adjustment Layer icon in the Layers panel are called *fill layers*. These unique layers enable you to add a color, gradient, or pattern to a layer stack. You can also easily adjust fill layers without changing the underlying photograph.

Understand how
ADJUSTMENT LAYERS WORK

Once you start working with adjustment layers, you will probably use them when beginning your adjustments on any photograph. The great advantage of using adjustment layers right away is that you can make changes to the photograph without making changes to the pixels. The result is that you can easily readjust any change you make without any harm to the photograph.

Sometimes you may want to adjust the picture directly, such as when working on a picture you do not need to change. Then you will not use an adjustment layer. But the plusses of using an

adjustment layer are so great you will find it worth learning to use them and putting them into your normal workflow.

With adjustment layers, you can always adjust and readjust a picture at maximum quality. This is quite simple to do. You double-click the adjustment layer icon with the gears in it. The Adjustments panel immediately reopens and you can make any changes you want. This enables you to tweak an image in the later stages of adjustment if you discover your first adjustments do not mesh with the later adjustments as well as you would like.

Apply an Adjustment Layer

1. Repeat the steps from the previous page to open the Hue/Saturation adjustment panel.

2. Select Colorize (■ changes to ☑).

3. Change the Hue and Saturation sliders so the picture looks like it was shot with a strongly colored filter.

4. Click the Eye icon at the left of the adjustment layer in the Layers panel.

● The new color goes away, yet the adjustment layer is still in the Layers panel.

5. Click the Eye icon again.

● The color comes back.

Clicking the Eye icon simply turns the visibility of a layer on and off.

⑥ Click the adjustment layer icon at any time and the Adjustments panel reopens.

⑦ Change the Hue and Saturation sliders to change the color again.

Note: The underlying picture seen as background is not affected, yet the appearance of the photograph has changed.

TIPS

Important!

When the Adjustment controls of the Adjustments panel are open, everything else in the Photoshop Elements interface is accessible. For example, you can click the Eye icon for a layer and change the layer visibility if the Hue/Saturation adjustment is open.

Try This!

Using Hue/Saturation to colorize an image can be an interesting way to create a one-color or monochrome photograph. You can change the hue to give the color a bluish cast, a sepia tone, and more. This is a simple way of changing the picture without actually getting rid of the original color picture.

Important!

When you have layers and save your photograph with a PSD or Photoshop file format, all the layers are saved with the file. You can close the image and open it days later — all the layers will still be there. In fact, you can double-click an adjustment layer and go back to exactly what you used before or you can change it.

WORK BLACKS AND WHITES
with a Levels adjustment layer

The workflow that you followed in the first part of this book for adjusting an image is still important: Set blacks and whites, adjust midtones, correct color, and so on. Now you will be making the adjustments with adjustment layers.

The photo you see here is of monkey flowers blooming in the chaparral of the Santa Monica Mountains National Recreation Area. The image has been saved as a Photoshop or PSD file. The Photoshop file format is ideal for working with layers. This same image will be used for several tasks to allow the Layer panel to gain multiple layers.

Start by adjusting blacks and whites using the Levels adjustment panel. Blacks and whites are critical to how the rest of the picture looks, from its contrast to its colors, so this is a good place to start your work on an image. Adjust blacks depending on the subject, your interpretation of that scene, and your experience with working on pictures. Whites are very sensitive and usually have a more limited range of proper adjustment. Naming this Levels layer Blacks-Whites is a good idea so you know what it is doing as you add layers later.

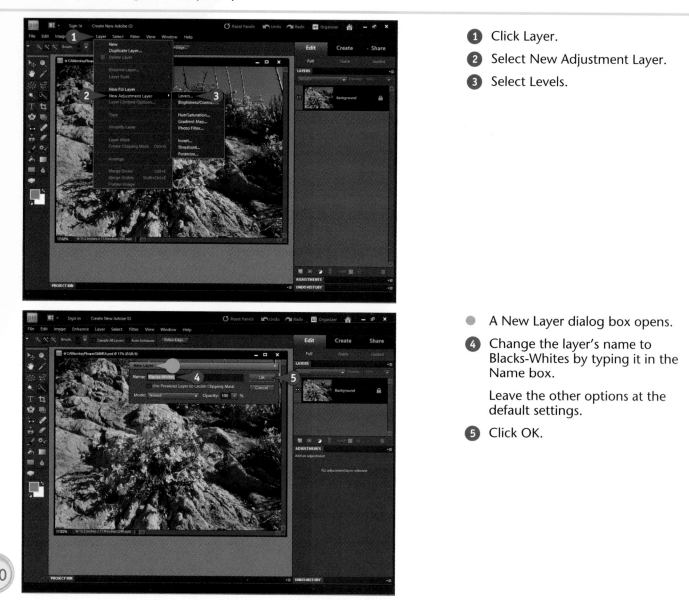

1 Click Layer.

2 Select New Adjustment Layer.

3 Select Levels.

● A New Layer dialog box opens.

4 Change the layer's name to Blacks-Whites by typing it in the Name box.

Leave the other options at the default settings.

5 Click OK.

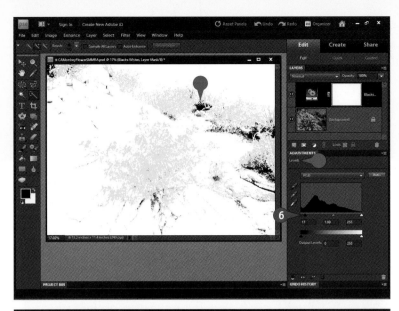

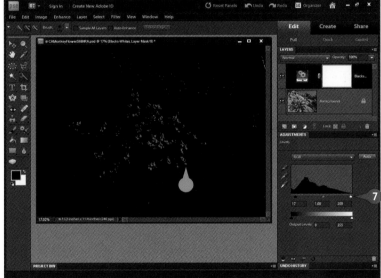

- The Levels adjustment panel opens; it looks nearly identical to the dialog box that you open by selecting Adjust Lighting in the Enhance menu.

6 Adjust blacks by pressing Alt/Option as you move the left, black, slider.

- A blacks threshold screen appears, showing you where the blacks and maxed-out dark colors occur as you adjust.

7 Adjust whites by pressing Alt/Option as you move the right, white, slider.

- A whites threshold screen appears, showing you where the whites and maxed-out light colors occur as you adjust.

TIPS

Did You Know?

Threshold screens show you where certain tones appear in a picture. This is easy to figure out when the tones are either pure black or pure white. The colors show maxed-out channels. Use them when a picture is filled with color and a pure black or white is hard to find.

Get Rid of Layers!

If you decide that the layer you are working on is messed up, you can easily get rid of it. Simply click that layer and drag it to the Trash Can icon at the bottom right of the Layers panel.

Did You Know?

The histogram, or graph, in the Levels adjustment panel gives you an idea of what needs to be adjusted for blacks and whites. A big gap at either side means that no data is there, which translates as no tones. Most photographs look best when no big gap appears on either side, which is what you aim for when adjusting blacks and whites.

WORK MIDTONES
with a Levels adjustment layer

You first adjust blacks and whites on your photograph with a Levels adjustment layer. Now you will add another Levels adjustment layer to change the midtones. Photoshop Elements does not offer Color Curves as an adjustment layer, so you have to use Levels for midtones. Levels offers a lot of flexibility when used as an adjustment layer.

Adjusting midtones is important because it affects the overall brightness or darkness of the picture. Do not use the black slider or white slider for this purpose, even though both seem to affect the overall brightness of the picture.

Because the middle slider appears in the first layer Levels, you might wonder why not adjust midtones there? By keeping your adjustments on separate layers, you gain more flexibility in readjusting parts of your picture later. It also allows you to precisely find the right layer affecting a particular part of your picture.

Name that Levels layer Midtones so that you can know exactly which layer is which simply by reading the names. If you follow a consistent workflow, the first layer above the original picture — also called the Background — will always be blacks and whites, and the second layer will be midtones.

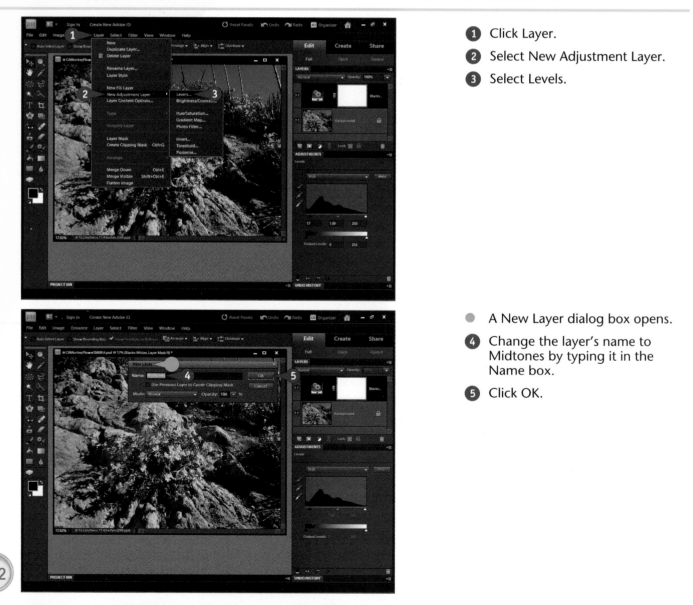

① Click Layer.

② Select New Adjustment Layer.

③ Select Levels.

● A New Layer dialog box opens.

④ Change the layer's name to Midtones by typing it in the Name box.

⑤ Click OK.

- The Levels adjustment panel opens; it looks almost identical to the dialog box that you open by selecting Adjust Lighting in the Enhance menu.

6 Adjust the midtones by moving the middle slider left or right.

The photograph and its midtones get brighter as you move the slider to the left.

The photograph and its midtones get darker as you move the slider to the right.

7 Double-click the bar to the right of the Adjustments panel tab. This collapses the panel.

Double-click the bar again to reopen the panel.

- Two adjustment layers now sit on top of the original picture and affect how it looks.

TIPS

Try This!
Cropping is important when you are working with layers. You can crop at any time using the technique described in task #15. Cropping occurs across all the layers and is a destructive form of processing, so limit your cropping at first to just getting rid of problems.

Important!
Name your layers. You will find this makes working with layers a lot easier as you add more layers during the process. It can get confusing as to which layer is doing what. In addition, named layers can help you see the process used in working on the picture — simply look at the layers from the bottom to the top.

Try This!
The Color Curves adjustment (see task #21) is a good one for midtones, but it is not available as an adjustment layer. Often you will find that your blacks/whites Levels adjustment is pretty standard and can be applied directly to the pixels of your picture. That way you can use the Color Curves adjustment for midtones and use adjustment layers for the rest of your image processing.

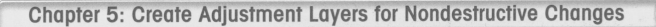

CORRECT COLOR
with an adjustment layer

Color casts — subtle colors that contaminate the colors and tones throughout the photograph — can be a problem with any type of photography. Examples include bluish landscapes at sunrise and greenish hair. Color casts were a serious problem when everyone shot film because they could be hard to get rid of. Film reacted to light in one way, but that one way depended on what kind of film it was. With digital photography, correcting color by removing problem color casts has become a lot easier.

When you correct color with an adjustment layer, you gain a great deal of flexibility. If you decide that a

previous color correction is not quite right as you continue to work on a photograph, you can always reopen the adjustment and do it again. This is a great advantage of the nondestructive nature of adjustment layers. In addition, you can use the opacity of the layer to change how strongly the adjustment affects the photograph.

A specific white balance, Cloudy, was chosen for this photo to add some warmth to the light from an early sun. The color-correction needs are minimal but the photo could be less warm. The rocks strongly show the effects of color correction to illustrate this task.

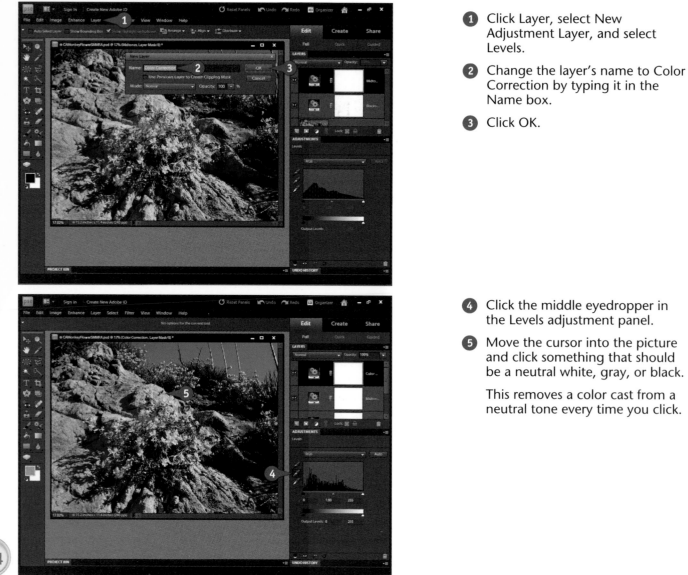

① Click Layer, select New Adjustment Layer, and select Levels.

② Change the layer's name to Color Correction by typing it in the Name box.

③ Click OK.

④ Click the middle eyedropper in the Levels adjustment panel.

⑤ Move the cursor into the picture and click something that should be a neutral white, gray, or black.

This removes a color cast from a neutral tone every time you click.

6 Try clicking different neutral grays throughout the photograph to see what you get.

Sometimes you get the right color on the first click, and sometimes it takes a number of clicks.

If you like the overall color, but it is too strong, you can change the opacity of the layer.

7 Position your cursor over the word Opacity.

The cursor changes to a hand with arrows.

8 Click and drag left or right to change the opacity of the layer.

TIPS

Did You Know?
Opacity is the opposite of transparency. Both terms refer to how much you can see through something, a layer in this case. Lower opacity for adjustment layers means the layers' adjustments lose some of their effect.

Important!
The first layers in the workflow described here are all Levels. Although all the adjustments could be made in one Levels control, this would give you a lot less flexibility. By separating the adjustments into separate layers, you can adjust each control individually. This means you can also readjust each control individually.

Did You Know?
As you make more adjustments with Levels, and sometimes with other controls, gaps begin to appear in the histogram in Levels. These are not necessarily a problem. They become a problem only when tonalities such as gradations in your photograph start to break up. This breakup will be very obvious, looking like steps where there are none, for example.

Chapter 5: Create Adjustment Layers for Nondestructive Changes

ENHANCE COLOR
with an adjustment layer

Colors in a photograph often need to be enhanced. The camera simply is not capable of seeing colors in the world the same way you do. Sometimes the camera and sensor capture colors that have an unpleasant color cast in them; correcting it was discussed in the previous task.

Other times, the colors are out of sync with what you saw in the scene — colors might be stronger or weaker than what you envisioned for the photograph. This is very common when you have a number of bold colors in a photograph and also when you have colors

that show up in both bright and dark areas of the photograph. Because of this, it is usually better to adjust colors individually rather than try to correct everything with one overall color adjustment.

Many times, you also need to give a slight boost to the color to make the picture livelier or more dramatic. You can do all these things with a Hue/Saturation adjustment layer. You use this control the same way it was used in task #24.

In this task, you learn a different way of opening an adjustment layer and renaming it.

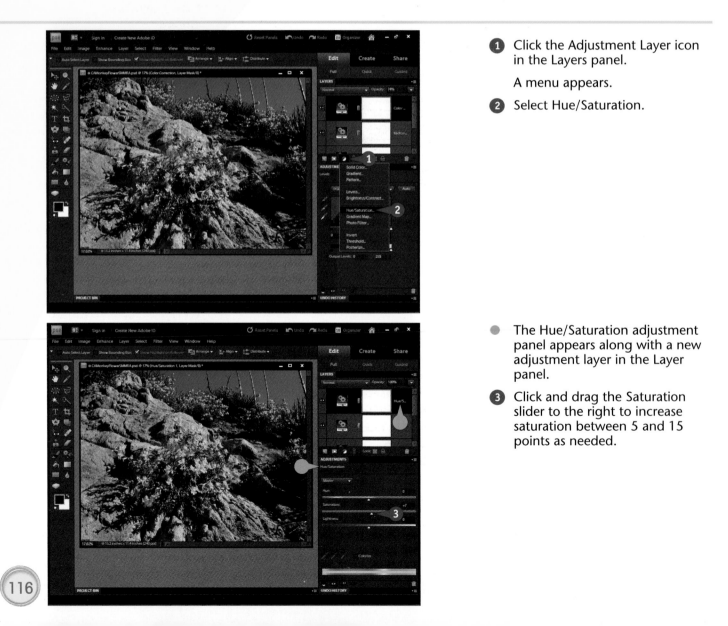

① Click the Adjustment Layer icon in the Layers panel.

A menu appears.

② Select Hue/Saturation.

● The Hue/Saturation adjustment panel appears along with a new adjustment layer in the Layer panel.

③ Click and drag the Saturation slider to the right to increase saturation between 5 and 15 points as needed.

4 Click the Master drop-down menu and select a specific color to adjust.

5 Move the Saturation slider to the right as needed.

You can increase saturation more when you work with individual colors and still avoid problems.

6 Click the Master drop-down menu again and select another specific color to adjust.

7 Move the Hue slider to the right or left to correct a color.

8 Move the Saturation slider to the right as needed.

You can increase saturation more when you work with individual colors and still avoid problems.

TIPS

Caution!

When working with Hue/Saturation, be careful that you do not oversaturate colors. This can make the picture look garish and unattractive very quickly. It is tempting to increase the saturation of your picture to make the colors look bright and lively, but this can also create a harsh quality for the image.

More Options!

You can readjust the panel bin to make it display the layers in your Layers panel better. For example, the Undo History panel does not need as much space as the Layers panel often does. You can click and drag the dividing line between these panels to make them smaller or larger.

Did You Know?

You can change the size of the layers in the Layers panel. You may want them bigger so that the icon appears larger. Do this by clicking the menu icon at the top of the panel, and then going to the bottom of that drop-down menu and selecting Panel Options. This gives you choices for the size of layers.

FIX PROBLEM EXPOSURES
with layer blending modes

At times your picture may be simply too dark or too light. The camera makes a mistake in exposure, or the photographer sets the camera wrong. You end up with a picture that needs immediate correction, either to make it brighter or make it darker.

Photoshop Elements gives you a way to do this in its layer blending modes. You need to add an adjustment layer to your photograph. It really does not matter which adjustment you choose because you will not be using the adjustment layer for its original adjustment purpose. You are simply using this layer so that Photoshop Elements has something to work with

when communicating between layers, which is what layer blending modes do. When you first open the blending modes, you see a long list of choices — ignore them and concentrate on two key modes for photographers: Multiply and Screen.

These photos were shot in the chaparral of the Santa Monica Mountains Recreation Area. These mountains are near Los Angeles, yet most Los Angeles photographers overlook this area and miss great shots. Often photographers overlook nearby places, but with an attitude of discovery you can find amazing areas for photography anywhere.

Fix a Too-Bright Photograph

① Click the Adjustment Layer icon and select Levels.

● The Levels adjustment panel appears along with a new adjustment layer in the Layers panel.

② Click the blending modes drop-down menu, which says Normal by default.

③ Click Multiply.

● The whole photo darkens by about one f-stop.

Fix a Too-Dark Photograph

1 Click the Adjustment Layer icon and select Levels.

● The Levels adjustment panel appears along with a new adjustment layer in the Layers panel.

DIFFICULTY LEVEL

2 Click the blending modes drop-down menu, which says Normal by default.

3 Click Screen.

● The whole photo lightens by about one f-stop.

TIPS

Caution!

These blending modes are no substitute for good exposure. They really can help when you run into problems and challenges with specific images, but you should not use them as a habit because they can only fix limitations in the picture and not capture what was originally in the scene.

More Options!

Noise can be a problem when you use Screen as a blending mode. Noise is always in a picture but is usually well hidden in the darkest parts of the image. Because Screen brightens those dark areas, it also often reveals noise. That is not a problem of Screen, but a fact of life for digital photography.

Did You Know?

Neither Screen nor Multiply have controls other than on or off. You either use them or you do not. However, the layers that they affect do have an important control that you can use, Opacity. With Opacity, you can reduce the effect of Screen or Multiply as you reduce the opacity.

Understand
HOW LAYER MASKS WORK

You may have wondered what the white boxes in the adjustment layers are. Those are layer masks. Layer masks allow you to choose how much of the photograph is affected by an adjustment layer. Very often a photograph needs to be adjusted in different ways across the image. It may be too bright in one area or the wrong color in another. Chapter 4 describes how to use selections to control adjustments in specific areas. Layer masks increase this type of control, and unlike selections, they can always be changed.

New to Photoshop Elements 9, layer masks can now be used with any layer. This allows you to control how much of a layer appears or disappears from your final image. Layer masks affect what a layer does or does not do. They do not affect anything in the photograph itself except as they change what their layer does.

White in a layer mask allows the layer to appear fully, whereas black blocks it. By applying white or black to a layer mask, you can then effectively control specific areas in a photograph and, in those areas, whether a layer works (white) or is not allowed to work (black).

❶ Click the Adjustment Layer icon and select Brightness/Contrast.

● The Brightness/Contrast adjustment panel appears along with a new adjustment layer in the Layers panel.

❷ Change the Brightness slider to −100 so that the picture gets very dark.

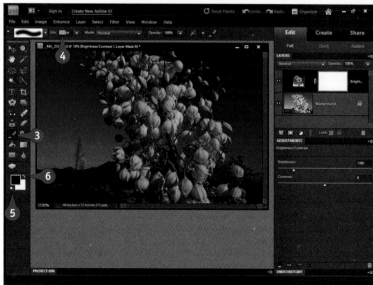

❸ Click the Paintbrush in the toolbox.

❹ Set the brush to a large size using the Options bar under the menu names.

❺ Click the small white-over-black icon below the colors at the bottom of the toolbox.

This resets your foreground, or top, and background, or bottom, colors.

❻ Click the curved arrow between the foreground and background so that black is on top.

The top color is the foreground color and the color for your brush.

7 Click and paint two lines across your picture to create an X.

● A dark X now appears in the layer mask icon.

You did not draw a dark X on the picture, but in the layer mask.

The black X in the layer mask then blocks the original adjustment, a darkening of the image, which creates the lighter X in the picture.

8 Click the curved arrow between the foreground and background colors so that white is on top.

9 Paint out the X in your photograph by painting white over the black.

● This removes the black, which then allows the effect of the adjustment layer to reappear.

TIPS

Did You Know?

Layers plus layer masks are an important benefit of Photoshop Elements and Photoshop. They can take some time to master, but it is worth it. Layers plus layer masks give you a high level of flexible, nondestructive adjustment. They totally isolate parts of a photo from other parts so that you can adjust only what you want adjusted.

Important!

Layer masks affect what a layer does, but not the actual adjustment. This is an important distinction. Putting black in a layer mask might block a darkening effect and make the picture brighter, or it could block a brightening effect and make the picture darker. You have to think in terms of black blocking an effect and not creating its own effect.

Practice!

Layer masks can be counterintuitive for the photographer. Yet they are an extremely important tool to understand. You can do it! It just takes practice. You have to add adjustment layers with different sorts of controls and then paint in black and white to see how the layer mask works to block or allow those adjustments.

Chapter 5: Create Adjustment Layers for Nondestructive Changes

COMBINE TWO PHOTOS
with layer masks

This chapter has been mostly about working with adjustment layers. Add layer masks to them and you gain a very powerful combination. But now, with Photoshop Elements 9, you can add a layer mask to any layer. You will learn more about using layers that are not adjustment layers in the next chapters. This task is about using solid photo layers so that you get a better understanding of how layers and adjustment layers work.

In this task, you will put one photo on top of the other. This is no different than if you were to take to

prints and put one print on top of the other. They show up as layers in the Layers panel, and the top layer blocks the view of the bottom layer, just as if these pictures were sitting on top of each other on your desk.

Suppose you wanted the top photo to stay on top, yet allow some of the bottom picture to show up. With the photos on your desk, you could cut a hole in the top picture. That would allow the bottom picture to show through, but it would also damage the top picture.

1 Open two photos from Organizer.

● They may come into Editor as tabs of a single display window, like a tabbed Web browser.

2 Click a tab and drag it down so that it separates as its own photo.

3 Click and drag the top bar of the photo to change its position on the interface so that you can see some of the second photo under it.

4 Click the Move tool at the upper left corner of the toolbox.

5 Press and hold Shift and then click and drag the top photo so that the cursor goes all the way over the bottom photo.

6 Release your mouse button and then the Shift key.

The top photo is now on a layer over the bottom photo. If you did the steps exactly as described and your photos were the same size, they will also be exactly lined up.

⑦ Click the X at the top right of the first photo to close it in Windows or the red button at the top left of that photo on a Mac. Just click that photo if you cannot see all of it.

● Now you can clearly see the layers representing the two photos.

You see only the top photo because it is covering and blocking view of the bottom photo.

⑧ Click the Layer Mask icon at the bottom of the Layers panel.

TIPS

Important!
The exact steps mentioned here are very important. You must press and hold Shift first, click and drag the top photo so the cursor shows up on the bottom photo, and release the mouse button and then the Shift key. If you do anything else, you get an error message or the photos do not line up correctly.

Important!
The Shift key is a constraint key with your computer. It modifies many things besides making letters capitals. In this task, you are using it to constrain the movement of one photograph onto another. If the two pictures are identical in size, the Shift key makes the move so that the top picture exactly lines up with the bottom.

Practice!
This cannot be overemphasized: You are simply not going to master layers and layer masks by reading this book and trying it a couple of times. Taking some time to master layers is worth it because once you do, you will find that your time in front of Photoshop Elements will be more efficient and effective.

COMBINE TWO PHOTOS
with layer masks

There are many situations where you might want to put one picture on top of another, cut a hole in the top picture, yet keep that top picture undamaged. That might sound like magic, but that is exactly what you can do in Photoshop Elements 9. By adding a layer mask to the top photo, you can create a hole in that top photo to allow the bottom picture to show through. This is the same as if you cut a hole in the top print on your desk, except that you do it with the layer mask so that this hole is not permanent.

As you learn to work with a layer and its layer mask, remember that the layer mask affects only what happens to its layer. Black blocks the layer, whereas white allows the layer and its effects to display. Black in the layer mask then allows you to cut a hole in the photo that represents that layer. If you do not like that hole, then you can paint white over that area to fill it back in. This is a great advantage of layer masks — you can block or restore any part of a layer at will.

● A white box appears in the layer and is the icon for the layer mask.

❾ Select the Paintbrush from the toolbox.

❿ Right-click the photo to get the Brush menu.

⓫ Choose a large soft-edged brush.

⓬ Make the brush larger or smaller by using the bracket keys to the right of the letter P.

⓭ Click the small white-over-black icon below the colors at the bottom of the toolbox.

This resets your foreground, or top, and background, or bottom, colors.

⓮ Click the curved arrow between the foreground and background so that black is on top.

The top color is the foreground color and the color for your brush.

15 Paint over the photo where you want to remove the top photo.

The top photo disappears, blocked by the black you painted into the layer mask.

The soft edge between the pictures comes from the soft brush and the size of the brush.

● Black appears in the layer mask.

16 Click the curved arrow between the foreground and background colors so that white is on top.

17 Paint back parts of the top photo by painting white over the black.

CONTINUED

TIPS

Important!
You must be in the layer mask to use it. That sounds obvious; however, it is easy to miss and end up on the photo itself. The difference between the photo on a layer and its layer mask being active is subtle. The difference is simply a white line around the active part. If strange things start happening to your picture, check your Layers panel to be sure that you are working in the layer mask.

Important!
Color on your photograph tells you that you are working on the photo rather than in the layer mask. When you are working in the layer mask, you should see no colors, just black or white appearing where you are painting your brush. If you do see colors, simply undo that brush stroke with Ctrl/⌘+Z, click the layer mask, and continue.

Try This!
When you are working with layer masks, you can make changes to your brush with your keyboard. You can make your brush larger or smaller by pressing the bracket keys to the right of the letter P. You can also switch back and forth between the foreground and background colors, usually black and white, by pressing the letter X.

REMOVE ADJUSTMENTS
with black

Once you start working with layer masks, you will learn the real power of adjustment layers. It is very common to do early adjustments in a picture and run into a problem with the range of tones. For example, when adjusting most of the picture properly, you may find one small area gets overadjusted. If you try to adjust for that one spot, the rest of the picture does not get the proper adjustment.

A good example is seen here in this photo of Joshua trees in the Mojave National Preserve in California.

This is the densest stand of Joshua trees anywhere. As the dark areas around the trees are brightened, the sky loses its color.

With the adjustment layer's layer mask, you can make the correct adjustment for the overall picture and ignore what happens with one small part. You simply use a black brush and paint over that problem part of the picture in the layer mask. That blocks the adjustment and gives you much more control over your picture.

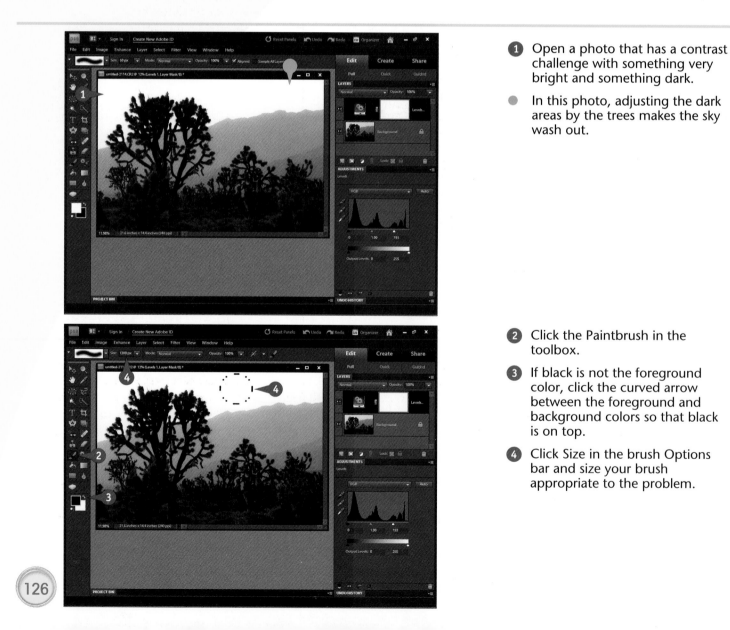

1 Open a photo that has a contrast challenge with something very bright and something dark.

● In this photo, adjusting the dark areas by the trees makes the sky wash out.

2 Click the Paintbrush in the toolbox.

3 If black is not the foreground color, click the curved arrow between the foreground and background colors so that black is on top.

4 Click Size in the brush Options bar and size your brush appropriate to the problem.

5 Paint black over the problem to block the adjustment.

● The layer mask icon indicates the painted area.

6 Change your brush size as needed to block or allow the adjustment in other areas.

TIPS

More Options!

You can change how strong the blocking effect of black is, or the effect of white, by changing the opacity of the brush. You make that change in the Options bar above the photograph. A number of other options are here for affecting how a brush works.

Remember This!

As you gain experience working on layer masks, you will discover that to get the best and most effective layer mask, you constantly have to change the size of your brush. That is normal. Do not try to keep using the same size brush that does not work. Remember the bracket keys to the right of the letter P — the opening bracket ([ ) makes the brush smaller and the closing bracket ( ]) makes it larger.

Important!

Once you start working with more than one adjustment layer, you have to be sure you are in the right layer and layer mask. As you make changes and move among layers, it is easy to get confused and end up on the wrong layer or the wrong layer mask. To be sure, you can simply click the layer mask icon in the correct layer in the Layers panel. The correct layer is also highlighted in black.

ADD ADJUSTMENTS
using black and then white

Sometimes you run into a photograph that simply needs an adjustment in one area but not in the rest of the image. You could try adjusting the whole picture and then blocking out everything in it, doing a lot of work with a black paintbrush. If there really is only a small area that needs to be adjusted, that can be a lot of work.

A better way is to first make the adjustment as best you can for the small area that needs the change. You ignore what happens in the rest of the photograph. Then you block the entire adjustment by filling the entire layer mask with black. Next you take a white paintbrush and bring the adjustment back in only in the areas where you want it. Essentially you are adding an adjustment to a very specific area without affecting the entire picture.

This technique is like using selections, only better, because you can add or subtract the adjustment as needed without having to make a new selection. In this photo of a birthday girl blowing out the candles, the cake is too bright in relation to the rest of the photo. This technique easily fixes that.

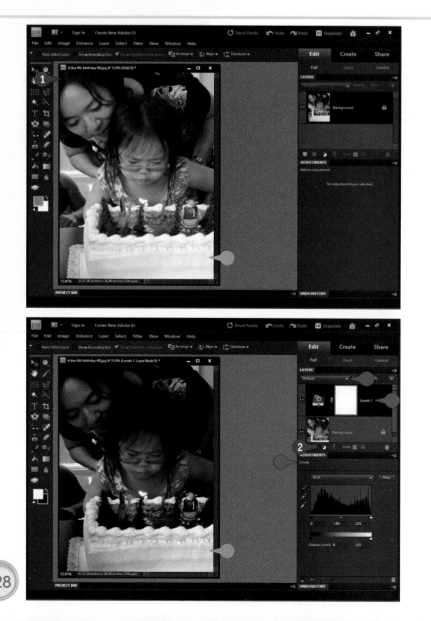

Identify the Problem

1 Open and adjust a photo that has a small area that needs adjustment compared to the rest of the picture.

● In this photo, the mother and child look good, but the white cake is too bright and takes attention away from them.

2 Add an adjustment layer to correct the problem area even though it makes the whole picture look wrong.

● A Levels adjustment layer was added to this photo without adjustment.

● Then the Multiply mode was selected.

● The cake looks much better now, but the rest of the picture is too dark.

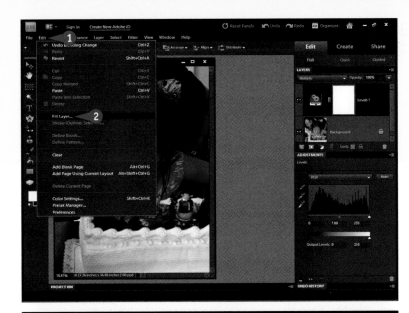

Add Black

1 Click Edit.

2 Select Fill Layer.

● The Fill Layer dialog box appears.

3 Click the Use drop-down menu and select Black.

Leave the other options at their defaults.

4 Click OK.

TIPS

Try This!

All photographers must deal with the challenge of how we see the world compared to the way the camera does. Simply pointing a camera at a scene and taking the picture is no guarantee that the resulting photograph will have the right balance of tones. It can help to check your LCD playback to better see what the camera is capturing.

More Options!

You may be working on a picture and find that the layer mask gets confusing. You cannot tell what you have or have not done. To start with a clean slate, you can fill the layer mask with white by using the Fill Layer command from the Edit menu but choosing white instead of black.

Try This!

When working with the Multiply or Screen blending modes, you may find that the first use of the mode helps but is not enough. If you duplicate this layer, you can increase the effect even more. Duplicate the layer by dragging it to the New Layer icon (▣), which is to the left of the Adjustment Layer icon (▨).

ADD ADJUSTMENTS
using black and then white

A common problem in photographs is a lack of balance among the tones. The camera wants to interpret the scene very differently than your eyes do. You can see all the detail from bright to dark areas just fine, but the camera cannot. To bring that picture back to balance, you need to make some adjustments in Photoshop Elements.

This is exactly what is happening in this image. Although the cake is naturally bright, the camera overemphasizes that brightness. Bright areas can take over an image and draw attention from the important parts of the photo. By balancing

brightnesses in a photo, you can help your photo better communicate.

This is where layer masks really shine. You can very carefully choose exactly what areas of the picture are going to be affected by any individual adjustment. That can mean either blocking an overadjustment or allowing a small area of a very specific adjustment, as shown in this example. You will sometimes hear people say that this is "cheating." That comes from a lack of understanding of how photography really works. You should be able to control your picture to interpret it closer to what you really saw.

● The photo now has a Multiply adjustment layer, but the black in the layer mask blocks its effect.

The picture looks as if no Multiply adjustment has been made at all.

Work with White

① Select the Paintbrush.

② Change the foreground color to white.

③ Change your brush size to match the area that needs to be adjusted.

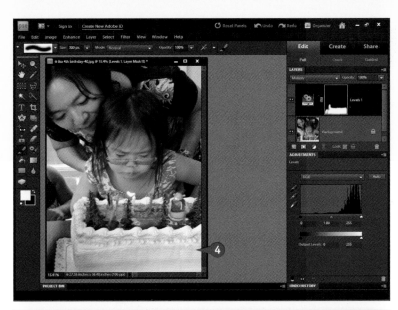

④ Paint the brush with the white foreground color over the area that needs to be changed.

The adjustment is now allowed, but only in that area.

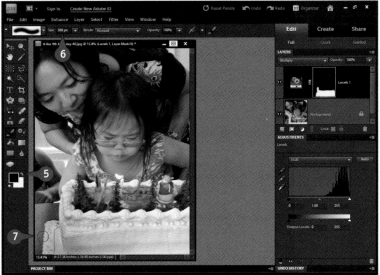

⑤ Change the foreground color to black.

⑥ Make the brush smaller.

⑦ Paint over problems along the edge between adjusted and unadjusted areas.

The black brush now blocks the adjustment again to fix the edge.

TIPS

Important!
Generally you want to use soft-edged brushes for the layer mask. Soft brushes enable you to better blend the adjusted and the unadjusted areas. Hard-edged brushes can cause problems by making your brush lines show up. Use them sparingly.

More Options!
Remember that you can only change the opacity of the layer to affect how strongly the layer works with your photograph. If, for example, you darken bright areas but they look too dark, instead of readjusting the layer, you can simply reduce the opacity of the layer.

Important!
Edges are very important. One thing that often gives away a poorly adjusted image is the edge between an adjusted and unadjusted area. Pay close attention to what is happening along that edge. Use smaller brushes for a tight edge or larger brushes for a soft edge. And when you have a very tight edge, use a selection, even changing the feathering.

COMBINE LAYER MASKS
with selections

Everything you learned about selections still applies when working with adjustment layers and layer masks. Although layer masks give you more options compared to a simple selection, selections are still very useful when working in Photoshop Elements. Sometimes it is easier to simply paint an effect on or off the picture by using white or black, but other times your workflow is more efficient if you create a selection first. When you create a selection and then add an adjustment layer, a layer mask is automatically created for you based on that selection.

A selection limits an effect to one area and blocks the effect outside that area. That certainly sounds familiar. The same sort of thing happens with a layer mask as it limits an effect to an area controlled by white and blocks the effect where the mask is black. Making a selection and then adding an adjustment layer creates a layer mask with white as the selected area and black outside the selection. Selections can be very helpful when very specific areas need to be adjusted, such as creating dark edges for a photograph.

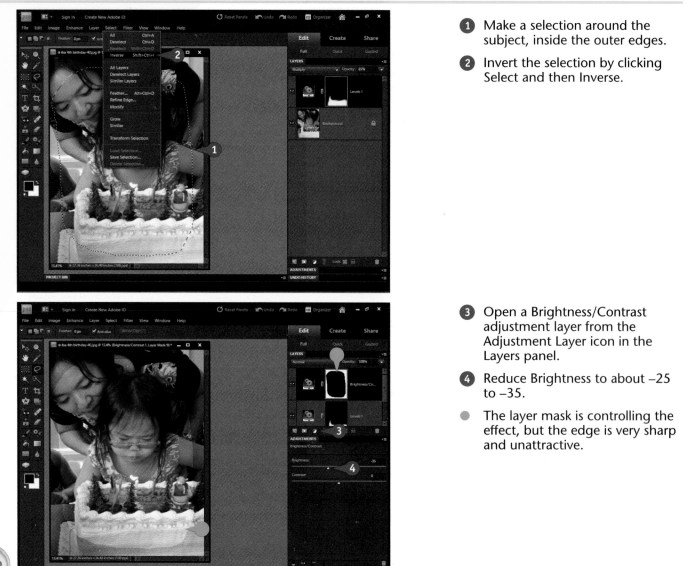

1 Make a selection around the subject, inside the outer edges.

2 Invert the selection by clicking Select and then Inverse.

3 Open a Brightness/Contrast adjustment layer from the Adjustment Layer icon in the Layers panel.

4 Reduce Brightness to about −25 to −35.

● The layer mask is controlling the effect, but the edge is very sharp and unattractive.

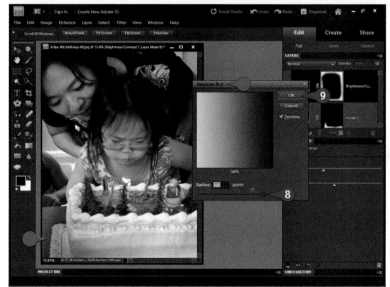

5 Click Filter.

6 Select Blur.

7 Select Gaussian Blur.

● The Gaussian Blur dialog box opens.

8 Click and drag the Radius slider to a high amount.

Depending on the photograph, this can be as low as 40 or as high as more than 200.

9 Click OK.

● A soft darkness is applied to the outer edges of the photo, emphasizing the subject.

TIPS

Did You Know?
Using Gaussian Blur for blending edges has a lot of advantages over using feathering with selections. Feathering must be done to a specific number, and then you click OK and look to see if the effect is what you want. With Gaussian Blur and a layer mask, you can change the Radius and watch the blending occur in real time.

More Options!
When you first open Gaussian Blur, the edge might not appear in the preview box. Simply move your cursor into the picture and click the edge. That immediately places the black-white edge inside the preview box so you can see what happens as Gaussian Blur is increased.

Important!
A great advantage of adjustment layers is the ability to change the adjustment. In this edge-darkening technique, for example, you can always click the Brightness/Contrast adjustment layer and reopen the Adjustments panel. You can then change that edge darkness as desired.

BALANCE COLORS AND TONES
in a picture

A common challenge photographers face is a picture not balanced visually to match the composition or the way that people really see a subject. If you look at a scene, for example, your eye balances out the brightness levels so that you can easily see and compare elements of that scene. The camera does no such thing. If the left side of a scene is brighter than the right, the camera shows it just that way, creating an imbalance in the tones of the picture compared to the way you see the scene. Colors can have a similar problem when one color starts to dominate the picture because it is too saturated compared to the others.

Through the use of adjustment layers and layer masks, you can fix this imbalance and help your photographs communicate something much closer to what you originally saw when you took the picture. Skies are a common problem for imbalance. Skies are typically brighter than the ground, as seen in this photograph of the Mojave mound cactus in the Mojave National Preserve. The clouds are just on the edge of loss of detail from overexposure, yet the cactus and flowers are still fine.

1 Click the Adjustment Layer icon to open a Levels adjustment layer to correct an imbalance in brightness.

2 Adjust the sliders until the problem area looks better, such as the sky in this photo.

● Ignore what happens in the rest of the photo because it will be overadjusted.

③ Click the Gradient tool in the toolbox.

④ Click the curved arrow between the foreground and background colors so that white is on top.

⑤ Click your cursor first in the area where you want to keep your adjustment.

⑥ Drag your cursor into the area where you want to remove the adjustment.

● The Gradient tool puts white in the layer mask up to the point you first click, black in the layer mask past the point you dragged to, and creates a blend between them.

The image now has its tonalities better blended.

TIPS

Did You Know?
If you get the white and black parts of the Gradient tool mixed up, do not worry. That is actually a common challenge when first learning to use the Gradient tool. If you click and drag and the black and white show up in the wrong places, simply do it again in the reverse direction.

More Options!
You may need to do multiple applications of the Gradient tool before the picture looks right. Sometimes the angle will be wrong, other times the gradient will be too short and too obvious, and other times the gradient will be too long and ineffective. Keep trying until your picture looks right.

Important!
Change the adjustment as needed after you use the Gradient tool. Sometimes you will guess wrong as to the correct amount of adjustment to properly balance the picture. When you apply the Gradient tool, the picture may look too dark or too light. Simply readjust that adjustment layer as needed.

BRING OUT SHADOW DETAIL
in specific areas

As you look to balance a picture's tonalities, you often discover small areas that are too dark. These are typically shadows that did not get the same light as the rest of the picture. Yet for the picture to really look right, for it to be interpreted closer to the way you saw a scene, these dark areas need to be increased in brightness.

This photo of a beavertail cactus in bloom shows exactly this challenge. This Mojave Desert flower is in bright sun and the camera exposed correctly for it.

However, the stalks of the plant are too dark and need to be opened up or brightened.

Once again the adjustment layer and its layer mask come to the rescue. You use a blending mode again, the Screen mode, to brighten the dark area, and then the layer mask to limit that change just to the area needed. Although this works very well, one thing you may notice occurring is an increase in noise in those dark areas. There is nothing you can do about that. Revealing detail in dark areas sometimes means revealing the noise there as well.

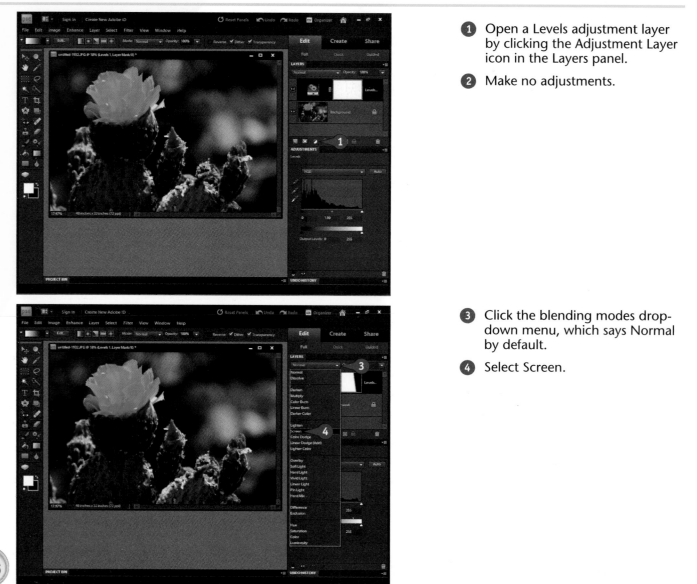

① Open a Levels adjustment layer by clicking the Adjustment Layer icon in the Layers panel.

② Make no adjustments.

③ Click the blending modes drop-down menu, which says Normal by default.

④ Select Screen.

The lightening effect of Screen is applied to the whole picture.

⑤ Open the Fill Layer dialog box from the Edit menu.

⑥ Select Black in the Use drop-down menu in the Contents area.

⑦ Click OK.

58

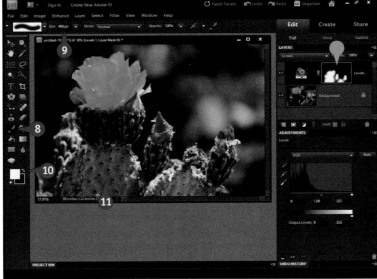

The lightening effect of Screen is blocked.

⑧ Click the Paintbrush in the toolbox.

⑨ Choose a brush size appropriate to the area being adjusted.

⑩ Choose white for the foreground color.

⑪ Paint in the lightening effect.

● The layer mask icon indicates the painted area.

TIPS

Important!
Edges are critical when you are dealing with small areas of change in a photograph and using a layer mask. A sloppily painted edge is very obvious in the picture and distracts the viewer even to the point of the truth of your picture coming into question. Sometimes blurring an edge with Gaussian Blur from the Filter and Blur menus helps.

Apply It!
Work your edges by going back and forth between white and black brushes. In addition, change the size of your brushes by using the bracket keys as you go. If you are really having trouble with an edge, try using a selection to control where the black and white go within your layer mask.

More Options!
You can actually see your layer mask in black and white over your photograph. Position your cursor over the layer mask icon in the layer you are working on. Press Alt/Option as you click the layer mask icon, and the layer mask appears where your picture is. Press Alt/Option and click again to get back to your picture.

DARKEN HIGHLIGHT DETAIL
in specific areas

As you continue to balance a picture's tonalities, you often find too-bright areas. These are typically highlight areas that received more light than your subject. When you expose properly for the subject, your photograph looks good where the subject is but these highlight areas look overexposed. Once again, for the picture to look right, such out-of-balance bright areas need to be balanced, this time brought down in tone.

This photo shows low-growing flowers of the desert star in Joshua Tree National Park in spring. Interesting shadows are around the flowers, but the correct exposure for the flowers makes the sand behind the flowers bright and distracting. That area is brighter than the area where the flowers are and wants to compete with them for attention.

You use an adjustment layer and its layer mask again, but this time using a Brightness/Contrast adjustment layer to darken the right area. The layer mask is used to limit that change just to the area needed. Luckily, no noise problems can come from darkening a bright area, but there are limits as to how much darkening you can do if the area is too overexposed.

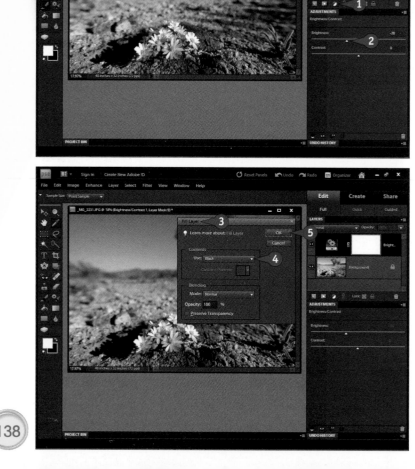

① Open a Brightness/Contrast adjustment layer by clicking the Adjustment Layer icon in the Layers panel.

② Make a darkening adjustment that tones down the overly bright area.

The darkening effect of the adjustment is applied to the whole picture.

③ Open the Fill Layer dialog box from the Edit menu.

④ Select Black in the Use drop-down menu in Contents.

⑤ Click OK.

The darkening effect of the brightness adjustment is blocked so the whole image goes back to its original brightness.

⑥ Click the Paintbrush in the toolbox.

⑦ Choose a brush size appropriate to the area being adjusted.

⑧ Choose white for the foreground color.

⑨ Paint in the darkening effect.

● The layer mask icon indicates the painted area.

TIPS

Important!
Exposure is very important when dealing with bright and highlighted areas in a photograph. If a bright area is too washed out, no amount of work in Photoshop Elements will bring in any detail. When bright areas in a picture absolutely have to have detail, they must be captured when you take the picture.

Did You Know?
Sometimes when you make a correction to a specific area in the photograph, the whole photograph changes in its appearance, maybe looking too bright or too dark overall. You can simply go back to your midtones adjustment layer, reopen the adjustment, and make a correction.

More Options!
You do not have to limit your adjustments to simply fixing a bright area or a dark area. If your photograph needs help in both areas, then use two different adjustment layers, one using Brightness/Contrast or set to Multiply and one set to Screen, and then use the layer masks appropriately to fix both places.

FLATTEN LAYERS
when done

After working on your photo, you will come to the point where you are more or less done with it. You can save and store this photo as a Photoshop PSD file, and keep all its layers. Sometimes, however, you may want a simpler file that you can quickly use for purposes other than adjusting it inside Photoshop Elements. The PSD file format and Photoshop layers are not generally recognized outside of Adobe programs, so even though you can save layers with a TIFF file, that will not do you much good. If you gave a TIFF file to someone else, they probably could not read it.

At this point, a good idea is to flatten the image, merging the layers together into a simplified image file, and then save the picture in a new file, in the appropriate format. If you are going to use a photo for the Web or e-mail, select a JPEG file. If you are preparing pictures for use in a brochure or other publication, you might decide to use a TIFF file. You can flatten an image using the Layer menu or through the Layers panel drop-down menu.

Use the Menu to Flatten

1 Click Layer.

2 Select Flatten Image.

All layers and their effects are now merged.

Use the Panel Menu to Flatten

1 Click the panel menu icon at the right of the Layers tab.

This icon is a set of horizontal lines and can be hard to see.

A drop-down menu appears.

2 Select Flatten Image.

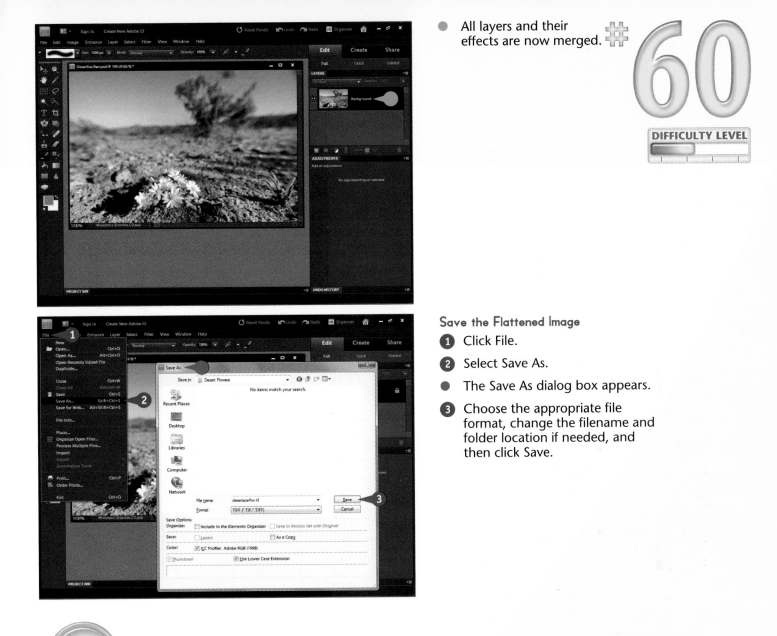

- All layers and their effects are now merged.

60

DIFFICULTY LEVEL

Save the Flattened Image

1 Click File.

2 Select Save As.

- The Save As dialog box appears.

3 Choose the appropriate file format, change the filename and folder location if needed, and then click Save.

TIPS

Did You Know?

Some photographers save all their layered files forever, just in case they want to revise the pictures. Other photographers find that saving all these layered files can get to be unwieldy and unnecessary for their workflow. There is no arbitrary right or wrong to this. It depends entirely on how comfortable you are with your work.

Important!

Once your file is flattened and closed, you have no access to the original layers. If you flatten the file, you can always undo this in the Undo History panel if the picture is still open. But if an image is flattened, saved and closed, that opportunity is gone and the layers are gone as well.

Try This!

You can combine all your layers and their effects into a single layer on top of the layer stack so that you have access to a "flattened file" and layers at the same time. Click the top layer and then press Ctrl+Shift+Alt+E or ⌘+Shift+Option+E. This merges the layers and then creates a new layer with that image on top of the layer stack.

Chapter 6

Solve Photo Problems

For most photographers, the fun is in taking the pictures. Photoshop Elements is a way to get the most from your pictures, but is rarely an end in itself for a photographer. For that reason, you will enjoy working with Photoshop Elements most after you have already taken the best possible picture with your camera. You do not want to have to fix problems in the picture that could have been avoided.

There will be problems in your photos that you are going to need to fix, such as dust on the sensor, unwanted light flare, blank skies, and more. They are not anyone's fault, but can crop up in a picture due to many factors, and can keep that picture from being all that it can be. Regardless, you want them out of your picture.

Photoshop Elements includes some excellent tools to deal with problems in the picture after you have done your basic processing. Some of them do take some time and practice to master, however. Do not be discouraged if you try something like the Clone tool and your results are not perfect at first. With practice and experience, you can master any tool in Photoshop Elements.

Top 100

#61 Clone Out Problems 144   DIFFICULTY LEVEL

#62 Remove People from a Scene with Photomerge Scene Cleaner. 148   DIFFICULTY LEVEL

#63 Remove Unwanted Objects with Content-Aware Spot Healing. 150   DIFFICULTY LEVEL

#64 Fix Problems due to Lens Distortion 152   DIFFICULTY LEVEL

#65 Fix Perspective Problems with Building Photographs. 154   DIFFICULTY LEVEL

#66 Remove Dead Space with Recompose. 156   DIFFICULTY LEVEL

#67 Make an Out-of-Focus Background. 158   DIFFICULTY LEVEL

#68 Remove Distracting Colors 160   DIFFICULTY LEVEL

#69 Improve Blank Skies 162   DIFFICULTY LEVEL

#70 Create the Focus with Gaussian Blur. 166   DIFFICULTY LEVEL

#71 Add a New Background for Your Subject 168   DIFFICULTY LEVEL

CLONE OUT
problems

Cloning works essentially by copying a small part of the photograph from one area and then pasting that copy onto a new location in the photograph. This occurs without you having to actually perform any copy and paste commands. All you have to do is tell Photoshop Elements where you want the cloning to start from, how big of a copy you want to make, and where to place the copy.

You set a "clone-from" point by pressing Alt/Option as you click over the good part of the photo. You tell Photoshop Elements how big a copy you want to

make by the size you choose for your brush. Finally, you click over your problem area and the program knows where to place the little copy under the cloning point.

The photo here shows mussels and gooseneck barnacles at low tide along the coast of Southern California. When the camera is down at the level of the shells, the setting is revealed in the background, but so are some people. This is a busy beach, so removing the people in Photoshop Elements is easier than trying to wait them out.

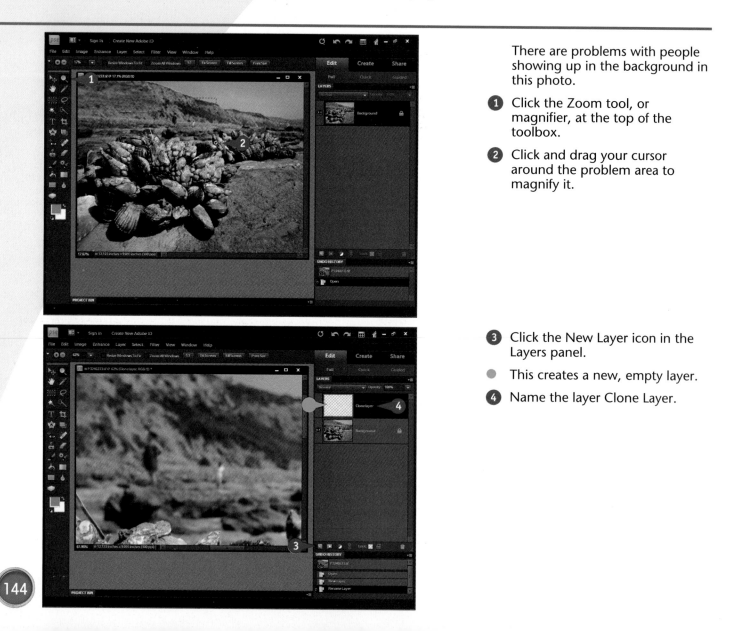

There are problems with people showing up in the background in this photo.

1. Click the Zoom tool, or magnifier, at the top of the toolbox.

2. Click and drag your cursor around the problem area to magnify it.

3. Click the New Layer icon in the Layers panel.

● This creates a new, empty layer.

4. Name the layer Clone Layer.

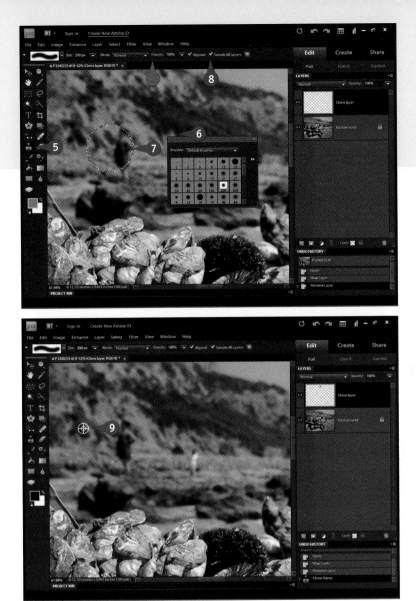

5. Click the Clone Stamp tool in the toolbox.

6. Right-click the photograph to open the brush menu to quickly select a specific size of brush.

7. Pick a brush size appropriate to the problem.

● Leave Mode at Normal, Opacity 100%, and Aligned selected.

8. Select Sample All Layers (■ changes to ✓).

9. Press Alt/Option as you click a problem-free area near your problem.

This sets the clone-from point.

TIPS

Did You Know?

For most cloning, you will use the Aligned option for the Clone Stamp tool. This keeps the clone-from and clone-to points at the same distance and angle from each other as you clone. If your clone-from area is very small, deselect Aligned so that the clone-from point always goes back to that area.

Try This!

If you run into trouble with the settings of any tool, including the Clone Stamp tool, you can quickly reset the tool back to its defaults. Click the small down arrow at the far left of the Options bar over the toolbox. This gives you a menu with the reset option. Usually you can just select Reset Tool.

Try This!

Once you magnify the area where you are cloning, you may need to adjust the position of that area slightly. If you press the spacebar, the cursor changes to a Hand icon. Keep pressing the spacebar and then click and drag the picture to move it around. This works with any tool in Photoshop Elements.

CLONE OUT
problems

It is not unusual to find unexpected objects in your photograph simply because you did not see them when you pressed the shutter. This can occur when you concentrate so hard on the subject that you do not see the rest of the photo. Such inadvertent objects can be very annoying and distracting. Other problems can include undesirable *lens flare* — the little light spots and circles near a bright light — or a misplaced piece of trash in the picture.

The Clone Stamp tool is a powerful way of covering up such problems. Click as you go for each clone spot rather than brushing continuously, reset your

clone-from point whenever you see problems, and change your brush size as you go. By doing these things, your cloning looks more natural, without repeating patterns called *cloning artifacts*.

Cloning takes practice. It also works best when you clone to a layer. By cloning to a layer you keep all of this work separated from the photograph itself. You can then work on that layer without messing up the original picture. This frees you to really concentrate on the cloning because you do not have to worry about doing something wrong that cannot be fixed.

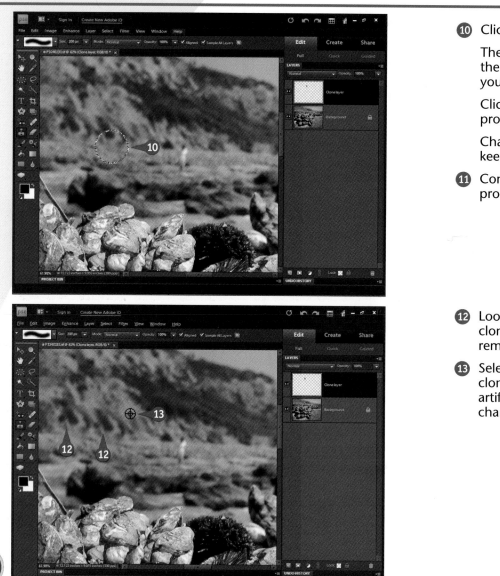

10 Click over the problem area.

The cursor shows the source of the clone as an overlay to help you find where to click.

Click multiple times to cover the problem.

Change your clone-from point to keep the clone work blending.

11 Continue clicking until the problem area is covered.

12 Look for repeating patterns, or cloning artifacts, that need to be removed.

13 Select a new clone-from point to clone back over the problem artifacts. You may need to change the cloning size, too.

Because you are on a layer, it does not matter if your cloning goes too far.

⑭ If it does, click the Eraser tool.

⑮ Choose a small brush size.

⑯ Erase the problem from the layer.

The rest of the photo is not affected.

⑰ Click and clone over additional problems in the same way.

TIPS

Try This!
If cloning starts to look messy, take the Eraser tool and erase the work. Because you are working on a layer, you are only erasing something applied *over* the actual picture. You can always turn the visibility of the layer on and off to see this by clicking the Eye icon at the left side of the layer.

Important!
To do cloning well takes practice. At first, it takes some time as you continually change your clone-from point and brush size so that the cloning blends well. Doing this is important because poorly done cloning draws attention to itself very quickly.

Did You Know?
Dust spots in the sky from sensor dust can be cleaned up using the Spot Healing Brush. This tool is in the group of tools just above the Eraser tool. With it, you simply click the dust spot and Photoshop Elements copies something nearby over that spot and helps it blend. You can also use this tool with layers — select Sample All Layers in the Options bar.

REMOVE PEOPLE FROM A SCENE
with Photomerge Scene Cleaner

So many wonderful photo opportunities are available in public areas. These places attract a lot of people as well. This often means that photographing without people getting into your shot can be difficult. A common challenge is a person talking on a cellphone in one spot, unfortunately in your shot, because of trouble getting service anywhere else, as illustrated by the photo seen here. This historic building is the old lightkeeper's house for the lighthouse at Point Fermin in San Pedro, California.

Sometimes you can wait until the person moves off or a gap occurs in the flow of the crowd so that you get

a picture without people. But often you cannot, especially if you are traveling with family who want to move on and see the other sights of the area.

The Photomerge Scene Cleaner in Photoshop Elements enables you to remove people from a scene. You have to shoot two or more pictures of that scene so that the people walking through it are not all in one place. Shoot from the same position, with the same exposure, and hold your camera as steady as possible so that the overall framing of your picture does not change much.

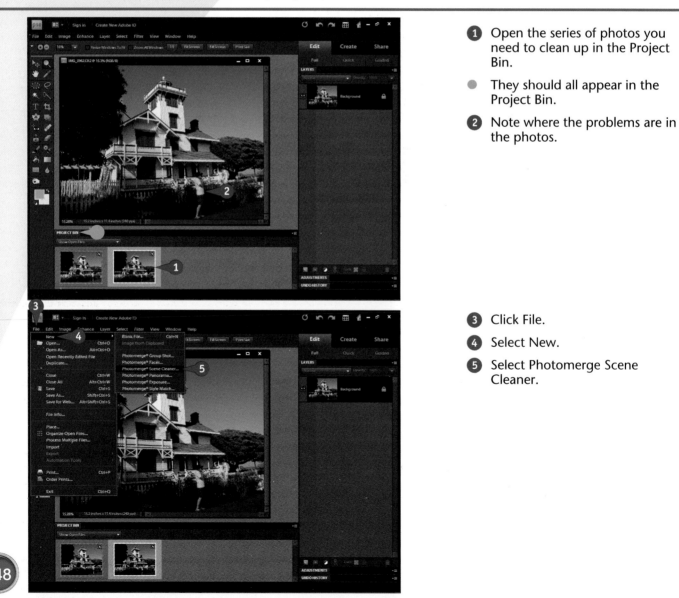

① Open the series of photos you need to clean up in the Project Bin.

● They should all appear in the Project Bin.

② Note where the problems are in the photos.

③ Click File.

④ Select New.

⑤ Select Photomerge Scene Cleaner.

The Photomerge Scene Cleaner opens with your first image.

● A how-to panel also appears.

⑥ Drag a different photo of your group into the Final photo window.

⑦ Click the Pencil tool in the how-to panel.

⑧ Draw around the object you want to remove in the Final frame.

A blue line appears in both the photos, and then the final photo line disappears as the photos are merged.

Note: When you are done circling areas, the program updates and shows you where the area came from that is doing the scene cleanup.

⑨ Alternatively, draw around an area in the Source window that you want to move to the Final frame.

Photomerge moves parts of the Source photo appropriately to the Final photo.

⑩ Click Done when you are finished.

The photo opens as a new image into Edit Full with layers holding the work you did.

TIPS

Did You Know?
Photoshop Elements includes some pretty amazing alignment work in its Photomerge feature. To match everything in the Scene Cleaner, the picture elements within the scene must line up. The program analyzes the pictures and lines them up for you. It helps to keep the image frame lined up as best you can while you shoot.

Try This!
The Scene Cleaner may not work immediately the way you want it to. Undo your work, and then try drawing around a different part of the picture, drawing tighter to an area, and drawing in both the Source and the Final images because you will get different results.

Try This!
Once you are done using the Scene Cleaner, you may discover that the photograph still has some imperfections. Instead of trying to do it all over again in the Scene Cleaner, it may be quicker and easier to use the Clone Stamp tool or the Content-Aware Spot Healing Brush to make small corrections as needed.

REMOVE UNWANTED OBJECTS
with Content-Aware Spot Healing

When you try to remove something that does not belong in the image, it can be challenging to make the correction match its surroundings. It can take a lot of work with the Clone Stamp tool or require just the right pair of pictures to use Photomerge Scene Cleaner.

The Content-Aware option for the Spot Healing Brush changes how you remove unwanted things in your image. This tool looks at what surrounds the problem, then it covers up the problem by using the texture, color, and lines of the surroundings so that everything matches. The Spot Healing Brush itself simply blends

a spot that you click into its surroundings. It does not look for things like texture and lines, so it cannot match them. That is the big change for the new Content-Aware function.

The photo here is of a stream in Sedona, Arizona. The camera is close to the water to emphasize the patterns of the water. However, it is so close that water droplets splash onto the lens, creating the annoying line at the lower right. This is a difficult scene to correct by cloning because of all the lines and texture in the water.

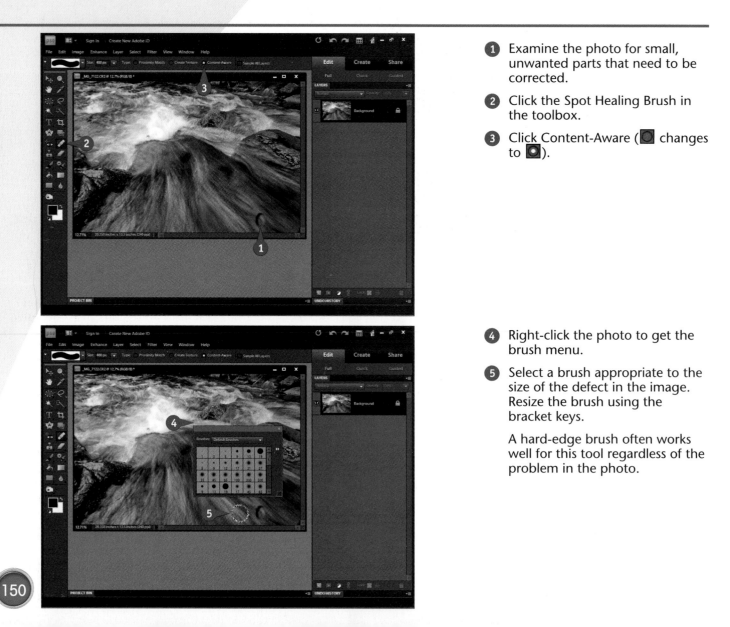

① Examine the photo for small, unwanted parts that need to be corrected.

② Click the Spot Healing Brush in the toolbox.

③ Click Content-Aware (⬚ changes to ⬤).

④ Right-click the photo to get the brush menu.

⑤ Select a brush appropriate to the size of the defect in the image. Resize the brush using the bracket keys.

A hard-edge brush often works well for this tool regardless of the problem in the photo.

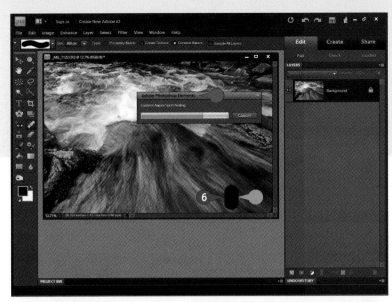

6 Brush over the problem.

● A dark area appears over the spot you have brushed.

● A status panel also appears.

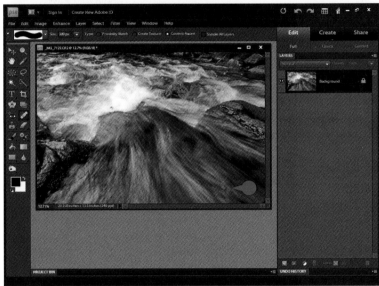

● The Content-Aware Spot Healing Brush moves parts of the photo appropriately over the problem and then matches what it has done to the photo.

TIPS

Important!
Content-Aware cannot be used for everything. Sometimes cloning is better because you have very specific control over what is moved into a particular area. Content-Aware spot healing sometimes pulls in the wrong things to match the area you are working with. However, the tool is so good that it is often worth using even if you end up undoing the change before trying something else.

Try This!
If you try using the Content-Aware Spot Healing Brush and your correction does not completely match, do not immediately undo it. Try using the tool again over roughly the same area. The algorithms underlying this tool look for slightly new things each time you do this.

Did You Know?
The Content-Aware Spot Healing Brush has some very complex algorithms working inside Photoshop Elements to make it do its job. Because of this complexity, the brush can take a bit of time to complete its work. The larger the area that you try to work on, the longer this can take. Slower computers take longer than faster computers.

Chapter 6: Solve Photo Problems 151

Fix problems due to
LENS DISTORTION

Many photographers have discovered the benefits of large-range zooms that go from very wide angles to extreme telephoto focal lengths, such as 18-200mm or 28-300mm. These lenses offer a lot of focal-length options in one lens, making them ideal for travel as well as a convenient way to be prepared for any subject. These lenses are available for digital single lens reflex (dSLR) cameras, and come built into many advanced compact digital cameras.

Such extreme focal-length changes in one lens, however, challenge lens manufacturers. Most of these lenses have something called *barrel distortion*,

especially common when shot at wider focal lengths. This causes an outward curving of straight lines near the top, bottom, or sides of the photograph. You can see this in the horizon of this photograph of a stranded jellyfish on a Florida beach at sunrise. The camera is being held just above the sand for this low angle shot.

You can correct this in Photoshop Elements in the Correct Camera Distortion filter, even though you are actually correcting lens distortion. You can apply this only to actual pixels of a photo, so this does not work on adjustment layers.

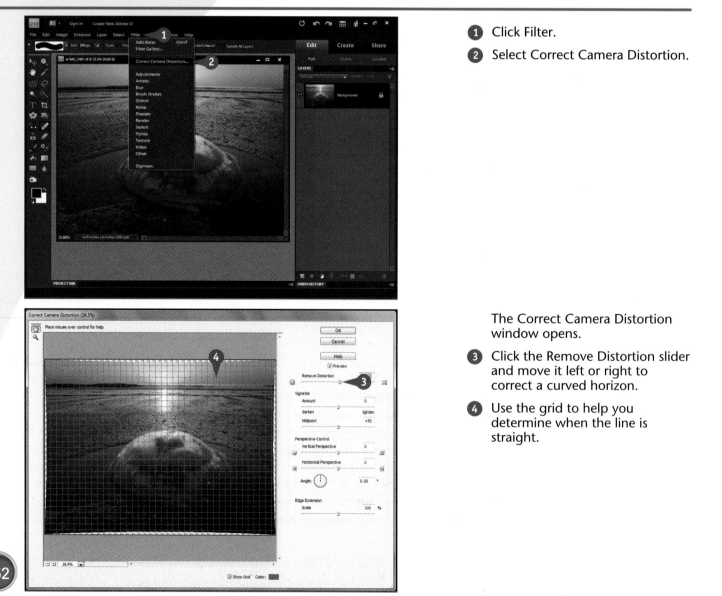

1 Click Filter.

2 Select Correct Camera Distortion.

The Correct Camera Distortion window opens.

3 Click the Remove Distortion slider and move it left or right to correct a curved horizon.

4 Use the grid to help you determine when the line is straight.

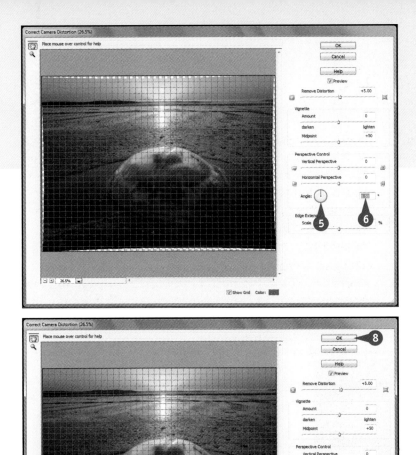

⑤ Correct any crooked horizons by clicking the Angle icon and dragging the pointer.

⑥ You can also correct crooked photos by typing a number in the angle degrees box.

⑦ Adjust the Edge Extension slider until the edges are solid, with no gaps.

⑧ When you have corrected the photo, click OK.

The photo opens into Edit Full with your work displayed as a single layer.

TIPS

More Options!

You can wait to fix the frame edges until the photo is back in the main Photoshop Elements work area. Sometimes this gives you more options for the final look of the image. In this case, do not use the Edge Extension slider. Instead, use the Crop tool in Photoshop Elements to crop out the distorted edges of the final photo.

Try This!

After you have used your camera and its lens or lenses, you will learn what focal lengths create the most distortion. You can then try to avoid the problem when shooting by keeping strong horizontal or vertical lines away from the edges of the photograph. You can also disguise those edges by having something in the photo cut across them, such as a tree or a rock.

Try This!

The Vignette controls in the Correct Camera Distortion window are designed to correct uneven brightness from the center to the corners of the picture. Some lenses, especially wide-angle focal lengths of long-range zooms, darken the outside parts of the picture; you can correct such images using the Vignette sliders.

FIX PERSPECTIVE PROBLEMS
with building photographs

Buildings stand tall, but when you photograph them, they often look like they are falling over backward. This is because when you get close to a building and point your camera up to photograph it, the camera and lens accentuate perspective so that the building appears smaller at the top than at the bottom. This is especially common with wide-angle focal lengths. In the past, you had to use very expensive gear to correct it, which meant architectural photography was not as accessible for the average photographer. In many situations, a leaning building weakens the look of the building.

Correct Camera Distortion once again comes to the rescue. Although the filter is commonly used for buildings, you can also use it for trees, cliffs, and other tall objects. By straightening up these objects, they gain a very majestic look in your photograph.

The image seen here shows an old hotel that has been converted into a very nice bed-and-breakfast in Independence, California. Independence is an historic small town in the Owens Valley part of California just east of the Sierra Nevada Mountains.

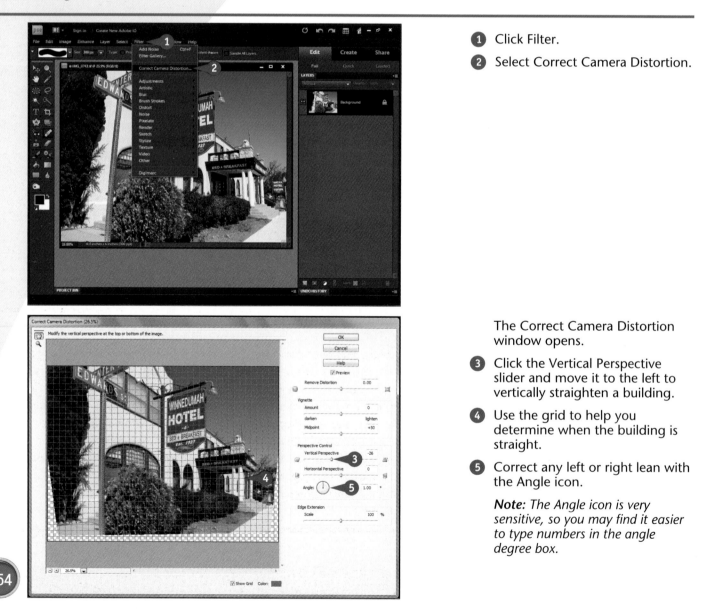

① Click Filter.

② Select Correct Camera Distortion.

The Correct Camera Distortion window opens.

③ Click the Vertical Perspective slider and move it to the left to vertically straighten a building.

④ Use the grid to help you determine when the building is straight.

⑤ Correct any left or right lean with the Angle icon.

Note: The Angle icon is very sensitive, so you may find it easier to type numbers in the angle degree box.

154

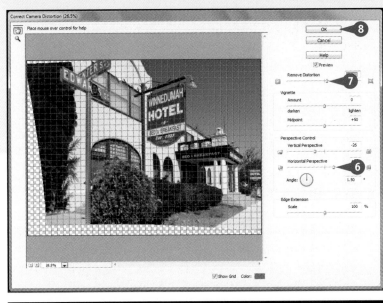

6 Click the Horizontal Perspective slider and move it to the left or right to adjust the horizontal perspective.

7 Click the Remove Distortion slider and move it to the left or right to fix any barrel or pincushion distortion from the lens.

8 When you have corrected the photo, click OK.

The photo opens into Edit Full with your work displayed as a single layer.

9 Click the Crop tool in the toolbox.

10 Use the Crop tool to crop out the distorted edges of the final picture.

11 Click the green check mark icon when you are finished.

TIPS

Did You Know?
To control perspective in the past, such as leaning buildings, photographers had to use special equipment. They would use perspective control lenses that allowed them to move the lens to get a whole building into the scene instead of tilting the camera. A view camera offered the same control.

Try This!
As you adjust the perspective of your picture, you may find you lose certain parts of the image. Often you can do nothing about that. In that case, use your Crop tool creatively. Instead of trying to get everything into the picture, which cannot be done, crop your picture so that it looks interesting.

Try This!
When you tilt the camera up at a tall building, perspective always makes it look as though it is falling backward. If you use a very wide-angle lens and get very close to the building, this can be a dramatic effect and not something you want to correct.

REMOVE DEAD SPACE
with Recompose

Sometimes people and objects do not cooperate when you photograph them. When you get extra space around your subject, you can use the Crop tool to remove pixels that do not belong in the picture. But what if those extra spaces are in between subjects, such as a mom and daughter standing too far apart, a soccer game where players and ball are separated too much compared to the reality of the game, and so on?

Or what if, as in this image of wind turbines near Palm Springs, California, cropping changes the image too much? These wind turbines are framed in a 35mm format that does not fit 8×10, for example. Cropping

to 8×10 would make the turbines look cramped, without the space that gives the open feeling to the image.

The Recompose tool enables you to deal with such problems simply and easily. When you are using this tool, Photoshop Elements very smartly examines your picture to find important objects in it. Then as you change the size of the picture, Photoshop Elements keeps the important objects at the same size while carving out dead space in between them. The results can be quite remarkable.

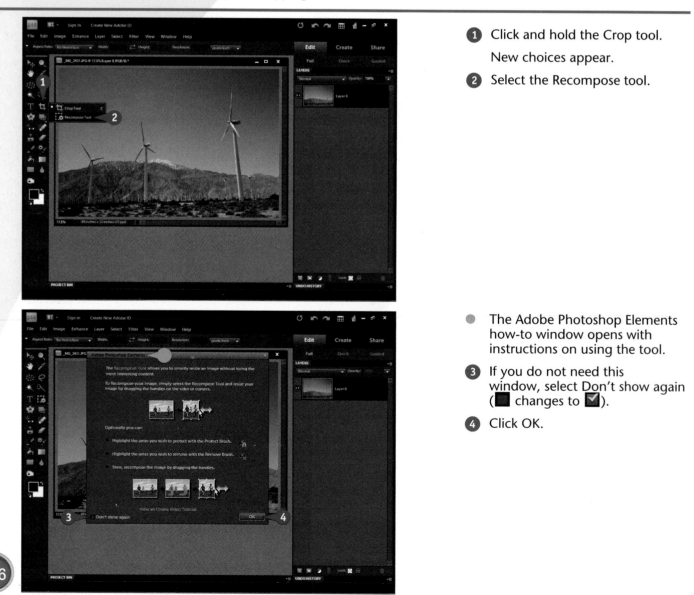

① Click and hold the Crop tool.

New choices appear.

② Select the Recompose tool.

● The Adobe Photoshop Elements how-to window opens with instructions on using the tool.

③ If you do not need this window, select Don't show again (■ changes to ✓).

④ Click OK.

⑤ Click a control box along the edge of the photograph.

When your cursor changes to a double arrow, you are over the box.

⑥ Drag the side in to have Photoshop Elements smartly crop and recompose the photo.

⑦ Click the green check mark icon when you are done.

Photoshop Elements processes the recomposition to make this change work.

The image appears as a layer.

⑧ Click and hold the Recompose tool to select the Crop tool from the toolbox.

⑨ Use the Crop tool to crop out the blank edges of the final picture.

⑩ Click the green check mark icon when you are finished.

TIPS

Caution!
Be careful of altering reality. Bringing man-made wind turbine towers closer together so they better fit a certain crop does not alter the basic relationships among the pictorial elements in the image. You can change the image so much that the photograph becomes a lie. Simply tightening up a photo where people were captured too far apart is altering a photo, but not reality if these people were originally closer together and the basic relationships stay the same. Change as much as you want if you are after a fantasy image; label it as such.

Try This!
For more precise control, use the green and red brushes (⬛ and ⬛). You will find them at the top of the photo in the Options bar for the Recompose tool. Choose the green brush, and then paint over areas you want to protect so Photoshop Elements protects them as you change the size of the photo. Choose the red brush and paint over areas you want to remove.

Make an
OUT-OF-FOCUS BACKGROUND

A good background in a photo can really showcase your subject. But for a variety of reasons, sometimes you simply cannot take a picture of your subject in front of a great background. This can be especially true if you are taking a snapshot of family with a little point-and-shoot camera you just happen to have in your pocket.

One way of improving backgrounds is to make them out of focus. Sometimes you can do this when you are taking the picture, but you can also blur the background behind your subject in Photoshop

Elements. The latter action can give you more control over your background, although making it look right can be a challenge. Although you can use selections to blur a background, you will find you get faster results and they look better when you use layers.

In this photo, the birthday girl has a great expression of joy. Yet the presence of background shapes and colors of other kids in the frame distract the viewer's attention. By blurring these areas to make them look out of focus, the birthday girl stands out better in the photograph.

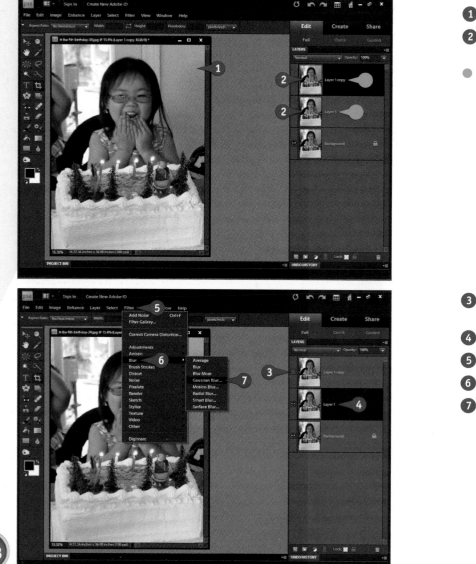

1 Click your flattened photo.

2 Press Ctrl/⌘+J twice to duplicate your layer twice.

● Duplicate layers appear over your original.

3 Click the top layer's Eye icon to turn it off.

4 Click the middle layer to select it.

5 Click Filter.

6 Select Blur.

7 Select Gaussian Blur.

- The Gaussian Blur dialog box appears.

8 Click and drag the Radius slider until the background looks out of focus.

9 Ignore what is happening to the subject.

10 Click OK.

11 Click the top layer's Eye icon to turn the layer back on.

 # 67

DIFFICULTY LEVEL

12 Click the top layer to select it.

13 Click the Layer Mask icon to add a layer mask.

14 Select a good-sized brush based on the area of the background, and change the size as you go.

15 Select black for the foreground color.

16 Click and drag the black brush to block the sharp parts of the top photo layer so the underlying blurred parts show through.

- Black brush strokes appear in the layer mask icon.

  If you go too far, change the foreground color to white and paint back the lost items.

TIPS

Caution!

Be careful of the amount of blur used. Too much blur and the photo looks surreal. Also, watch the edges as you erase. Change your brush size and hardness as you go around important edges on your subject. You may also need a selection to protect an important edge.

Try This!

If you want to keep your layers, you can use the merge and copy layers technique discussed in task #60. You need a flattened "photo," but a flattened layer representing that photo will do. Select the top layer and then press Ctrl+Shift+Alt+E in Windows or ⌘+Shift+Option+E on a Mac to create a merged-flattened layer above it that can be used for this task.

Try This!

You can also make a selection around your subject, feather it appropriately, and then press Delete or Backspace to reveal the background. On some photos, this provides better results than the Eraser technique, especially if the subject has a lot of intricate edge detail. On other photos, making a selection just takes more time, and the Eraser technique is more efficient.

Remove
DISTRACTING COLORS

Color is important for most photographs. Color is not, however, arbitrary and constant. Any color is influenced by other colors around it, dark or bright areas near it, people's feelings about it, and how a particular sensor and camera deal with it. Colors are never a constant.

When you have a distracting color within the image area, it can detract from your picture. This probably happens most commonly with bright colors such as red and yellow. Bright colors draw the viewer's eye away from other parts of the picture. This is especially true if the subject does not have bright

colors that can compete with it. In this image of simple rose flowers, the yellow trumpet flowers in the background want to fight a bit with the roses. The yellow and red are both strong colors and so both attract a viewer's eyes. In addition, the yellow color interacts with the red roses in the image in a less than pleasing way.

Any color can be a problem, too, when it is bright and saturated and draws attention away from the focus of the photo. Toning down or even removing problem colors can be an important adjustment for your photograph.

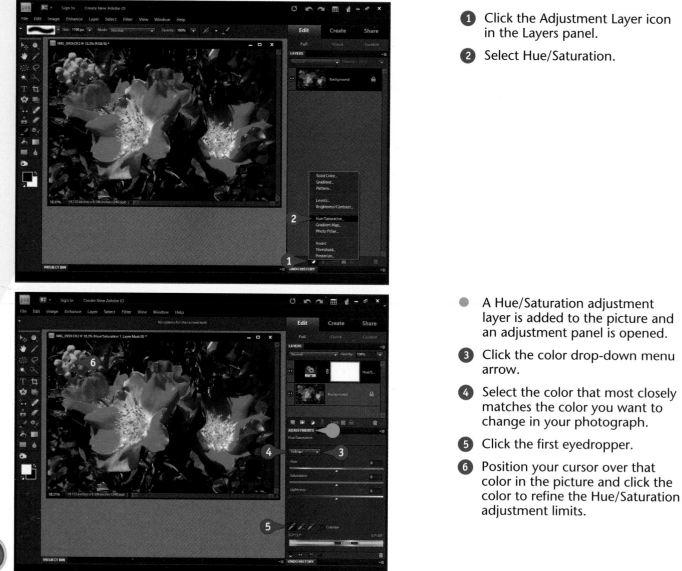

① Click the Adjustment Layer icon in the Layers panel.

② Select Hue/Saturation.

● A Hue/Saturation adjustment layer is added to the picture and an adjustment panel is opened.

③ Click the color drop-down menu arrow.

④ Select the color that most closely matches the color you want to change in your photograph.

⑤ Click the first eyedropper.

⑥ Position your cursor over that color in the picture and click the color to refine the Hue/Saturation adjustment limits.

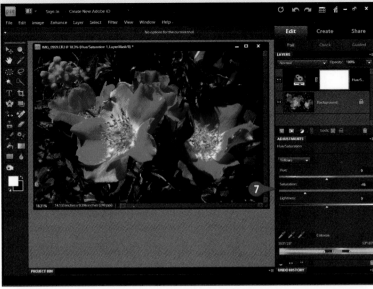

 # 68

DIFFICULTY LEVEL

⑦ Adjust the Hue, Saturation, and Lightness sliders until the color becomes less dominant in the picture.

Usually, the Saturation slider provides the greatest change, but try them all.

In this photo, reducing the yellow has hurt the centers of the roses.

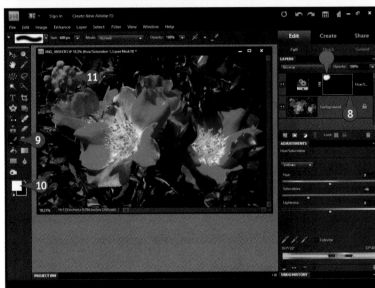

⑧ Press Ctrl/⌘+I to invert the white layer mask to black.

⑨ Click the Paintbrush tool.

⑩ Change the foreground color to white.

⑪ Paint white over the problem color area.

This enables you to limit the color adjustment to only one part of the picture.

● White brush strokes appear in the layer mask icon.

TIPS

Did You Know?
You can change the layer mask between black and white in a couple of ways. One is to press Ctrl/⌘+I to invert a color mask from white to black or black to white. Another is to click the Edit menu and then select Fill Layer to completely fill the layer mask with black or white, which replaces any work done in the layer mask. The layer mask has to be selected and active for any of this to work.

Try This!
Use this technique to tone down a color in the background of your photograph that cannot be removed any other way. You may find that you cannot crop that color out nor can you blur it without adversely affecting the rest of the picture. Yet, by simply toning it down, you make it less dominant.

Try This!
If several colors are giving you problems, use a separate adjustment layer for each one. Although you can do more than one color with a single adjustment layer, that can be confusing. Using single layers for each color makes it easy to go to the exact layer needed for any adjustment. Name your layers by the color affected.

Improve
BLANK SKIES

During the day, skies are bright. Typically, they are much brighter than anything on the ground. If you try to photograph the sky so that it has good color, you usually end up with a silhouette for a subject. If you expose to get good detail in the subject, then the sky becomes blank, or white. Another problem occurs when photographing on days with a hazy sky. The sky often looks blank in the photograph then, as well.

You can see such a blank sky in this photo of California buckwheat flowers in the Santa Monica Mountains. The sky is important because it does

define the edge of the mountains, yet such a blank white is distracting. No single exposure can hold detail in the flowers and the sky at the same time.

You could select the sky and simply fill it with a blue. This usually does not look very good, even to the point of looking quite artificial. Skies are not a consistent shade of blue. They are darker higher in the sky, and get lighter closer to the horizon. You need to duplicate this when fixing a blank sky so that it looks right.

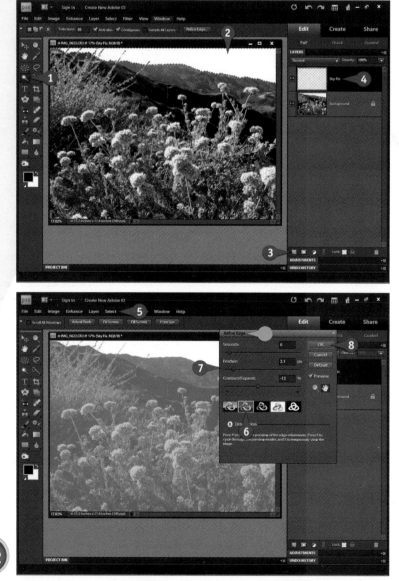

1 Click the Magic Wand selection tool.

2 Click the sky to select it.

Shift+click multiple times to get all the sky.

3 Click the New Layer icon in the Layers panel to add a blank layer.

4 Rename your layer Sky Fix.

5 Click Select and choose Refine Edge.

● The Refine Edge dialog box appears.

6 Click the red icon to create an overlay to better show the edges of your selection.

7 Adjust the Smooth, Feather, and Contract/Expand sliders until the edges along the sky look good.

8 Click OK.

9 Click the foreground color to open the Color Picker (Foreground Color) dialog box.

10 Click the center color bar to pick a good sky-blue color.

11 Click in the big color box to refine your color selection.

12 Click OK.

DIFFICULTY LEVEL

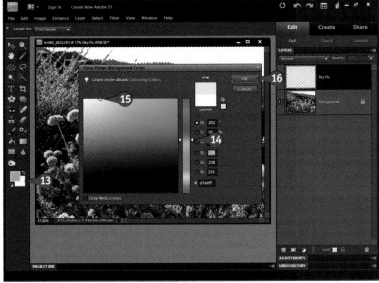

13 Click the background color to get the Color Picker (Background Color) dialog box.

14 Click the center color bar to pick a good sky-blue color.

15 Click in the big color box to get a color lighter than the foreground color.

16 Click OK.

TIPS

Did You Know?

Refine Edge is a useful control in Photoshop Elements for refining a selection edge. All the controls in Refine Edge have long been available in Photoshop Elements, but before Photoshop Elements 7 they were not so convenient or accessible. Being able to add an overlay that clearly shows what edges will look like based on the selection is also a great benefit.

Try This!

When you deal with skies that are broken up by the subject, by trees in the background and other pictorial objects, you may find it helpful to use the Magic Wand selection tool with Contiguous unselected. This enables the program to look for the sky throughout the picture even if it is not directly connected to the area that you click on.

Did You Know?

The Color Picker that appears when you click the foreground or background color enables you to choose all sorts of colors. The central color bar is for selecting hue, and the large box enables you to select the brightness of a color from left to right and the saturation from top to bottom.

Improve
BLANK SKIES

Placing a sky fix in a separate layer over your picture has several advantages. It enables you to change and tweak the sky as much as you want without affecting the underlying picture. In addition, it enables you to tone down the intensity of the fixed colors by simply modifying the opacity of the layer. You can also change the color of the sky by using Hue/Saturation on the layer.

Finally, a separate layer is very important because it enables you to add noise to the fixed sky. All

photographs have some sort of noise at some level. When Photoshop Elements adds color, it adds it in a pure form, without any noise whatsoever. This can make the sky look unnatural, even though a real sky has no noise. You need to add some noise to the sky fix so that it matches the rest of the photograph.

By adding color to the blank sky of this photograph, the picture gains a little bit more of a feeling of reality. This makes the image closer to what you see instead of being limited by the sensor of the camera.

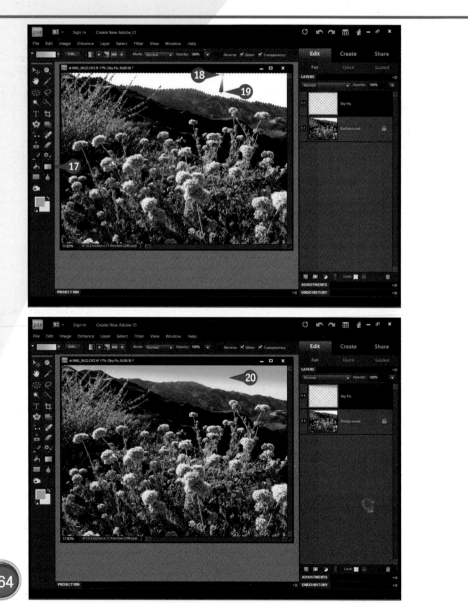

17 Click the Gradient tool.

18 Click high in the sky to start the gradient.

19 Drag your cursor down to the bottom of the sky and release to end the gradient.

A new sky appears; it will usually be too intense.

Try this multiple times until the gradient looks reasonable.

20 Deselect your selection by pressing Esc.

21 Adjust the opacity of the sky layer until the sky looks natural.

22 Click the Zoom tool or magnifier and then click the photo to enlarge a small section of sky in the original photo.

23 Click the Hand tool and then click and drag your photo to get a good view of both the noise in the original photo and the new sky.

24 Click Filter, select Noise, and then select Add Noise.

● The Add Noise dialog box opens.

25 Add a small amount of noise so the sky is a closer match to the original photo.

26 Click OK.

TIPS

Caution!
Be sure you are in the right layer when you add the sky. You do not want to add the sky to the original image or to any other layer that you might be using. This will cause you problems, although if you accidentally put the sky in the wrong place, you can undo it using the Undo History panel.

Try This!
Often you will find that it takes several tries with the Gradient tool to get a good-looking gradient for the sky. You may find that one time the sky looks crooked, another time it does not seem to match the way the rest of the scene looks, and another time the blend is too high or too low. Keep trying the tool until the sky looks good.

More Options!
The Gradient tool has a number of options in the Options bar. Most photographers use this tool at its default settings. However, you can choose some other interesting gradients in the Options bar. You might like experimenting with them for special-effect purposes. Use the Reset Tool function at the far left to get back to the defaults.

CREATE THE FOCUS
with Gaussian Blur

Photographs look their best when the image is clearly structured for the viewer. You want the viewer to be able to understand what your picture is about or at least understand your interpretation of the scene. Composition, filters, depth of field, and other shooting techniques are used to help define and structure the picture so that it affects the viewer.

A trendy effect photographers have been using for this purpose is a unique use of sharpness. By using special lenses, they create a small area of sharpness within the picture to define exactly what they want the viewer to look at. You can do something similar in Photoshop Elements. You create a blur over most of the picture that blends nicely to a sharp area. By choosing this sharp area carefully, you create a strong way of communicating your focus to your viewer.

The tortoise seen here is the endangered desert tortoise. You sometimes see them in the Mojave National Preserve at the side of the road. The picture has pretty much the same tone and color, so adding a region of sharp contrast with blur makes the photo more interesting.

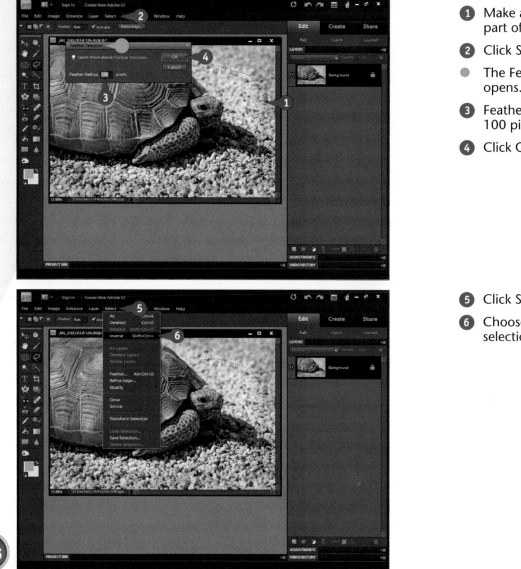

① Make a selection around a key part of your subject.

② Click Select and choose Feather.

● The Feather Selection dialog box opens.

③ Feather the selection by at least 100 pixels.

④ Click OK.

⑤ Click Select.

⑥ Choose Inverse to invert the selection.

7 Press Ctrl/⌘+J to copy the selected area to a new layer.

● You will see a layer with a hole in it over your original image.

70

DIFFICULTY LEVEL

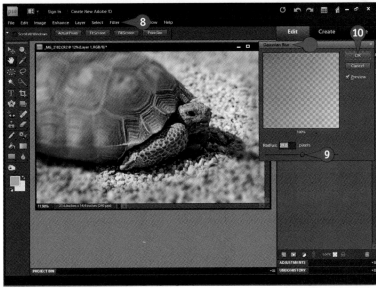

8 Click Filter, select Blur, and select Gaussian Blur.

● The Gaussian Blur dialog box opens.

9 Click and drag the Radius slider until you get a nice blurred effect on the top layer.

10 Click OK.

The hole in the top layer enables the sharp photo underneath to show through only in that area.

TIPS

Try This!
You can refine your final picture by using the Eraser tool. Choose a soft-edged brush for the eraser and erase parts of the top blurred layer. Press Ctrl/⌘+Z to undo anything you do not like. You can also change the opacity of the eraser to get a more blended effect as you erase an edge.

Did You Know?
A checkerboard pattern on a layer thumbnail in the Layers panel shows you that no pixels are there. This pattern occurs only on pixel layers. This can help you know when a layer has holes or gaps in it so that you can choose the right layer to work on. It also gives you an idea of the shape of the hole.

Try This!
If you are having trouble finding the edge of a layer's pixels as you erase on that layer, try turning off the layer below it. Click the Eye icon to turn the layer off; that way you see only the layer you are working on. A checkerboard pattern shows up when the pixels are gone.

ADD A NEW BACKGROUND
for your subject

How often have you taken a picture of friends or family, and you have liked the subject but not the background? This happens all the time. Sometimes the liveliest photos that really give an interesting interpretation of the person are captured informally, even spur of the moment, with a point-and-shoot camera. In these situations, you rarely have the chance to choose a great background for your subject.

You can change the background in Photoshop Elements. You can create everything from a very simple background to something with rich texture and color. You can even put your subject in front of a totally different real-world background. The technique is the same for both types of backgrounds. Changing backgrounds lets you practice your selection skills and your use of layers. The possibilities are endless and can keep you up late at night trying them all out!

The image seen here was processed in task #19 to work on blacks and whites using Levels. This young girl could look quite nice against a plain background, making this casual shot almost look like a studio shot.

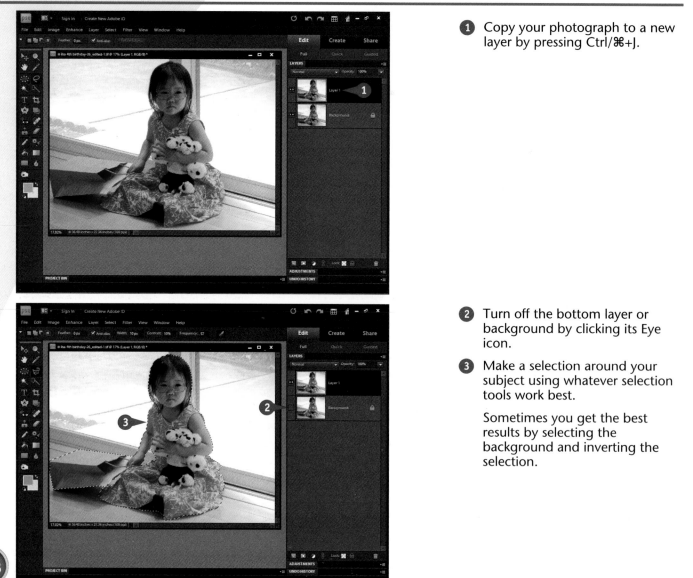

① Copy your photograph to a new layer by pressing Ctrl/⌘+J.

② Turn off the bottom layer or background by clicking its Eye icon.

③ Make a selection around your subject using whatever selection tools work best.

Sometimes you get the best results by selecting the background and inverting the selection.

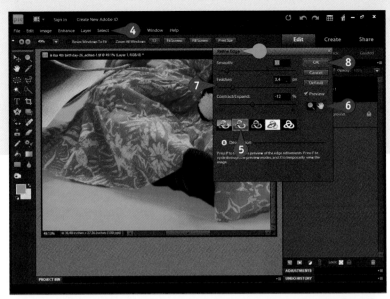

4. Click Select and then choose Refine Edge.

• The Refine Edge dialog box opens.

5. Click the Red icon to get an overlay that better displays the edge.

6. Use the Zoom and Hand tools as needed to magnify the image and move it around so you can better see the edge.

The Zoom tool zooms in by default. Pressing and holding Alt/Option plus the Zoom tool zooms out.

7. Adjust the Smooth, Feather, and Contract/Expand sliders to refine the edge of the selection.

8. Click OK.

9. Press ⌘/Ctrl+0 to display the image fitting fully inside the work area.

10. Click the Layer Mask icon to add a layer mask to the top layer.

The selected subject now floats against a checkerboard pattern. A checkerboard pattern says the area has no pixels in it and nothing can appear there when the bottom layer is turned off.

#71

DIFFICULTY LEVEL

TIPS

Important!

Watch those edges as you go around your subject. The edge really has a big impact on how well the background works with your subject, and the selection gets you started. Select your subject using whatever selection tools work best for you and the subject. Add to and subtract from that selection by pressing Shift and Alt/Option.

Did You Know?

The red overlay that appears when you use the overlay button in Refine Edge helps you see changes in the selection edge. The red is where nothing is selected; you clearly see the selected area that has no red. This edge shows blending, feathering, and so on, which is not visible with the normal selection edge.

Did You Know?

Selections work well with layer masks. Think of a selection as a precursor to a layer mask. Anything selected is "allowed" and therefore is white in the layer mask. Anything not selected is "blocked" and therefore is black in the layer mask. Selections can help create a layer mask, and then the layer mask can make the selection easily modified.

ADD A NEW BACKGROUND
for your subject

So what can you put as a new background for your subject? Bright colors work great with young people. Muted colors work well with gentle portraits. White and gray create a more formal, elegant look, whereas black is dramatic. Textures give dimension to a background, and Photoshop Elements offers a lot of them if you experiment with the filters in the Filter menu.

You can open a totally different photograph and use it for a background. An easy way to do this is to make a new layer in that photo by pressing Ctrl/⌘+J, and

then select the Move tool at the upper left of the toolbox. Click the layer and drag it to the photograph of your subject that needs a new background. Be sure that your cursor has gone completely over the edges of the photograph and then release the mouse button. This picture is dropped onto your picture, over the active layer. Move it up and down in the layer stack by clicking and dragging as needed. Move it around the layer with the Move tool, and then blur it so that it looks more natural.

⑪ Click the bottom layer to select it.

⑫ Pick an interesting foreground color by clicking it and using the Color Picker (Foreground Color) dialog box.

In this image, light gray was chosen for an elegant look.

⑬ Pick an interesting background color by clicking it and using the Color Picker (Foreground Color) dialog box.

In this image, white was chosen for an elegant look.

White and light gray colors are now available for use.

⑭ Click the Eye icon for the bottom layer to make it active.

⑮ Select the Gradient tool from the toolbox.

⑯ Click at about the middle of the photo and drag down slightly and release the mouse button to create a gradient.

Because the bottom layer is active and selected, the gradient occurs there.

A new background appears behind the subject. The Gradient tool gives the background some dimension.

#71 CONTINUED

⑰ Add a layer by clicking the New Layer icon at the bottom of the layer panel.

⑱ Select the Paintbrush tool from the toolbox.

⑲ Choose a moderate-size, soft-edged brush.

⑳ Click the default colors for foreground/background colors to get black as the foreground color.

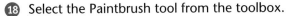

㉑ Paint the black on the middle layer to create a shadow for the subject.

Paint whatever seems right for a shadow with the light on the subject.

● Black brush strokes appear in the layer mask icon.

㉒ Use the Eraser tool and a soft edge to remove this shadow from where it does not belong.

㉓ Change the opacity of the layer to make the shadow less strong.

TIPS

Important!

Watch your edges. They can make or break this type of work in Photoshop Elements. Your selection was only the start of working that edge. Once you have a layer mask, you can refine that edge as much as you want by simply using small black or white brush tools to block or allow parts of the edge.

Try This!

Once you start putting backgrounds behind your subject, be aware of sharpness. Normally you want your subject to be sharp and the background to be less sharp. Because the background is new, you can blur it as much as you want with Gaussian Blur. Usually you should have at least a slight blur on that new background.

Try This!

Freely experiment with backgrounds. You can discover all sorts of backgrounds by using different colors and different images, and then just trying a lot of filters in the Filter menu. You can even copy your original picture below your subject and apply filters to that layer just for the effect.

Size and Sharpen Photos

Whenever you want to use a photograph for something, you always have to size it. Even when using film, you had to make a print sized specifically for the need or use of the photograph. With film, you simply put the negative into an enlarger and make the picture bigger or smaller as needed. Digital is a little harder because you have to be very specific in how you create a size for the image. Things like resolution and physical size must be treated separately.

In general, do all of your processing work on a photograph using a master Photoshop or PSD (Photoshop Document) file, and then save that master file for any future resizing purposes. Create a new file for every major change in size of picture you need. Do not resize your master file because you cannot get back to the original size from the saved file.

Some photographers resize an image for every small change in size that they need. This is rarely needed. You do not find a lot of quality difference changing from an 8×10-inch photo to a 5×7-inch photo, for example. But you do see a difference if you try to use an 8×10-inch photo for a 2×3-inch wallet-size image or vice versa.

Top 100

#72 Basic Workflow for Image Sizing .174   DIFFICULTY LEVEL

#73 Size Photos for Printing. 176   DIFFICULTY LEVEL

#74 Size Photos for E-mail 178   DIFFICULTY LEVEL

#75 Sharpen Photos with Unsharp Mask 180   DIFFICULTY LEVEL

#76 Sharpen Photos with Adjust Sharpness 182   DIFFICULTY LEVEL

#77 Sharpen Photos When You Have Layers 184   DIFFICULTY LEVEL

#78 Selectively Sharpen Parts of Your Photo 186   DIFFICULTY LEVEL

BASIC WORKFLOW
for image sizing

Photoshop Elements puts the key photo-sizing controls in one place: Image Size under Resize in the Image menu. To use the image-sizing options effectively, it helps to understand how Photoshop Elements structures the resizing of an image. You can make a picture bigger or smaller by either changing how many pixels are in a picture or changing the spacing of the pixels in an image file. You can also size a layered or flattened file.

The program uses some rather complex algorithms to make an image file bigger or smaller in pixels, yet retain the best possible quality for the picture. You

have to tell Photoshop Elements how to handle your particular picture, which is what the options in Image Size enable you to do. The right choices are fairly straightforward; however, some options can create problems if you are not careful. This should not deter you, but you do need to pay attention to what you are doing.

The photos seen in this chapter come from the Guadalupe Dunes along the middle part of the California coastline along the Pacific Ocean. This is a beautiful and sensitive area filled with high dunes and shifting sands.

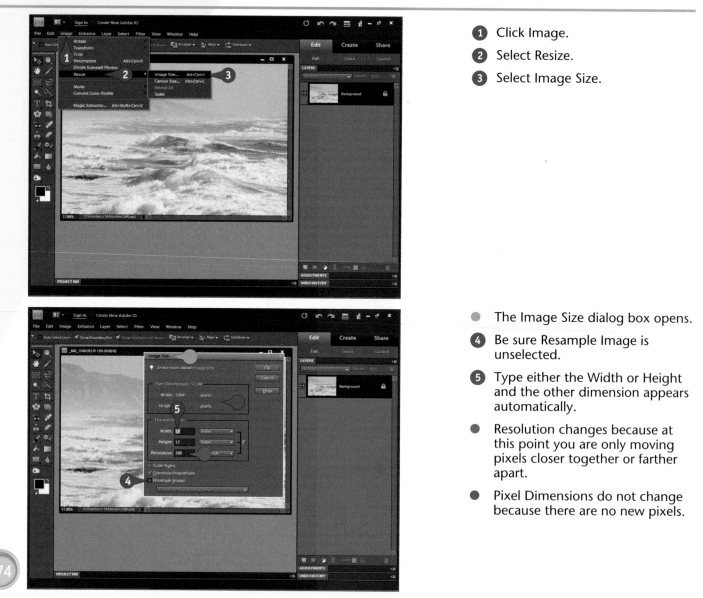

① Click Image.

② Select Resize.

③ Select Image Size.

● The Image Size dialog box opens.

④ Be sure Resample Image is unselected.

⑤ Type either the Width or Height and the other dimension appears automatically.

● Resolution changes because at this point you are only moving pixels closer together or farther apart.

● Pixel Dimensions do not change because there are no new pixels.

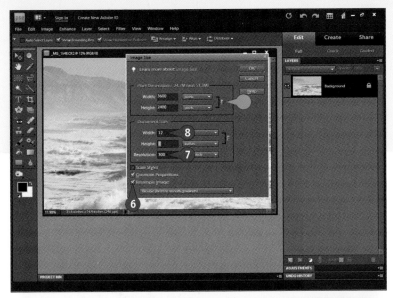

6 Select Resample Image (⬛ changes to ☑).

This tells the program to add or subtract pixels to change an image size.

7 Type a Resolution.

8 Type a new width or height.

● Pixel dimensions change because new pixels will be created.

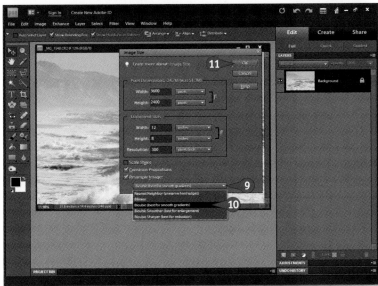

9 Click the drop-down menu below Resample Image.

10 Select Bicubic Smoother if your photograph will be enlarged; that is, Pixel Dimensions increase.

Select Bicubic Sharper if your photograph will be reduced in size.

11 Click OK to resize the picture.

![TIPS]

Did You Know?

Image sizing is not designed to give you a specific size such as 8×10 inches or 11×14 inches. It is designed to make your overall picture larger or smaller. If you want a very specific size, you need to use the Image Size dialog box to get a correct height or width, and then use the Crop tool to get the final size.

Caution!

In general, you should always leave the Constrain Proportions box checked. This means your picture resizes according to the original proportions of the photograph. If this box is unchecked, you get wildly distorted photographs from your resizing.

Did You Know?

When you enlarge an image size and pixels are created, the differences between those pixels must be smoothed out so your photo has maximum quality. That is why you use Bicubic Smoother. When you reduce the size of an image, detail is thrown out but you want to retain the sharpest detail. That is why you use Bicubic Sharper.

Size photos
FOR PRINTING

Inkjet printers do a fantastic job creating superb photo quality for your prints. But to get the optimum quality, the image file must be sized properly for a given print output size. You do not get the best results if you simply print any and all image sizes from one master file that has a specific size and resolution. In fact, print image quality can decline from too little or too much resolution.

Resolution is a very important part of image sizing for a print. You need to create an image with a printing resolution. All inkjet printers create a high-quality

print using resolutions between 200 and 360 ppi (pixels per inch). If you can resize your image without resampling the picture and stay within this range, you can use your master image file for printing. You do not need to make and save new copies of this image until you start resampling the picture.

Photos like these waves at Guadalupe Dunes will show a lot of detail as the image is enlarged. When you photograph a changing subject, timing is really important. You should be sure you get the best movement, in this case waves, for the photograph.

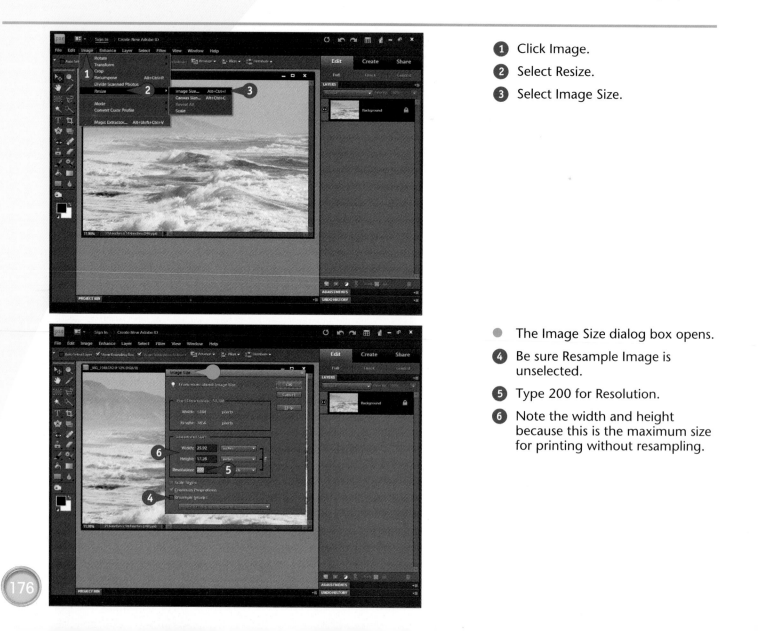

1 Click Image.

2 Select Resize.

3 Select Image Size.

● The Image Size dialog box opens.

4 Be sure Resample Image is unselected.

5 Type 200 for Resolution.

6 Note the width and height because this is the maximum size for printing without resampling.

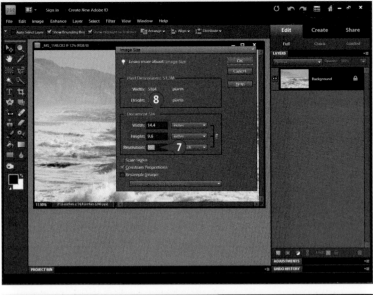

7 Type 360 for Resolution.

8 Note the width and height because this is the minimum size for printing without resampling.

You now know how big or small you can print without increasing or decreasing the number of pixels.

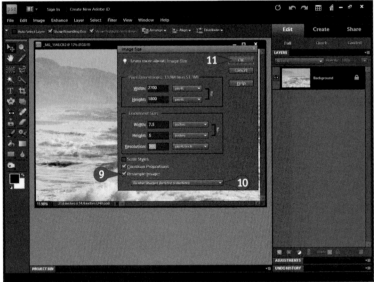

9 Select Resample Image when you want to change the size of your picture beyond the range represented by 200 to 360 ppi (■ changes to ✓).

Use 200 ppi for bigger pictures and 360 ppi for smaller pictures.

10 Choose Bicubic Smoother if your photograph will be enlarged, that is, Pixel Dimensions increase.

Choose Bicubic Sharper if your photograph will be reduced in size.

11 Click OK to resize the picture.

TIPS

Important!

The resolution of an image is not the same thing as the resolution of a printer. Image resolution refers to the way pixels create tones and details in a photo. Printer resolution has to do with how the printer puts down ink droplets on the paper. They mean very different things.

Did You Know?

Pixels per inch, or ppi, is a standard way of measuring the density of pixels in a picture, which is also a measure of resolution. Pixels alone are not enough information. To understand resolution, you must have pixels combined with inches, which is an indication of how many pixels fit in a linear dimension.

Did You Know?

The type of paper used for printing affects the ppi needed in the original image. Matte finishes can handle lower resolutions quite nicely, whereas glossy papers tend to require higher resolutions. Do your own tests and see how resolution affects the look of an image on the papers that you use.

Size photos
FOR E-MAIL

Sharing photos via e-mail is a great way to get your pictures in front of friends, family, and others. You can, for example, take pictures of your kids playing soccer in the afternoon, and then send off copies of those pictures to the grandparents that night. Even if the grandparents live nearby, this is not possible with film.

However, a common problem with e-mail pictures occurs when people simply download the image files from the camera and send them attached to an e-mail. The high-megapixel cameras of today have quite sizable files, even when using JPEG. This can cause problems for the recipient of the e-mail. Files this size can take too long for recipients to download or even crash their e-mail software. You can avoid this problem by sizing your pictures properly for e-mail purposes.

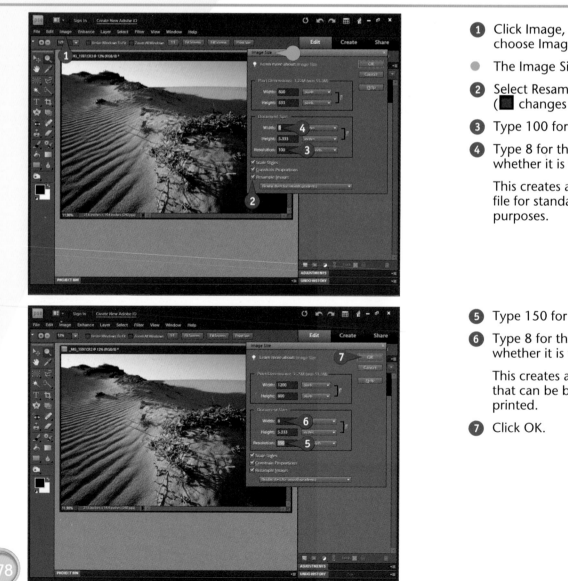

1 Click Image, Resize, and then choose Image Size.

● The Image Size dialog box opens.

2 Select Resample Image (■ changes to ☑).

3 Type 100 for Resolution.

4 Type 8 for the longest side, whether it is width or height.

This creates a good, small image file for standard e-mailing purposes.

5 Type 150 for Resolution.

6 Type 8 for the longest side, whether it is width or height.

This creates a small image file that can be both e-mailed and printed.

7 Click OK.

Your image now appears smaller in size in the Photoshop Elements workspace.

Make it fill the workspace again by pressing Ctrl/⌘+0.

⑧ Click File and select Save As.

● The Save As dialog box appears.

⑨ Give the file a name.

⑩ Select JPEG for the file format.

⑪ Click Save.

● The JPEG Options dialog box appears.

⑫ Click and drag the Quality slider to set a moderate JPEG Quality setting between 6 and 9.

⑬ Click OK to resize the picture.

TIPS

Did You Know?

A resolution of 100 ppi is easy to remember and works fine for displaying pictures that have been sent by e-mail. Few monitors display at 72 ppi anymore, which used to be the recommended resolution for e-mail.

Did You Know?

For optimum printing quality, you should generally choose a resolution of at least 200 ppi. However, 150 ppi gives an acceptable, photo-quality print while at the same time enabling you to have a significantly smaller image size for e-mailing.

More Options!

When you save an image as a new JPEG file, a dialog box with options for JPEG settings appears. As you change the Quality setting, you see a number appear below the Preview check box. This number is the size of your image based on the quality setting you selected. For e-mail, quality numbers between 6 and 9 are common and work fine. Look for a setting that provides a final file size less than 300KB (the number appears below the Preview check box).

SHARPEN PHOTOS
with Unsharp Mask

Photoshop Elements has an excellent sharpening tool, but it can only be used to sharpen something with pixels. You must sharpen a flattened file saved for a specific purpose or use a technique that creates a pixel-based layer for sharpening.

Photos with detail like this view of a sand dune at Guadalupe Dunes need to be sharpened properly. If you have sharpened in the Camera Raw part of Photoshop Elements, you do not need to sharpen now; otherwise, you must do at least some sharpening now. Sharpening in Photoshop Elements is designed to get the optimum amount of sharpness from your original

image based on a sharp picture to begin with. It does not help blurred or out-of-focus pictures.

For a variety of reasons, images coming from a digital sensor are not optimally sharp. Most cameras apply some sharpening to a JPEG file as it is processed inside the camera. No sharpening is applied to a RAW file. Yet, no matter what image comes into Photoshop Elements, it usually needs some degree of sharpening. The name Unsharp Mask comes from a traditional process used to sharpen photos for printing plates in the commercial printing industry. It is not about making unsharp pictures sharp.

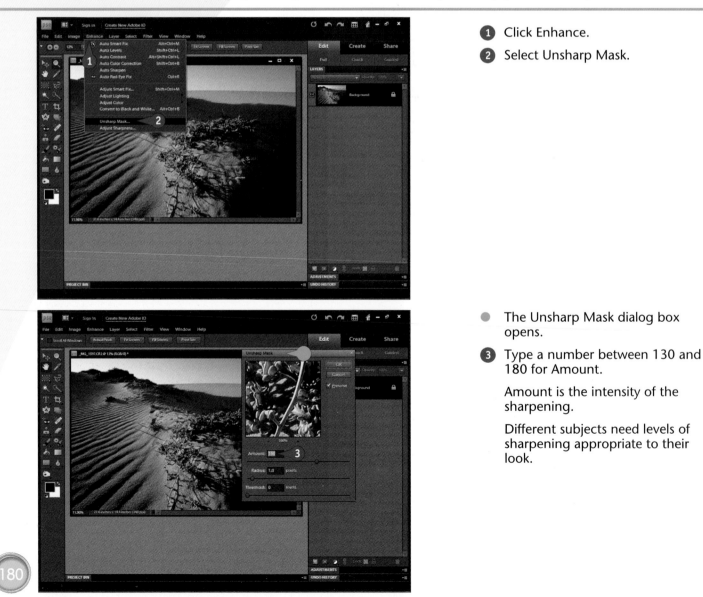

① Click Enhance.

② Select Unsharp Mask.

● The Unsharp Mask dialog box opens.

③ Type a number between 130 and 180 for Amount.

Amount is the intensity of the sharpening.

Different subjects need levels of sharpening appropriate to their look.

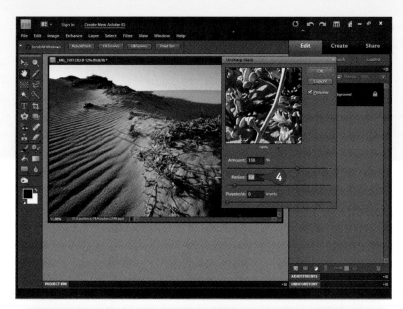

4 Type a number between 1.0 and 1.5 for Radius.

Radius affects how sharpness is enhanced around an edge.

Be careful of overdoing this control — watch for unnatural halos of brightness around contrasted edges.

5 Type a number between 3 and 6 for Threshold.

Threshold affects how small details such as noise are sharpened.

Set this higher for images showing more noise, and lower for those showing less.

6 Click OK to sharpen the picture.

TIPS

Caution!

Be wary of using high Threshold numbers. Threshold is very useful in minimizing the impact of sharpening on noise and other image detail problems called *artifacts*. But it can also affect small important detail. Keep your Threshold setting below 6 when you can, and go up to only a maximum of 12.

More Options!

The Preview window in the Unsharp Mask dialog box can be very helpful. Click part of the picture to show its detail in the preview. Click on and off the preview picture to see how sharpening is being applied. Click the preview picture and drag to move its position around so it displays key sharp parts of the image.

More Options!

Change your sharpening based on the subject. Landscapes and architecture typically do well with higher sharpening numbers for Amount and Radius. Photos of people, especially close-ups of faces, usually need less sharpening, even as low as 100 for Amount and less than 1 for Radius.

SHARPEN PHOTOS
with Adjust Sharpness

Adjust Sharpness uses advanced algorithms for sharpening to get the maximum detail possible from a photograph. This is the same control as Smart Sharpen in Photoshop. You might wonder why you would not use this method to sharpen photos all the time. The reason is because of noise and Threshold.

Adjust Sharpness does not have a Threshold control. This means if you have noise in your picture, that noise is likely to be sharpened just as much as anything else in the picture. As a result, the noise becomes more visible. Luckily, today's digital cameras do keep noise to a minimum. You find more noise in

small cameras with small sensors and high megapixels. You also find more noise with higher ISO settings. It certainly does not hurt to try Adjust Sharpness in those conditions. If noise shows up too much from that, then go back to Unsharp Mask.

Adjust Sharpness works well for highly detailed pictures, such as landscapes and architecture, but when you need more gentle sharpening, such as with people, you may find Unsharp Mask works better. Getting the most detail of someone's facial pores may not be the most flattering thing to do.

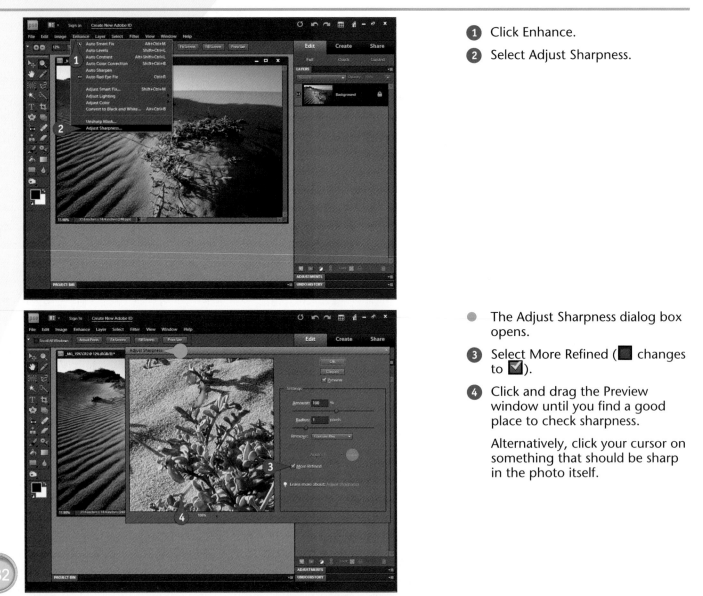

① Click Enhance.

② Select Adjust Sharpness.

● The Adjust Sharpness dialog box opens.

③ Select More Refined (■ changes to ☑).

④ Click and drag the Preview window until you find a good place to check sharpness.

Alternatively, click your cursor on something that should be sharp in the photo itself.

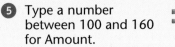

5 Type a number between 100 and 160 for Amount.

Amount acts slightly different from Amount in Unsharp Mask.

6 Type a number between 1.0 and 1.5 for Radius.

Radius also acts slightly different from Radius in Unsharp Mask.

7 Click OK to sharpen the picture.

TIPS

Important!

Because noise can become more obvious in Adjust Sharpness, looking for it is important. Enlarge the picture in the Preview window by clicking the plus button underneath the Preview window. Check areas such as dark parts of an image that have been brightened and the sky. They usually show noise before other areas.

More Options!

The Remove drop-down menu instructs Adjust Sharpness how to handle sharpness. Click it and a drop-down menu appears. Sometimes sharpening pictures with motion blur is easier by selecting Motion Blur. And sometimes you can get sharper pictures with an out-of-focus subject by selecting Lens Blur.

More Options!

If you read anything about Photoshop and Photoshop Elements, you will find a variety of formulas for Unsharp Mask and Adjust Sharpness. Generally, they all work and can be worth a try. Every photographer uses different formulas because sharpness truly depends on the subject and on the personal tastes of the photographer.

Sharpen photos
WHEN YOU HAVE LAYERS

The sharpening features of Photoshop Elements must have pixels to work on. This presents a challenge when you are working with layers because first, you need to have pixels in a layer to sharpen it, and second, even if you do have pixels in a layer, you can sharpen only one layer at a time. Once you have finished working on a photograph using layers, you normally sharpen the whole picture, including everything that adjustment layers might do to it.

The way to do this is to create a special layer on top of all your other layers that merges those layers together into one pixel layer. You then sharpen this layer. Label it the sharpened layer so you know what it is. You can later go back and adjust anything underneath that layer, although you must create a new sharpened layer if you do.

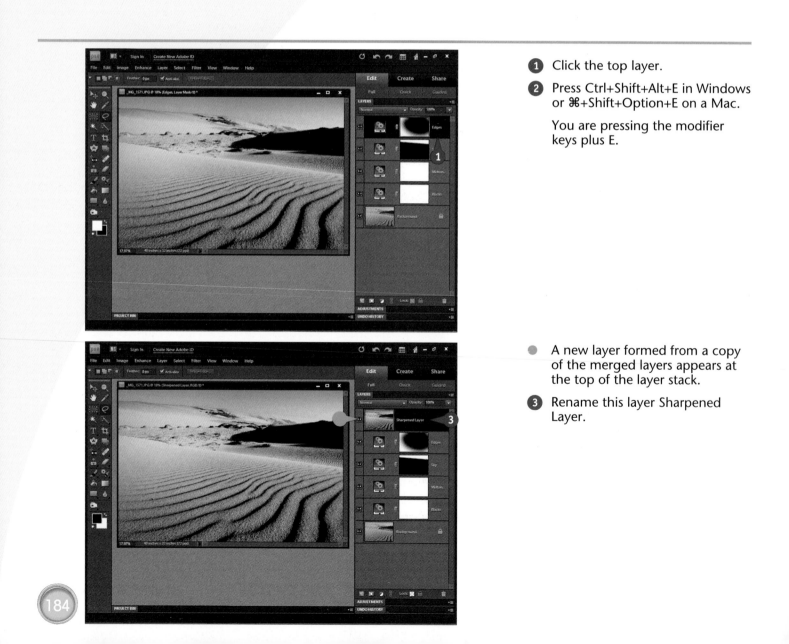

① Click the top layer.

② Press Ctrl+Shift+Alt+E in Windows or ⌘+Shift+Option+E on a Mac.

You are pressing the modifier keys plus E.

● A new layer formed from a copy of the merged layers appears at the top of the layer stack.

③ Rename this layer Sharpened Layer.

4 Click Enhance, and then select Adjust Sharpness.

● The Adjust Sharpness dialog box opens.

5 Type a number between 100 and 150 for Amount.

6 Type a number between 1.0 and 1.5 for Radius.

7 Click OK.

DIFFICULTY LEVEL

● The layer named Sharpened Layer is now sharpened, but nothing else in the photo is sharpened.

TIPS

Caution!

Beware of oversharpening. Although you can increase the Amount and Radius to make a blurry picture look sort of sharp or make sharpness look intense, this can also damage your photo in a lot of ways. It makes tonalities look harsh, and you lose fine tones and colors in the picture.

Did You Know?

Unsharp Mask can be very useful when you are sharpening the layer created from merged layers in a many-layered file. When a lot of adjustment layers are applied to a photograph, especially a JPEG picture, you may find noise and other image artifacts begin to appear. You can minimize them using a Threshold setting, which does not exist in Adjust Sharpness.

Did You Know?

The Merge and Make New Layer command, Ctrl+Shift+Alt+E in Windows or ⌘+Shift+Option+E on a Mac, is a fairly well-known command, but it does not show up in any menus. You have to know it exists and what it does to use it. This command is the same in both Photoshop and Photoshop Elements. Be very careful that you click the top layer before using the command.

SELECTIVELY SHARPEN
parts of your photo

If you have a photograph with a close-up of a flower, and that flower is sharp whereas the background is out of focus, you really only need to sharpen the flower. If you have a portrait with an out-of-focus background, the face needs to be sharp, but not the background.

In fact, there are good reasons that you should not try sharpening out-of-focus areas at all. A big reason is noise. Noise tends to show up more in out-of-focus areas and does not need to be sharpened. Another reason is that odd little details can be sharpened in the out-of-focus area, degrading the visual quality of

the area. If you restrict your sharpness to only the areas that need to be sharp, you will not have these problems. Selectively sharpening works best for pictures with a distinct difference in sharpness between the subject and the rest of the image.

This image is also from Guadalupe Dunes. Trash has become sadly ubiquitous, even in beautiful natural areas. This Coke bottle is frosted from its exposure to the sand and waves. Sharpening just the bottle and its immediate surroundings helps emphasize it in the photograph.

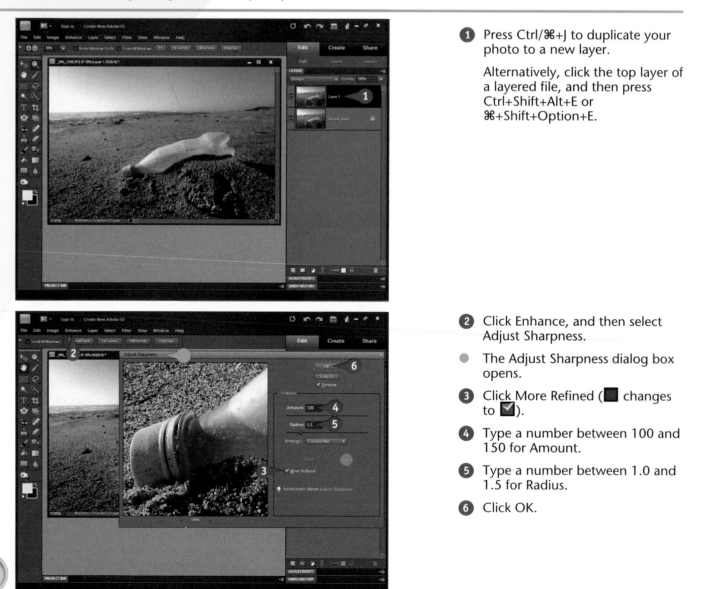

1 Press Ctrl/⌘+J to duplicate your photo to a new layer.

Alternatively, click the top layer of a layered file, and then press Ctrl+Shift+Alt+E or ⌘+Shift+Option+E.

2 Click Enhance, and then select Adjust Sharpness.

● The Adjust Sharpness dialog box opens.

3 Click More Refined (■ changes to ☑).

4 Type a number between 100 and 150 for Amount.

5 Type a number between 1.0 and 1.5 for Radius.

6 Click OK.

7 Press Alt/Option as you click the Layer Mask icon.

This creates a black layer mask which blocks the sharpened layer.

8 Select a large, soft-edged brush.

9 Choose white for the foreground color.

10 Click the Eye icon for the bottom layer, Background, to turn it off.

11 Paint white over the parts of the picture that need to be sharpened.

● The layer mask icon indicates the sharpened area.

By turning off the bottom layer, you can more easily see what you are erasing.

Change your brush size as needed to go around your sharp subject, and press Ctrl/⌘+Z to undo any mistakes.

12 Click the Eye icon for the bottom layer, Background, to turn it back on.

The top layer is now a sharpened layer, but only where the original picture was sharp.

TIPS

Caution!

If you are shooting JPEG, be very wary of oversharpening your photo. Many cameras already apply a high amount of sharpening on their JPEG files, especially lower-priced cameras. Watch out for gentle, pleasant tonalities becoming harsh and unpleasant.

Did You Know?

You typically do sharpening at the end, or at least toward the end, of your image processing workflow in Photoshop Elements. The reason is that sharpening affects things like noise and other details that can be changed as you process the image. Sharpening too early can cause problems with these things.

Attention!

Think about your subject as you sharpen your photograph. Sharpening is not a one-size-fits-all adjustment. Some subjects look great with high sharpness, such as rocky landscapes. Others look better with lower amounts of sharpness, such as people's faces.

Chapter 8

Go Beyond the Basics

Digital photography can be a lot of fun. Once you start mastering Photoshop Elements, you may start looking for new things to do with your pictures. One great option is to convert your pictures to black-and-white. Not all that long ago, color was the special type of photography and black-and-white was rather ordinary. At that time, black-and-white was commonly seen in every publication. Today, color is the most common way that pictures are printed. Black-and-white has become a very special way of dealing with pictures, giving images a unique look in contrast to very common color photos. In addition, black-and-white gives you multiple ways to deal with a subject.

Another fun thing you can do with digital photography and Photoshop Elements is create a panoramic photograph. This type of photograph is created from a series of images. The width or height of the scene is too great for your lens to include when you are shooting, so you make up for it by taking pictures across the scene. Alternatively, you may like the format of a panoramic image, but want a photograph that is bigger than possible from simply cropping a panoramic format from a single image. Photoshop Elements supports the multi-image panoramas quite well.

Top 100

#79 Convert Color Photos to Black-and-White. 190   DIFFICULTY LEVEL

#80 Adjust Your Photos in Black-and-White 192   DIFFICULTY LEVEL

#81 Create Toned Images 194   DIFFICULTY LEVEL

#82 Use the Smart Brush for Creative Effects 196   DIFFICULTY LEVEL

#83 Create a Hand-Colored Look. 198   DIFFICULTY LEVEL

#84 Photograph a Scene to Get More Exposure Detail. 202   DIFFICULTY LEVEL

#85 Merge Photos for More Photo Detail. 204   DIFFICULTY LEVEL

#86 Photograph a Scene for a Panoramic Image 206   DIFFICULTY LEVEL

#87 Merge Photos for a Panoramic Image 208   DIFFICULTY LEVEL

#88 Group Images on a Page 212   DIFFICULTY LEVEL

#89 Transfer Styles between Photos. 216   DIFFICULTY LEVEL

Convert color photos to
BLACK-AND-WHITE

With many digital cameras, you can set the camera to take a black-and-white photograph. The advantage to this is that you are able to see exactly what you get from a scene when it is turned into black-and-white. The disadvantage is that the black-and-white image is locked into a JPEG file and cannot be changed.

Any black-and-white photo is created by changing the colors of the world into tones of black-and-white. When you convert a color image to black-and-white in Photoshop Elements, you have a lot of control over how the colors change into tones of black-and-white. This can be an extremely important factor in your

work because sometimes colors that stand out in a color image blend together when turned into black-and-white equivalents. Because you can change how this conversion occurs in the computer, you have a lot of power and flexibility when working with black-and-white.

This colorful image of geraniums and the Point Fermin Lighthouse in San Pedro, California, can be interpreted in black-and-white in many ways, both good and bad. The challenge is to create a black-and-white photo that appears as lively in black-and-white as the color version.

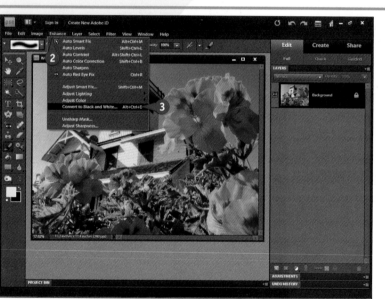

① Process the color image as you normally would.

② Click Enhance.

③ Select Convert to Black and White.

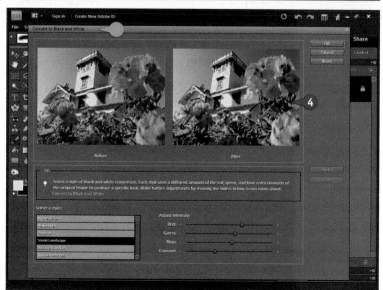

● The Convert to Black and White dialog box opens.

④ Compare the color and black-and-white images to see if you like the interpretation of the scene.

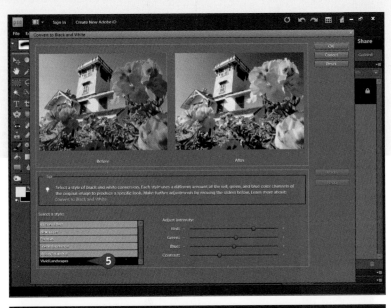

5 Click different styles, or interpretations, of conversions and see how they work with your photo.

6 Modify a style by changing the brightness of tones by adjusting the intensity of colors.

7 Click OK.

Photoshop Elements converts the photo to black-and-white.

TIPS

Important!

The default black-and-white conversion of your image by Photoshop Elements should be seen purely as a starting point. Sometimes it will look fine, but most of the time you will need to at least adjust the color sliders to refine how colors are changed into tones of gray.

Did You Know?

Strong adjustments to a picture as it is converted to a black-and-white image can cause some undesirable effects. Watch out for noise appearing in areas that have had an extreme change. Also beware of breaks in the tonality, which will look like steps of tones, in smooth-toned areas such as skies.

Did You Know?

RAW files always come into Camera Raw in Photoshop Elements as color images even if you shot them as black-and-white in the camera. One advantage to RAW for black-and-white is you can use a 16-bit file. This allows for stronger tonal adjustments without breaks in smooth-toned areas.

Adjust your photos in
BLACK-AND-WHITE

The tonalities and gradations of grays are what bring a black-and-white image to life. This is why these tonalities and gradations are very important. The first way to get them is when you make the conversion from color to black-and-white. Do not be satisfied with simply changing the picture to black-and-white. Be sure that such a conversion does well with changing colors to certain shades of gray. For some photos, this is all you will have to do.

Often, however, you need to do more using the controls that have been discussed in the rest of this

book. Because a good, strong black is very important to a good-looking black-and-white image, it can be very helpful to reexamine the blacks in your photograph. You may want to set them to a higher point within the range of dark grays for a dramatic effect. Midtones are also very important, so you may want to use Color Curves to see various effects. All black-and-white images are interpretations of the world because humans do not see the world this way. Your interpretation is important and is affected by these adjustments.

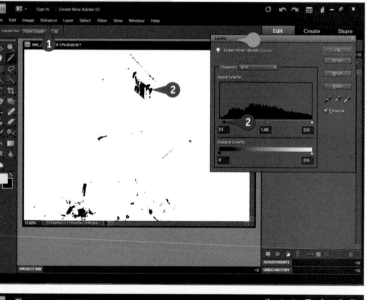

① Click Enhance, select Adjust Lighting, and then select Levels.

● The Levels dialog box opens.

② Press Alt/Option as you move the black slider toward the right until you like how your blacks look.

You can also do this using a Levels adjustment layer. See task #47.

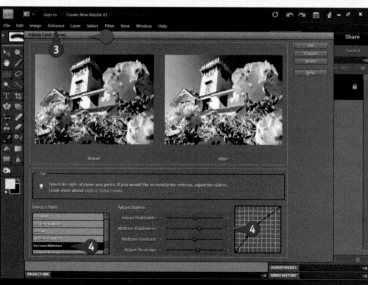

③ Click Enhance, select Adjust Color, and then select Adjust Color Curves.

● The Adjust Color Curves dialog box appears.

④ Adjust the Styles, plus the shadows, midtones, and highlights until you like the overall brightness of the picture and how the tonalities look.

5 Examine your photo for tonal imbalances or areas that should be darker.

6 Click the Adjustment Layer icon and select Brightness/Contrast.

7 Adjust the Brightness slider to darken the picture.

80

DIFFICULTY LEVEL

8 Press Ctrl/⌘+I to invert the layer mask to black and block the darkening effect.

9 Use a soft white paintbrush to brush in the darkening where needed in the picture.

TIPS

Important!

Grayscale and Remove Color in the Enhance menu are two additional black-and-white adjustments in Photoshop Elements. They are very limited and not recommended for most black-and-white conversions because they change color to black-and-white tones in one, and only one, way. You cannot change this.

Did You Know?

You sometimes hear black-and-white images called grayscale. *Grayscale* is a term that simply refers to the way an image deals with color, in this case a scale of gray tones. The term tends to be used more by computer people than photographers.

Did You Know?

Another term for black-and-white is *monochrome*. Although this is somewhat trendy, monochrome actually refers to any image based on one color. Monochrome is not limited to gray and can include red, blue, or any other color.

Create
TONED IMAGES

One of the classic ways photographers worked in the traditional darkroom with black-and-white images was to tone them. This meant adding a slight color to a black-and-white image. It was rare, for example, for photographers like Ansel Adams to leave a print totally neutral in color. The most common toning color was a warm tone called sepia tone. Another common toning color was a slight blue for a cool effect. Either color often added a richer tonality and color effect for the print.

Toning can also be an effective way to enrich your black-and-white images. In addition, toned photos are often easier to print on inkjet printers. You have a whole range of possibilities here, from a subtle effect that provides a hint of color to the picture to a strongly colored effect for special purposes. One advantage of a toned image is that it usually prints very nicely on any inkjet printer as compared to a pure black-and-white photo.

Photographers sometimes create dramatic posters using a strongly colored black-and-white image. For this sort of effect, they often create rather dramatic black areas and white areas in the photograph that go beyond a simple black-and-white conversion.

1 Click the Adjustment Layer icon and select Hue/Saturation.

2 Select Colorize (■ changes to ✓).

● The image now has a color and is a monochrome image based on that color.

● For a sepia-toned image, use a number between 35 and 50 points for Hue to get a warm tone you like.

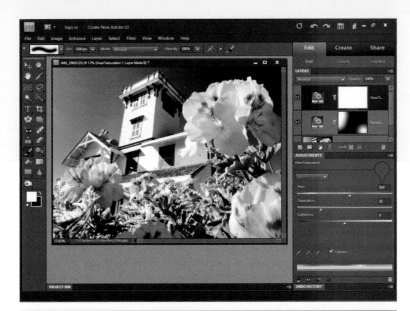

- For a cool-toned image, use a number between 180 and 210 points for Hue.

- In Saturation, use a lower number for a less intense color or a higher number for a more intense color.

- Use the layer Opacity to reduce the effect of the color as needed.

TIPS

More Options!

As you make a color image into a black-and-white photo, you may find it helpful to save different versions of your pictures. An easy way to do this is to select Duplicate in the File menu. This option creates an immediate copy with a new name saved to the same folder as your original. Now make the changes to the copy.

Try This!

You can modify the toning effect using layer blending modes. Click the blending modes box, displaying Normal at first, and then try the blending modes grouped under Overlay. Some of them can be pretty extreme, but all of them can create interesting effects with your photograph.

More Options!

Have fun with toning colors. There is no right or wrong, only what you like or dislike. Although most black-and-white photographs probably do not look their best with extreme colors, it can be fun to try unexpected colors to create unique images that elicit attention for special purposes.

Use the Smart Brush
FOR CREATIVE EFFECTS

You get a fun special effect when you adjust one area of your picture one way and another area completely differently. A good example of this is a photograph with the subject in color, and the background black-and-white. Color in a black-and-white photo could also include a very small part of the picture, such as a red rose being held by a young girl, with only the rose in color. That very effect is shown here by going back to the original color image of the Point Fermin lighthouse. A very interesting black-and-white image results when most of the picture is black-and-white, but the flowers retain their color.

You can create special effects like this with layers: Copy a photo to a layer, apply a unique effect to the top layer, and then in that layer, erase wherever you want to reveal of the original image underneath. There is a simpler way to do this. You can literally paint the effect onto your picture using the Smart Brush. The Smart Brush adds an adjustment layer to your photograph, and then uses the Quick Selection tool with the layer mask to smartly place the adjustment where you brush.

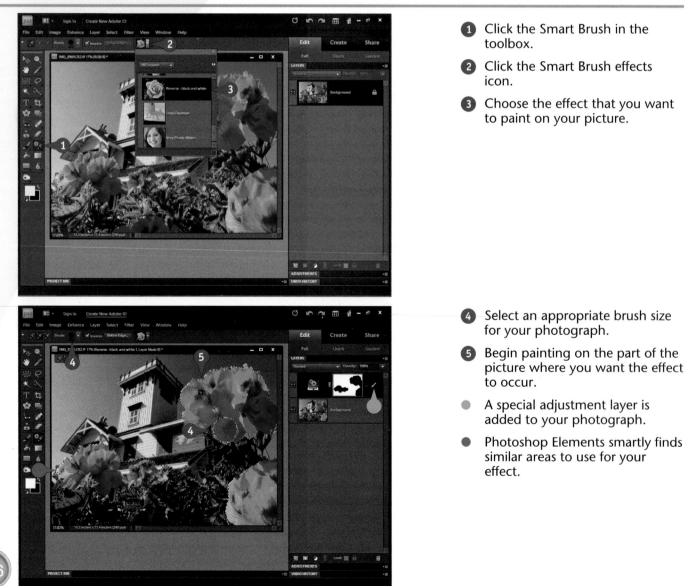

① Click the Smart Brush in the toolbox.

② Click the Smart Brush effects icon.

③ Choose the effect that you want to paint on your picture.

④ Select an appropriate brush size for your photograph.

⑤ Begin painting on the part of the picture where you want the effect to occur.

● A special adjustment layer is added to your photograph.

● Photoshop Elements smartly finds similar areas to use for your effect.

82

Sometimes the tool selects too much and applies the effect where you do not want it.

6 Change the effect brush to an effect removal brush by clicking the rightmost brush icon in the upper left corner of your photograph.

7 Adjust the brush size to fit the area that you want to change.

8 Click in that area.

It often works better to click in areas to remove an effect and then brush over the area.

9 Press Ctrl/⌘+H to hide the selection edge so that you can better see what is happening to your picture.

10 Revise the effect as needed. Reduce the size of your brush to fix small areas.

11 Click the Select menu and then choose Refine Mask.

● The Refine Mask dialog box opens.

12 Feather and smooth the edge so the effect blends naturally.

TIPS

Important!
Unless your background is very simple, you will find you must change brush sizes as you use the Smart Brush. A large brush works well at first, but then begins to capture too much of a photograph. When this happens, switch to a smaller brush. Remember to use the [and] keys to quickly change your brush size.

Try This!
Because everything you do with a Smart Brush uses an adjustment layer plus a layer mask, changes to your picture are not permanent. This means you can freely experiment with the Smart Brush effects. If you do not like the way the effect is working, simply drag the layer to the Trash Can icon to delete it.

More Options!
You can use the Smart Brush to make a lot of interesting adjustments to your picture. They all work the same way in that an effect is applied to your picture in specific areas as you paint over the image. Explore the complete list of Smart Brush choices and you may find a few that will probably work with your types of pictures.

Create a
HAND-COLORED LOOK

A classic effect for black-and-white photography was made by taking a black-and-white print and then painting colors by hand onto that print. Most of this was done in a very realistic way, but some of this hand coloring was done in quite unusual ways as well. Either way, it required a bit of an effort to do because you had to have prints made and the right paint for working on the images. If you made a mistake, you had to throw out the print and start all over again.

You can duplicate this effect in Photoshop Elements, yet you do not have to worry about making mistakes

and do not need special paints. In addition, you have a great deal of flexibility in the colors you use, and you can change any of them whenever you want. This can be a fun way of creating a striking new look for your photographs.

This effect is being applied to the same lighthouse photo used for black-and-white effects. This allows you to compare different black-and-white techniques possible in Photoshop Elements. The hand-colored look is still based on a black-and-white image.

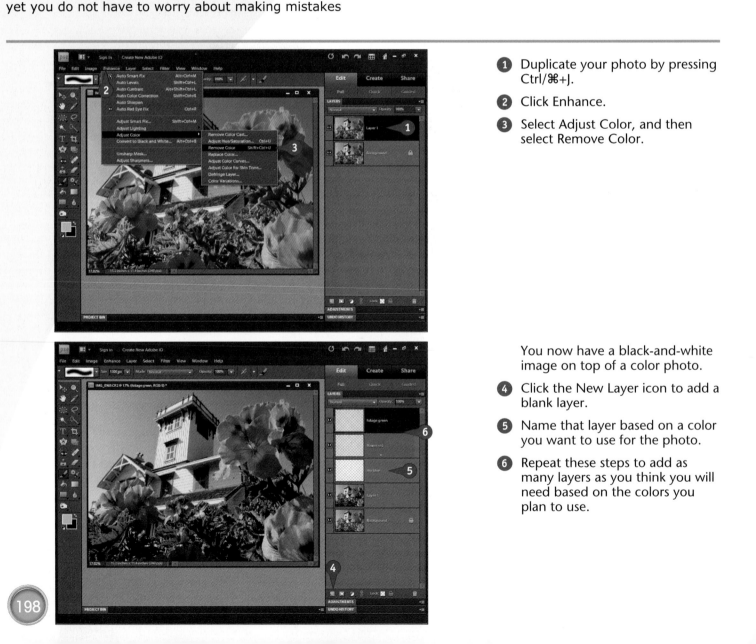

① Duplicate your photo by pressing Ctrl/⌘+J.

② Click Enhance.

③ Select Adjust Color, and then select Remove Color.

You now have a black-and-white image on top of a color photo.

④ Click the New Layer icon to add a blank layer.

⑤ Name that layer based on a color you want to use for the photo.

⑥ Repeat these steps to add as many layers as you think you will need based on the colors you plan to use.

7 Click the Eye icon for the black-and-white layer to turn it off.

8 Click the Eyedropper in the toolbox.

9 Click a color in the picture that you want to use.

● This color now appears as the foreground color.

10 Click the Eye icon for the black-and-white layer to turn it back on.

83

DIFFICULTY LEVEL

11 Click the layer you want to use for this color.

12 Click the Paintbrush in the toolbox.

13 Choose a good-sized, soft-edged brush.

14 Select Color for the layer blending mode.

15 Paint over the photo where you want this color to appear.

TIPS

Did You Know?
You may wonder if it is better to create the black-and-white layer using Remove Color or by making your own black-and-white adjustment as explained in task #80. This really depends on personal taste and individual photographs. There is no right or wrong way to do it.

Try This!
A quick and easy way to get to the Eyedropper tool when you are in any other tool is to simply press Alt/Option. This immediately changes whatever cursor you are using to the Eyedropper. You can then click a color and it will appear in the foreground color; then you release Alt/Option and the original tool returns.

More Options!
Not having the right number of layers when you get started on this technique is okay. The only reason for adding layers at the beginning is to get you started with a set of layers that will separate your colors. You can add or subtract layers later if your plans change as you work on the image.

Create a
HAND-COLORED LOOK

The hand-colored, or hand-painted, look has a lot of possibilities. There is no one way to use this technique. You can choose realistic colors, or you can decide to color your subject and its surroundings in some totally new way. You can make this effect look very pale and pastel by both the choice of your colors and keeping the layers at a low Opacity setting. You can also make this effect look very intense by choosing very saturated colors and keeping the layers at 100% Opacity.

It helps to work from the bottom color layer up to the top. By building up color one layer at a time, you can

often fix mistakes of an underlying layer simply by brushing on new color in an upper layer.

You also do not have to color the entire photograph. Sometimes it can be interesting to add only one or just a few colors to a picture. Or you can color everything, including using different colors than were in the original. You can also be as precise in your coloring as you want, but many photographers find that the effect looks quite interesting if the edges are not precise.

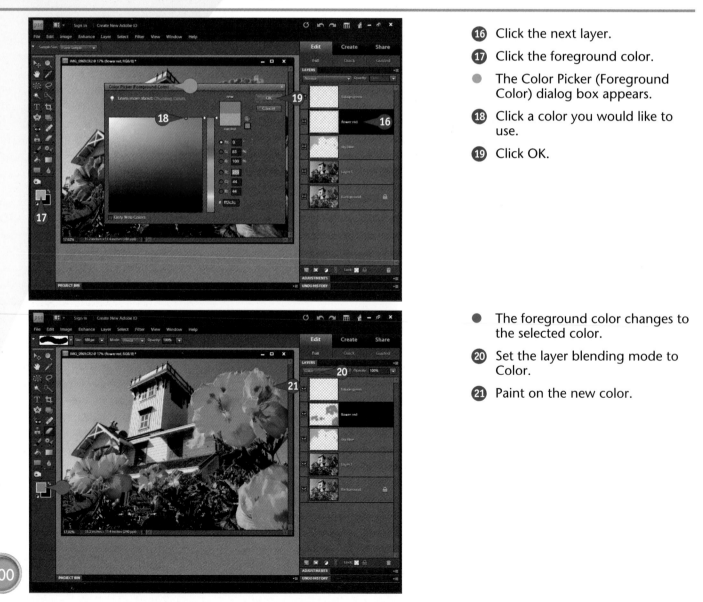

⓰ Click the next layer.

⓱ Click the foreground color.

● The Color Picker (Foreground Color) dialog box appears.

⓲ Click a color you would like to use.

⓳ Click OK.

● The foreground color changes to the selected color.

⓴ Set the layer blending mode to Color.

㉑ Paint on the new color.

22 Change the opacity of the layer until the color looks right.

23 Continue this process, layer by layer, until you have finished painting color on your image.

Use selections if needed to confine color to certain areas.

TIPS

Try This!
You can get the colors you use for painting from two places, as you have seen in this task: from the original picture or from a foreground color setting. Try both techniques to see which one gives you the colors that best suit your needs and your photograph.

Important!
In this technique, you have been using a separate color layer for each color. You can put more than one color on a layer, but this is not recommended. You are more likely to have problems adjusting colors if you have more than one color on a layer. Keep them separate and you will find that your image work has more flexibility, too.

More Options!
As you paint a color onto your photograph, change the brush size as you go to better match changes within the photograph. In addition, use the Eraser tool at different sizes to remove areas of color that have spilled onto places where you do not want it.

Photograph a scene to
GET MORE EXPOSURE DETAIL

Your camera and sensor do not see the world the same way as your eyes and brain. This can cause a problem for photographers when they try to photograph something that they see perfectly well, but the camera cannot.

Sometimes photographers think that they are not getting the correct exposure when such pictures do not seem to work out. The camera simply cannot give an exposure that equals what the eyes see. That is very true for the photo of pond lilies seen here. Although the reflection of the flowers shows up quite well in real life, the camera cannot handle the tonal

range between the bright leaves and the flowers' reflection.

The answer to that is to use more than one exposure. Shoot an image with an exposure that makes the bright areas look their best and not overexposed. Then shoot an image with an exposure that makes dark areas look good even if the bright areas are overexposed. You can put these two images together into a final shot with Photomerge in Photoshop Elements that is more accurate to what the world truly looks like.

Often a scene looks very good to your eyes, such as these pond lily leaves and the reflection of the flowers.

The camera cannot match your eyes and brain for seeing the real world.

1 Take one photo with an exposure that favors the main part of the subject even if the bright areas look too bright.

2 Change your exposure to get good highlights. A simple way to do this is by adjusting your exposure compensation.

#84

3 Take a second photo with an exposure that favors the bright areas even if the dark parts of the photo look too dark.

You can put these two images together into a final shot in Photoshop Elements.

TIPS

Try This!

Use the playback capability of your digital camera when doing this technique. Play back both of the photographs on your LCD that you have taken to be sure that you have one that adequately captures the bright areas and another that adequately captures the dark areas.

Important!

A tripod can be very helpful when you are taking multiple exposures of a scene in order to get more exposure detail. Photoshop Elements can, to a degree, line up images that are not shot on a tripod, but this can take time and it does not always work.

More Options!

HDR or *high dynamic range* photography is becoming increasingly popular. With this type of photography, you take three or more exposures of the same scene so that you have a whole range of exposures showing off everything from the dark parts of the scene to the very brightest parts of the scene. You then bring these images into the computer and process them into one final photo that combines all of the good parts of the images by using HDR software.

MERGE PHOTOS
for more photo detail

Once you have taken your two exposures, you need to be able to combine those two images into one final photo that is closer to what you saw. Photoshop Elements does this in its Photomerge Exposure feature. The best way to learn how to use this feature is to shoot two exposures of a scene as described in the previous task and then try to merge them. This will better help you understand what sorts of images work best with this technique and what images do not.

This photo of pond lily pads and flower reflections works very well with this feature of Photoshop Elements because the pond lily pads and reflections are fairly separated from one another. When the bright areas and the dark areas that need to be adjusted are mixed with each other, Photomerge Exposure does not work as well and is rather challenging to even use. You will help yourself a lot if you make sure the bright areas and dark areas in your composition are in distinctly separate parts of the photograph.

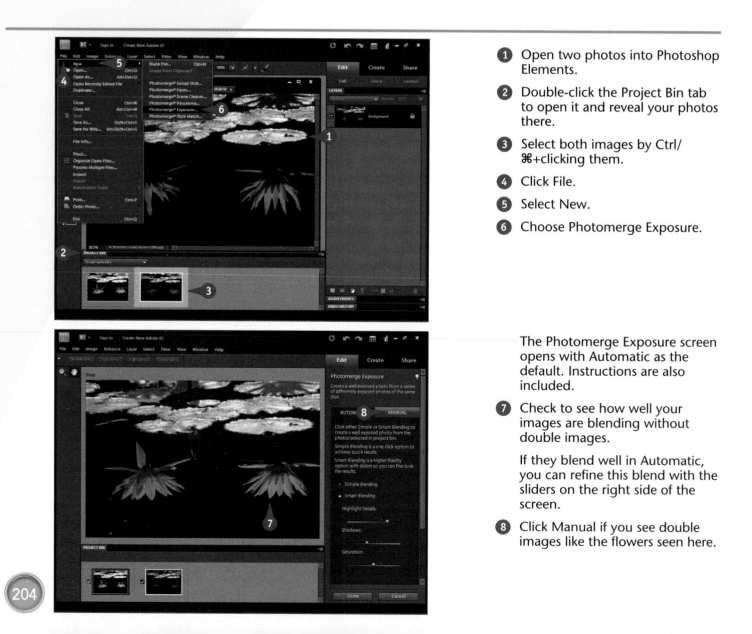

1 Open two photos into Photoshop Elements.

2 Double-click the Project Bin tab to open it and reveal your photos there.

3 Select both images by Ctrl/ ⌘+clicking them.

4 Click File.

5 Select New.

6 Choose Photomerge Exposure.

The Photomerge Exposure screen opens with Automatic as the default. Instructions are also included.

7 Check to see how well your images are blending without double images.

If they blend well in Automatic, you can refine this blend with the sliders on the right side of the screen.

8 Click Manual if you see double images like the flowers seen here.

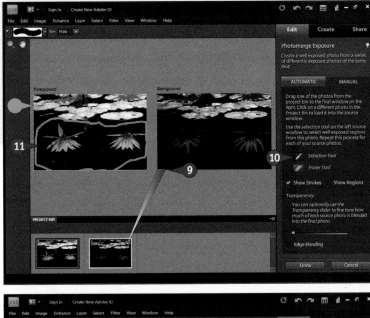

- One image will appear at the left.

9 Drag the second image to the box at the right.

10 Click the Selection tool.

11 Circle around the good exposures of the left image that need to replace the bad parts of the right image.

#85

DIFFICULTY LEVEL

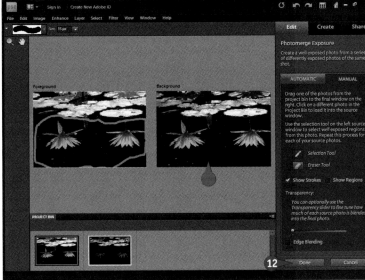

- The photos are combined in the right image.

12 Click Done.

TIPS

Did You Know?

Why not simply use Shadows/Highlights to adjust the dark and bright areas of one image? You gain a couple of things by merging two exposures as seen in this task. First, less noise. Simply brightening a dark area often increases noise in that area and reduces image quality. Second, better color. Your sensor records the best color in the middle of its range so by exposing your colors in that range, you get better color than if they are under- or overexposed.

Try This!

Adjust your photos for optimum color and contrast before using Photomerge Exposure. This enables you to be sure that your highlights do indeed look their best in the highlight exposed image and the shadow tonality and color look their best in the darker exposed photo.

More Options!

You can use Photomerge Exposure with multiple changed exposures rather than just two. This gives you similar results to HDR or high dynamic range photography. The difference is that you get a blended file rather than a true HDR file that can be readjusted or "tonemapped" in multiple ways.

Photograph a scene
FOR A PANORAMIC IMAGE

The panoramic image is like a wide-screen movie — physically, it is a photo that is very wide compared to its depth. It is possible to crop a photograph to give a panoramic look to an image. In that case, however, your picture can never be very big because it is limited by the maximum size of the image file.

Digital photography makes it relatively easy for anyone to create a panoramic image. You create a multi-image panoramic photo by shooting two or more images across a scene, and then merging them together in the computer. This type of panoramic shot gives you a very large image because your original image file size is actually quite a bit smaller than the final photo. This means you can make very large prints without any loss in quality. In addition, you can shoot a wider view of the scene than is possible otherwise, including a full 360-degree photograph.

The location seen here is in Alabama Hills below the Eastern Sierras in Lone Pine, California. The jumble of rocks is fascinating, and it is the rocks going across the area, not the blank sky or dull foreground, that is most interesting. That is what the panoramic captured.

Before taking your panoramic photo, find a scene with distinctive photo elements from the left to right.

1. Find a beginning.
2. Include an interesting middle.
3. Finish with an end.

Set up your tripod.

4. Level the top of the tripod below the tripod head.
5. Level the camera.

6 Set your camera to Manual exposure.

7 Set one exposure for the scene to be used for all images.

8 Shoot a series of pictures across the scene.

9 Overlap the pictures by 30 to 50 percent so that they can blend well in Photoshop Elements.

TIPS

Try This!
You can do verticals in a panoramic format, as well. This creates a tall, narrow image. The process is the same except that you shoot a series of images that overlap from top to bottom, rather than left to right. This can be a great way to photograph a waterfall, for example.

Important!
Manual exposure, including setting a specific white balance, is very important when you are shooting panoramic images. If you shoot your camera on automatic, you get variations of exposure among the series of photos you take across the scene. This exposure variation makes the photos much more difficult to blend together.

More Options!
You can do several things to level your tripod and camera. A simple, compact level from the hardware store can help get you started. You can also get a level that fits into your camera's flash hot shoe that will help you level the camera. Some cameras even have a level that can be displayed on the LCD.

MERGE PHOTOS
for a panoramic image

Now that you have shot your photos, you are ready to merge them in Photoshop Elements. Photomerge for Photoshop Elements includes several ways you can merge multiple photos, from working with different exposures to cleaning up scenes to the powerful Photomerge Panorama. Photomerge includes a number of possibilities for your panoramic images.

The basics are simple. You tell Photoshop Elements which pictures to work with. These are photos you shot using the techniques from task #86. The Alabama Hills photos come together as one long image in this task. Alabama Hills is an area of rocks

and mountains that has long been used by Hollywood for westerns, science fiction, and "foreign" locations.

Photoshop Elements examines your set of pictures, comparing the overlapping areas, and aligns the images. This is why getting a good overlap with your photographs as you take them is so important. The program lines up the images so the overlapped areas match, which is why leveling your camera is important; otherwise, the matched individual pictures will line up crookedly. Finally, Photoshop Elements puts these pictures together as a panoramic image.

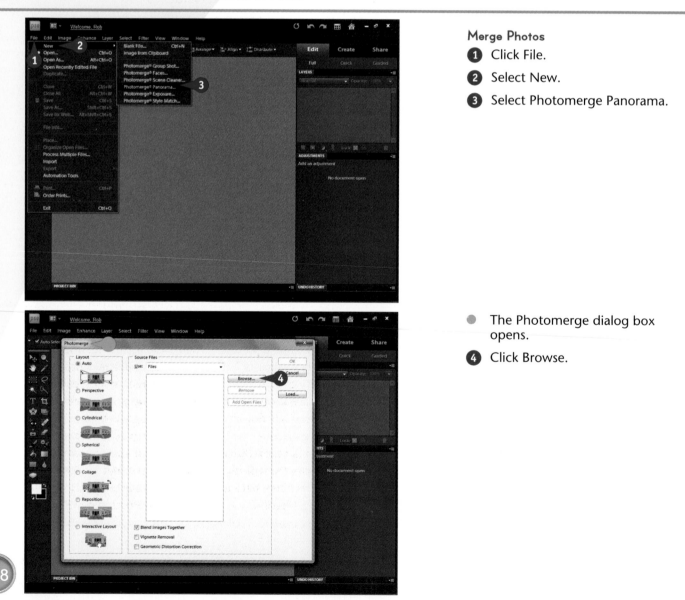

Merge Photos

① Click File.

② Select New.

③ Select Photomerge Panorama.

● The Photomerge dialog box opens.

④ Click Browse.

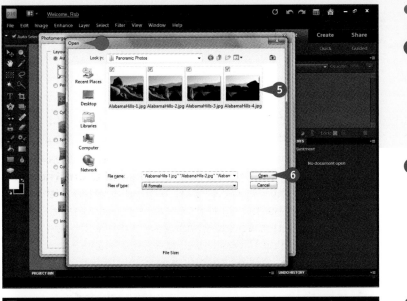

● The Open dialog box opens.

⑤ Select the series of images that make up your panorama.

Clicking the first one and Shift+clicking the last one selects the ones in between.

⑥ Click Open.

⑦ Select Reposition in the Layout area (○ changes to ◉).

⑧ Click OK.

TIPS

Try This!

Sometimes you will find that individual pieces of your panoramic image do not blend together as well as you would like. Because Photoshop Elements puts the individual pictures for a panoramic into layers, you can adjust individual pictures to make them better match the rest. Simply select that area's layer and work on the picture there directly.

Try This!

When is the best time to process individual panoramic images? Before or after putting them into the panorama? The answer is not simple. Sometimes working on individual pictures before combining them is easier. Other times working with the individual photos in layers is better because it gives you a lot of flexibility.

More Options!

When you open Photomerge Panorama, you can choose either Folders or Files in the Use drop-down menu. Some photographers merge a lot of images into one. To keep track of them all, they often find it easier to put each panorama group into its own folder. That way they can go directly to the folder when they are in Photomerge Panorama.

MERGE PHOTOS
for a panoramic image

Photoshop Elements does most of the work for a panoramic for you. You may discover that the newest aligning and blending algorithms in Photoshop Elements are so good that you need to do little cleanup work. The program offers several different options for putting together your panoramic image. A common look for a panoramic is to use the Reposition option, which is the one used here. This simply lines up the pictures where they overlap and blends them together in a straightforward manner.

The Perspective option puts the pictures together with perspective effects that make the image look like a bow tie. If you are photographing so that parts of your picture are in front and directly to the sides of you, this option may line things up better. The Cylindrical option maps the image onto imaginary cylinders, which sometimes helps things line up better in really wide panoramic shots. The Spherical option maps the images to the inside of a sphere. It is similar to Perspective, but gives some curved perspective lines. Collage is a funky option that allows for some changing of sizes and angles to the shots. The Interactive Layout option lets you do it all yourself.

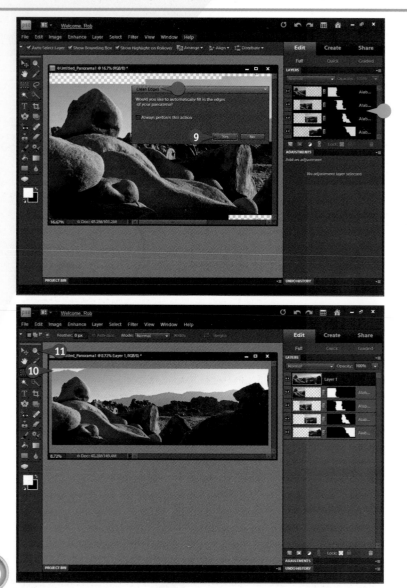

A panoramic image is created based on your group of photos. Depending on the speed of your computer and size of the original files, this can take some time.

- Each photo is placed into a layer with an automatic layer mask to help blend it with the others.

- The Clean Edges window appears. This uses the same technology as Content-Aware for the Spot Healing Brush to fill in the gaps along the edges.

⑨ Click Yes.

   If you do not like the results, you can always crop the image later.

⑩ Look both at the top and bottom to check for poorly filled areas and on the photo itself to check where the overlap occurs between pictures to see if any problems need to be fixed.

⑪ Use the Zoom tool as needed to magnify the image to better see and work on problems.

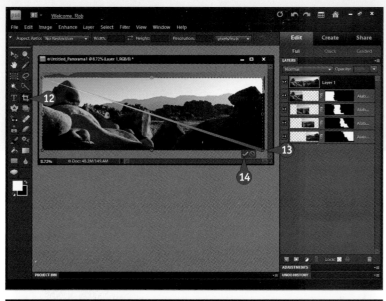

Fix Defects

⑫ Click the Crop tool in the toolbox.

⑬ Click and drag your cursor to create a crop box over the image.

⑭ Press Enter or click the green check mark icon.

Fix Gaps and Overlap Problems

⑮ Click the New Layer icon to add an empty layer over the panoramic.

⑯ Click the Clone Stamp tool in the toolbox.

⑰ Select Sample All Layers in the Options bar (■ changes to ☑).

⑱ Select a reasonable brush size to deal with the edge gap on a panoramic image.

⑲ Press Alt/Option and click once to set a clone from a point near the problem area.

⑳ Clone over the gap.

TIPS

Important!

Today's Photoshop Elements uses some very advanced processing algorithms to line up and merge the different photos into a final panoramic photo. You will often find you get excellent results right from the start. If you see any problems, however, you still have the layers to work with. You can go back and use a black or white paintbrush in the layer masks to better blend problem layers.

Try This!

Sometimes it is hard to see how the edges overlap in the Photomerge output. It can help a lot if you click layers on and off. This helps you to better see edges and what they are doing in your image. You will often find problems with, as well as opportunities for, your image when you do this.

Important!

When your panoramic image is basically complete, you can continue to adjust tonalities and colors. At this point, however, you should adjust them with adjustment layers. An adjustment layer above the top photo in your panoramic image will now adjust the entire panorama. You can limit adjustments to certain layers by using the layer mask.

GROUP IMAGES
on a page

Photographers have traditionally used one photo at a time to show their images. Even if photos were used in a slide show or a stack of prints, they were still presented and used one at a time. Photoshop Elements offers the capability of showing more than one picture at a time on a screen or a page.

The photos here are from Sedona, Arizona. Any one of these photos might have been fine, but look at the impression that you get when you see all of them as a group. You begin to see a story about a rainy day that goes beyond simply seeing single pictures. When

arranged in a certain order and varying in size across the page, they gain additional possibilities in how they relate to each other and tell that story.

You can create stories through groupings of your own pictures for everything from birthday parties to vacations. Although you can also do something like this task through the collage section of the Create tab, these steps will help you better understand layers and layer masks, as well as give you more flexibility.

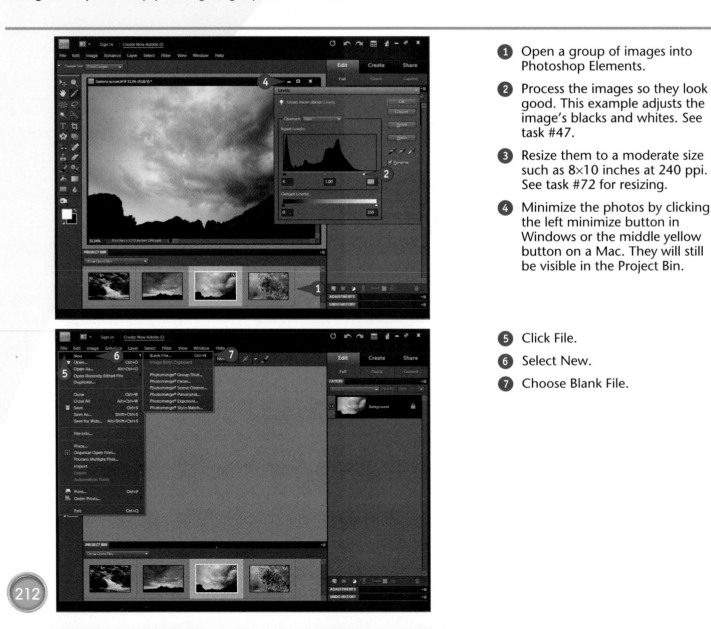

① Open a group of images into Photoshop Elements.

② Process the images so they look good. This example adjusts the image's blacks and whites. See task #47.

③ Resize them to a moderate size such as 8×10 inches at 240 ppi. See task #72 for resizing.

④ Minimize the photos by clicking the left minimize button in Windows or the middle yellow button on a Mac. They will still be visible in the Project Bin.

⑤ Click File.

⑥ Select New.

⑦ Choose Blank File.

- The New dialog box opens.

8 Type in a name for your group page.

9 Choose a preset size in Preset and go to step 13 or select Custom and continue below.

10 Type a width and height as well as a printing resolution such as 240 ppi.

11 Select RGB color for Color Mode and choose White for Background Contents.

12 Click OK.

A blank white page opens as an image file.

13 Click and drag a photo from the Project Bin onto the new blank image.

14 Select the Move tool from the toolbox.

15 Select Auto Select Layer and Show Bounding Box in the Options bar.

16 Click and drag the photo to a rough placement on the blank white page.

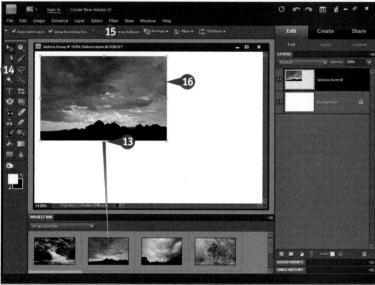

TIPS

Important!
If your images only show a tab and you cannot find the minimize button, they are not floating. Click and drag the tab toward the center of the display and the photo will float if General Preferences have been set to allow floating images. Preferences are under the Edit menu in Windows and under the Photoshop Elements menu on a Mac.

Important!
How big a page to make for your overall size of your group photo page depends on your final use of that page. Size appropriately according to whether you are going to use this for display on a computer monitor or you are going to print it out. For display purposes, size by the number of pixels the display supports. For prints, size based on the paper you plan to use.

Important!
Size your photos to a size that is some fraction of the final size of your page. It gets confusing if your pictures are at their original size and you drag them onto the new blank page. Usually, the pictures are so big they just cover each other up and you have a hard time working with them.

GROUP IMAGES
on a page

Experiment with your photos grouped onto a single page. When the Move tool has Auto Select Layer selected, all you have to do is click and drag individual photos to move them around. As you will see in this task, you can also use the picture's bounding box to resize the image in relation to the others. Try different positions and sizes for your photographs to see which arrangement tells the best story.

Because Western languages are read from left to right, top to bottom, position your photos to roughly

follow that so as to create a story from beginning to end. You can also help emphasize certain photographs by making them larger than the others.

Each photo comes in on its own layer as you drag pictures from the Project Bin to the blank page. This means that you can adjust any one of these individually to make it better match the others, plus you can drag any image up or down in the layer stack to make it show up above or below other photos. Overlapping images in this way can create a very interesting group of photos on a page.

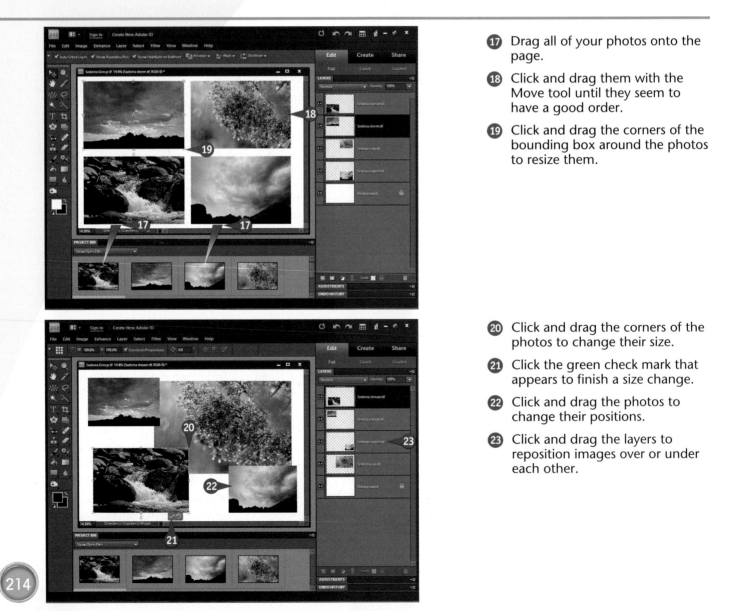

⑰ Drag all of your photos onto the page.

⑱ Click and drag them with the Move tool until they seem to have a good order.

⑲ Click and drag the corners of the bounding box around the photos to resize them.

⑳ Click and drag the corners of the photos to change their size.

㉑ Click the green check mark that appears to finish a size change.

㉒ Click and drag the photos to change their positions.

㉓ Click and drag the layers to reposition images over or under each other.

24 Click the Type tool in the toolbox.

25 Click the drop-down menu arrow to the right of the color in the Options bar.

26 Choose a color for your text by clicking a color in the menu.

27 Click in the image where you think text would look good.

28 Type your text.

29 Change the text like you would use a word-processor, by selecting the text and then changing font and size in the Options bar.

30 Use the Move tool to click and drag your text into new positions.

TIPS

Try This!

The group of photos on a page capability has been greatly enhanced with the new layer mask capabilities of Photoshop Elements 9. You can now add a layer mask to any layer. This allows you to use a brush on the layer mask, for example, to add or remove certain parts of a photo.

Try This!

For precise positioning of photos on your blank page, you can turn on the Photoshop Elements grid. You can find this under the View menu by choosing Grid. You can change the Grid by going to Preferences, Guides & Grid and then changing the options for Gridline and Subdivisions. You can also snap the movement of your photos to this grid by going to Snap To in the View menu.

More Options!

The Move tool has two very important options. Auto Select Layer allows you to click something with it in your page or photo area and the layer of that object is automatically selected. Show Bounding Box creates an outline around your photo that you can click and drag its corners to resize the photo. Dragging sides changes the proportions of the image.

TRANSFER STYLES
between photos

Like most photographers, you will discover that certain photographs have a look that you would like to duplicate to a new image. Photoshop Elements allows you to do this through something called styles. You start processing an image in Photoshop Elements, and then you use Photomerge Style Match. There are some images that have distinctive styles to get you started. Even though the images are black-and-white, you can apply them to color photos.

You can also import your own photos to use for style matching. You might, for example, have spent a lot of

time on an image and you really like the final results. You would like to duplicate that same result in other photos without going through all of the work you did on the first photo. You can click the green plus button in the Style Match work area and follow the directions to add your own image.

The photo seen here is of a cottonwood and other trees in a canyon near Sedona, Arizona. A lot of moisture and haze was in the air, but a style from one of the black-and-white images that comes with Photoshop Elements gave it the drama it deserved.

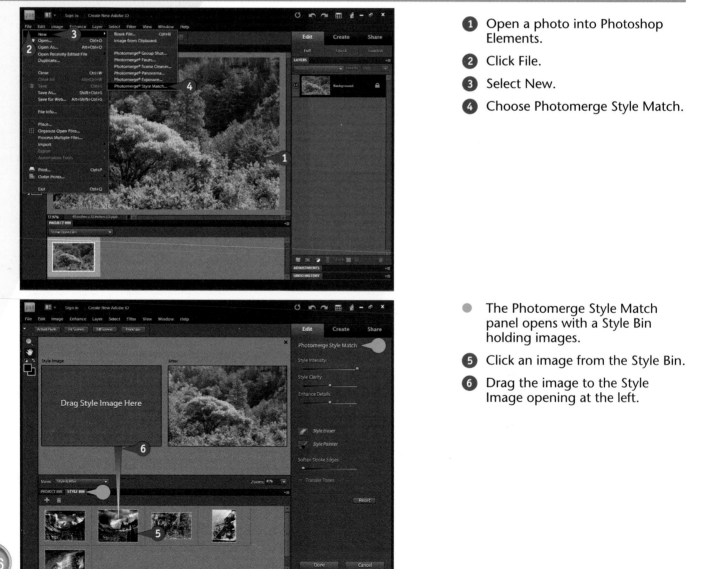

1 Open a photo into Photoshop Elements.

2 Click File.

3 Select New.

4 Choose Photomerge Style Match.

● The Photomerge Style Match panel opens with a Style Bin holding images.

5 Click an image from the Style Bin.

6 Drag the image to the Style Image opening at the left.

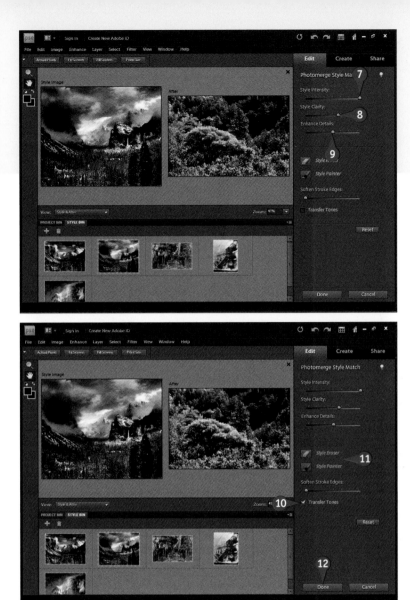

Your original photo on the right is changed to match the style of the photo at the left.

⑦ Adjust Style Intensity to affect how boldly the style is matched.

⑧ Change Style Clarity to affect the softness or hardness of the image.

⑨ Adjust Enhance Details to affect how intensely details show up.

⑩ Click Transfer Tones to make a color image match the black-and-white tones of the style image (■ changes to ✓).

⑪ Use the Style Eraser and Style Painter tools to change where the style is applied to your photo.

⑫ Click Done.

TIPS

Try This!

Play around with the extremes of the Style Clarity and Style Intensity sliders. They do similar things though the results are not identical. Both left give an almost painterly look to the image. Clarity left and Painter right give a very stylized look to your image. Both right give an extreme contrast that is very bold but may look harsh for many images.

Important!

Style Match requires intensive processing on the part of your computer as it compares the two images. Do not be surprised if this processing takes a little time. Even changing the options sliders can put your computer into thinking mode as it works through the algorithms to make this change.

More Options!

The Style Eraser and Style Painter tools are brush controls; you can change them the same as any brush in Photoshop Elements. The easiest way to change the size of these brushes is to use the bracket keys to the right of the letter P on your keyboard. You can also quickly set a brush by right-clicking the photo to get a brush menu.

Software Plug-ins Make Work Easier

Spending more time at the computer than you have to makes no sense when there are photos to be taken! As you have seen in this book, Photoshop Elements has a lot of power, but plug-ins can help you harness that power and make your work in that program more effective.

Plug-ins are software programs that fit inside a host program and help it do something different, better, or both. They are sometimes referred to as Photoshop plug-ins, but they usually work in Photoshop Elements, too.

One of the big benefits of using a plug-in within Photoshop Elements is that it can expand your efficiency and the power of the program. Many photographers discover that by using a few plug-ins, they can easily create work equal to that of more sophisticated photographers using Photoshop. And they can do this at a fraction of the cost of buying Photoshop!

In this chapter, you learn about a variety of plug-ins that offer a range of features for Photoshop Elements users. Few photographers will need or even want all of them. You can always try out any of the plug-ins discussed here by downloading trial versions from the manufacturers' Web sites. This way you can decide how valuable a given plug-in might be for you at no cost.

Top 100

#90 Use Viveza for Quick Creative Adjustments . . . . 220 DIFFICULTY LEVEL

#91 Use Color Efex Pro for Efficient Photo Work. . . . . 222 DIFFICULTY LEVEL

#92 Remove Noise with Dfine . . . . 224 DIFFICULTY LEVEL

#93 Get Dramatic Black-and-White with Silver Efex Pro . . . . . . 226 DIFFICULTY LEVEL

#94 Use Bokeh for Easy Depth-of-Field Effects . . . . 228 DIFFICULTY LEVEL

#95 Try PhotoTune for Fast Color and Tonal Adjustments . . . . . 230 DIFFICULTY LEVEL

#96 Use Snap Art for Creative Effects . . . . 232 DIFFICULTY LEVEL

USE VIVEZA
for quick creative adjustments

Nik Software (www.niksoftware.com) is a company that specializes in plug-ins for photographers, plug-ins that really seem to speak to photographers' needs. Their Viveza 2 is a remarkable plug-in that intelligently helps you process your images. Did you think that layer masks were difficult to learn? Maybe you are still working on that. Viveza 2 offers a unique, easy-to-use approach that uses a control point on the photograph. This control point looks for similar tones, colors, and textures within a defined circle. Then as you make adjustments to that control point, such as brightness or contrast, Viveza 2 makes those

adjustments to only the parts of the picture it sees as similar. For example, if you put a control point in the sky, adjustments affect the sky but not the clouds around it, and this is without you having to do anything other than click in the picture and start making adjustments.

In addition, Viveza 2 includes a unique control that no other program has called Structure. This control alone can be worth the price of the program for landscape and travel photographers. It creates a midtones contrast that really can make a photograph come alive.

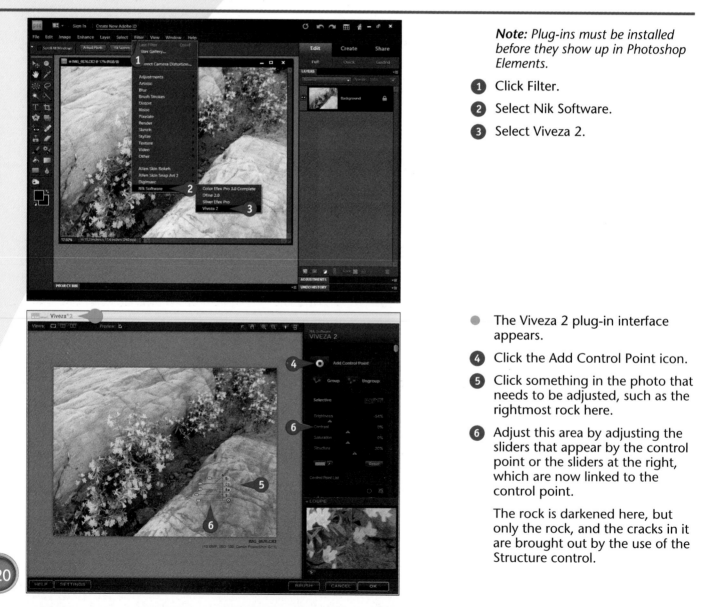

Note: Plug-ins must be installed before they show up in Photoshop Elements.

① Click Filter.

② Select Nik Software.

③ Select Viveza 2.

● The Viveza 2 plug-in interface appears.

④ Click the Add Control Point icon.

⑤ Click something in the photo that needs to be adjusted, such as the rightmost rock here.

⑥ Adjust this area by adjusting the sliders that appear by the control point or the sliders at the right, which are now linked to the control point.

The rock is darkened here, but only the rock, and the cracks in it are brought out by the use of the Structure control.

7. Click the Add Control Point icon.

8. Click another part of the photo that needs to be adjusted.

9. Adjust this new area by adjusting the sliders that appear by the control point or the sliders at the right.

The back rock is darkened now, but only the rock, and the cracks in it are brought out by the use of the Structure slider.

10. Click the unmarked slider coming from the control point. This affects the area of coverage.

11. Adjust the area of coverage as needed. Viveza 2 is not looking at everything within that area, only things that match the location of the control point.

12. Click OK.

TIPS

Did You Know?

Control points are a special part of Nik Software programs. They are points you set on your photograph to add or subtract a plug-in effect. They enable you to quickly control where these effects go, without using layer masks.

Did You Know?

The Structure control is a very powerful part of Viveza 2. It affects the contrast of midtones in a very natural way and gives them a sense of presence. They almost seem to become dimensional, as if they were present right before you. This can be very effective with landscapes and buildings.

Important!

Most plug-ins must have pixels to work with. This means they need to work on a flattened image file or on a layer made up of pixels. You can apply a plug-in to a layered file by creating a single layer from all of your layers using the keyboard command Ctrl+Shift+Alt+E in Windows or ⌘+Shift+Option+E on a Mac.

USE COLOR EFEX PRO
for efficient photo work

One thing Nik Software Color Efex Pro does for you is make your work more efficient. You can apply many of the adjustments and effects in this plug-in in Photoshop Elements. Color Efex Pro enables you to make these adjustments faster, more easily, and more efficiently.

Color Efex Pro is a plug-in with an entire range of ways to adjust your photographs. They include very direct effects, such as ones to change the brightness balance of certain colors, add a graduated neutral density filter effect, and get more richness from foliage. They also include adjustments that can fix

problems in the picture, such as a dynamic skin softener, a skylight filter, and a white neutralizer. Very creative effects are also included, such as effects that mimic the look of infrared film, create a glamour glow look, and make a pastel image from your original.

In this image of barrel cactus in the Mojave National Preserve in California, the background and sky show off the location but need to be brought into balance with the cactus. The cactus should be seen clearly as the star of the photo.

1 Click Filter.

2 Select Nik Software.

3 Select Color Efex Pro 3.0 Complete.

● The Color Efex Pro plug-in interface appears.

4 Select Graduated Neutral Density Filter from the left side.

● The effect appears in the center window.

5 Adjust the Blend slider to 0 to make the edge show up better while you do these adjustments.

6 Use the Upper Tonality slider to adjust how the sky and top of the photo will be darkened.

7 Use the Lower Tonality slider if the bottom of the photo needs darkening.

Use these controls to darken part of the photo to balance other sections, though you can also use them to brighten these areas.

8. Adjust the Vertical Shift slider to make the effect start higher or lower in the image.

9. Rotate the adjustment to fit the photo by using the Rotation slider.

10. Adjust the Blend slider to make the effect blend nicely in the image.

11. Readjust the Vertical Shift slider if needed.

12. Click OK.

TIPS

Important!

Do your basic image processing before you use a plug-in. You want to be sure that your blacks are set properly, the midtones look good, and the colors are corrected before you start making major changes to the photograph. Start with a good photograph before using the processing power of a plug-in.

Did You Know?

Color Efex Pro also includes the capability to define a specific color for a graduated filter effect. This can be very helpful in matching sky color or to create a late-afternoon mood by darkening everything except the light coming from near the horizon. The combination of Viveza 2 and Color Efex Pro adds a lot of power to Photoshop Elements.

Check It Out!

You can learn more about Color Efex Pro and other software plug-ins from Nik Software by going to its Web site, www.niksoftware.com. The site has trial versions to download as well as a complete listing of all the features in its programs. Plus you can see some great examples and tutorials of how the software can be put to work.

REMOVE NOISE
with Dfine

Noise can be a problem with digital photos. Sometimes noise shows up when an underexposed image is brightened to normal levels in Photoshop Elements. Other times it shows up when you need to use a high ISO setting on your camera because of low light levels or when you need a fast shutter speed to stop motion with a lot of action. Although Photoshop Elements includes some very basic noise reduction controls, they do not work very well when you have the challenge of strong noise in a picture.

For optimum noise reduction, you need a dedicated noise reduction software program. Nik Software Dfine is a plug-in that works to control noise without hurting other detail in the photograph. Dfine also allows you to specifically define areas based on color to determine how much noise reduction you do. This gives you more control over how details are affected.

The image seen here was shot with a compact digital camera on a cloudy day. The conditions were such that a high ISO was needed for a sharp picture. This image was shot at ISO 1600 and has a lot of noise.

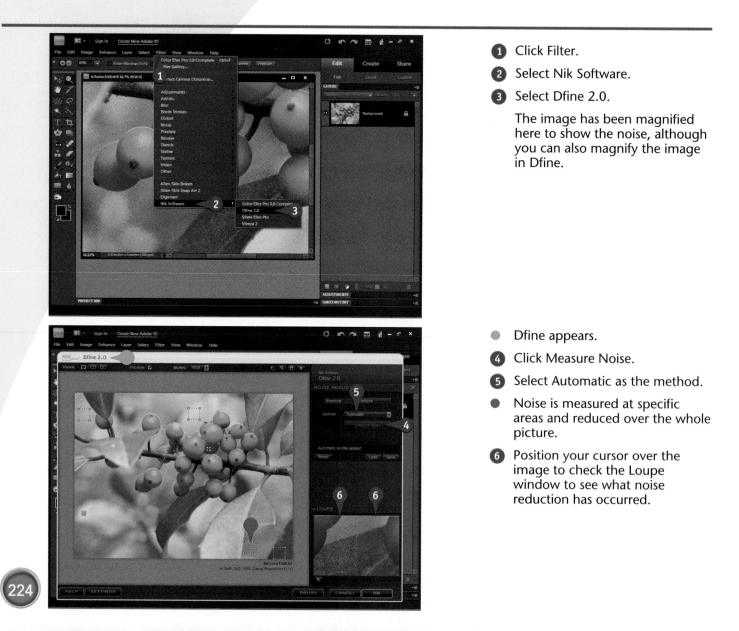

① Click Filter.

② Select Nik Software.

③ Select Dfine 2.0.

The image has been magnified here to show the noise, although you can also magnify the image in Dfine.

● Dfine appears.

④ Click Measure Noise.

⑤ Select Automatic as the method.

● Noise is measured at specific areas and reduced over the whole picture.

⑥ Position your cursor over the image to check the Loupe window to see what noise reduction has occurred.

7 Click the Method drop-down menu if more noise reduction is needed and choose Manual.

8 Click the add rectangle button below Manual.

9 Draw a rectangle over an area with a noise problem.

10 Click Measure Noise.

DIFFICULTY LEVEL

11 Click Reduce.

12 Click the Method drop-down menu and select Color Ranges.

13 Click an eyedropper next to a color.

14 Click a color in the photograph that you want to affect.

15 Adjust the slider to change how much noise reduction is done for that color.

16 Repeat steps 13 to 15 for other important colors.

17 Click OK.

TIPS

Important!

Use the Loupe window to watch small detail and see how the noise reduction affects it. Noise is essentially small detail. Dfine does a good job of controlling noise without hurting small detail, but sometimes it has trouble telling the difference. Reduce the amount of noise reduction when this happens.

Did You Know?

It can help to take noise reduction off of blacks and very dark parts of the picture. These areas often create a certain structure for sharpness and a slight bit of noise in them can actually help. As long as these areas remain dark in your processing, noise will probably not be a problem.

More Options!

Nik Software includes a number of views of how your picture is being affected. On the left in the upper toolbar, you will see Views with several icons. The first shows you the picture as it is changed. The others may show before-and-after images, plus split views showing before and after in the same picture.

Get dramatic black-and-white
WITH SILVER EFEX PRO

Black-and-white photography is a real art, not simply a matter of changing a color picture to grayscale or a monochrome. It is about how different brightness values and colors in a photograph are changed to tones of gray. You can, of course, create a fine black-and-white image in Photoshop Elements, as shown in Chapter 8.

But for the photographer who really wants to get the most out of black-and-white, Nik Software Silver Efex Pro offers a superb amount of flexibility and control. The plug-in uses the same type of interface as other Nik Software programs. Silver Efex Pro adds controls

that make it easier to look at how a color picture changes to black-and-white. Preset effects are shown as small sample images to make your options easier to choose. Just click what you want. In addition, a range of controls enable you to make adjustments as needed.

The photo seen here shows Joshua trees in the Mojave National Preserve. The picture is okay in color but has a lot more potential in black-and-white. Some scenes just look better in black-and-white than they do in color.

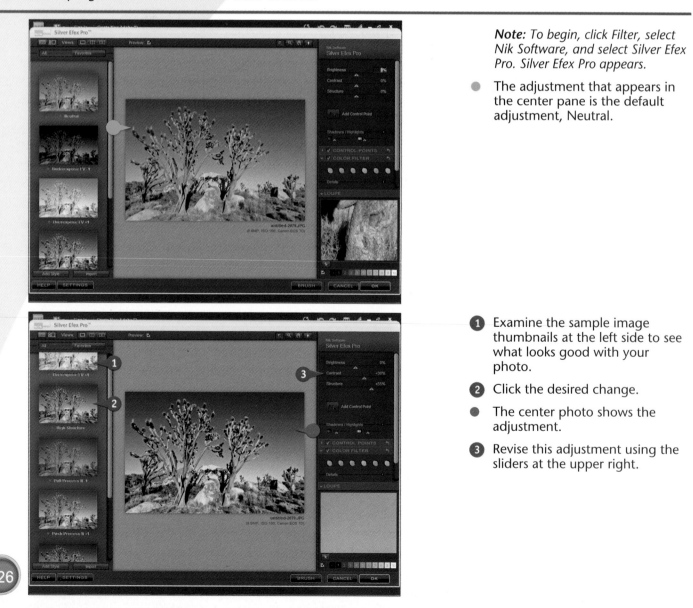

Note: *To begin, click Filter, select Nik Software, and select Silver Efex Pro. Silver Efex Pro appears.*

● The adjustment that appears in the center pane is the default adjustment, Neutral.

① Examine the sample image thumbnails at the left side to see what looks good with your photo.

② Click the desired change.

● The center photo shows the adjustment.

③ Revise this adjustment using the sliders at the upper right.

④ Click a color filter to change how colors translate to black and white.

⑤ Click the Details drop-down menu arrow.

⑥ Change the Hue slider to see how colors are affected.

⑦ Vary the Strength slider to adjust the effect.

⑧ Click the Add Control Point icon.

⑨ Click something in the photograph that you want to adjust separately from the rest.

⑩ Change the Control Point sliders to affect that area.

⑪ Click OK.

TIPS

Did You Know?

The Structure control in Silver Efex Pro is an adjustment that affects the finer gradations of tonalities. It is similar to the Contrast control, and definitely affects contrast, but it is a more refined control. Structure looks at and adjusts small midtone changes in tonalities for more or less drama in the details of a picture.

Did You Know?

Control points allow you to make very specific changes to your photograph without ever having to deal with layers or layer masks. In Silver Efex Pro, you can selectively control the tonality and structure of an object or area. This really helps you define parts of a photograph.

More Options!

Silver Efex Pro includes a Film Types section that enables you to simulate the looks of 18 black-and-white films. Many photographers still prefer the look of a specific black-and-white film they used when they shot using traditional cameras. This part of the plug-in allows you to try out some of these looks on your photograph.

Use Bokeh for
EASY DEPTH-OF-FIELD EFFECTS

Alien Skin Software (www.alienskin.com) is another company that makes photographer-friendly plug-ins for Photoshop and Photoshop Elements. Bokeh is a plug-in that enables you to perform some interesting effects with sharpness in your picture. A good technique for emphasizing your subject is to shoot with a very limited amount of sharpness in the photograph so that only the subject is sharp. This is called *selective focus*.

Bokeh makes it a lot of fun to play around with selective focus and other depth-of-field effects. To duplicate some of these effects without the program would

require an expensive tilt-and-shift lens. Plus, performing those effects at the time the picture is taken locks them into the image. With Bokeh, you can change your depth-of-field effects quickly and easily in Photoshop Elements. The program uses unique blur settings based on how real lenses render out-of-focus areas.

Bokeh is not just the name of this software. It is also a relatively new term becoming more widely used to refer to the way a lens renders out-of-focus parts of the scene. You will hear photographers referring to the bokeh of the background in a photograph, for example.

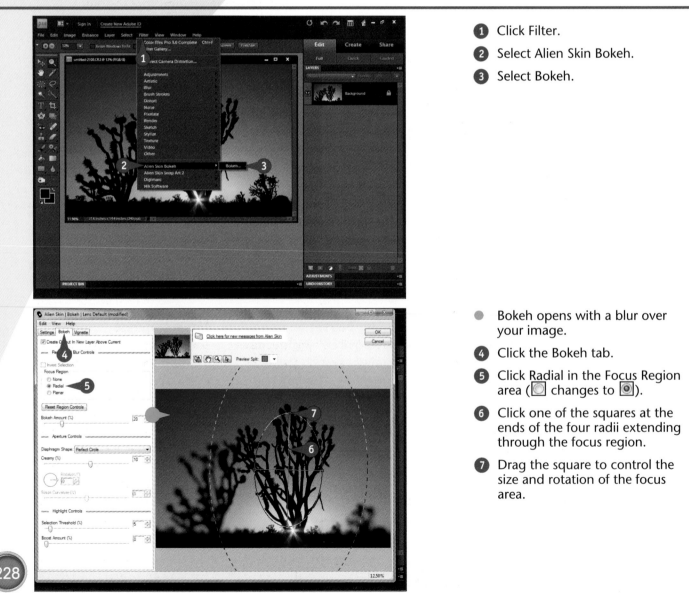

① Click Filter.

② Select Alien Skin Bokeh.

③ Select Bokeh.

● Bokeh opens with a blur over your image.

④ Click the Bokeh tab.

⑤ Click Radial in the Focus Region area (○ changes to ◉).

⑥ Click one of the squares at the ends of the four radii extending through the focus region.

⑦ Drag the square to control the size and rotation of the focus area.

8 Change the amount of blur with the Bokeh Amount slider.

9 Adjust the Aperture controls to affect the appearance of your blur.

10 Change the Highlight controls to change how the blur affects bright areas.

11 Click the Settings tab.

12 Click any preset to affect the blur differently, including using specific lenses and f-stops.

13 Click OK.

TIPS

Important!

You cannot add sharpness to a photograph. If you need something to be sharp in the picture, it must be sharp when you take the picture. Bokeh needs sharpness to work with so that something contrasts against the blur. The plug-in can help a photograph with sharpness problems as long as the subject itself is sharp.

Did You Know?

If you really like playing around with unusual focus effects, you might like trying that same thing as you take pictures. The Lensbaby system of lenses allows you to bend and twist the lens to change where the plane of focus goes through the photograph. In addition, you can use different types of lenses for different focus effects.

More Options!

Bokeh offers some additional creative options for you. You can create a motion blur to make your subject look like it is moving quickly. You can also add a vignette to make the blurred areas lighter or darker. If the image has no blur, you can simply use the vignette to quickly and easily darken outside parts of the picture.

TRY PHOTOTUNE FOR
fast color and tonal adjustments

Although Photoshop Elements truly has a good variety of controls to adjust the color and tones of your photo, sometimes they seem too much of a good thing. Where do you start? Even if you know how to find them and use the controls from this book, you still have to think about what to do. How much of an adjustment do you make? How much of a change to color is appropriate to the subject?

PhotoTune from onOne Software (www.ononesoftware. com) is designed to focus on changes in your photo, not changes in sliders. The program gives you sample images with adjustments built into them that you choose, just like going to the eye doctor, where you choose which correction is better: a or b. The plug-in also comes in a Professional version designed to help pros with adjustments such as precise skin color and tone when doing portraits.

PhotoTune is not a plug-in for everyone, but if you really like the idea of comparing "better or worse" images rather than always looking for controls to change, you may find this a welcome addition to Photoshop Elements.

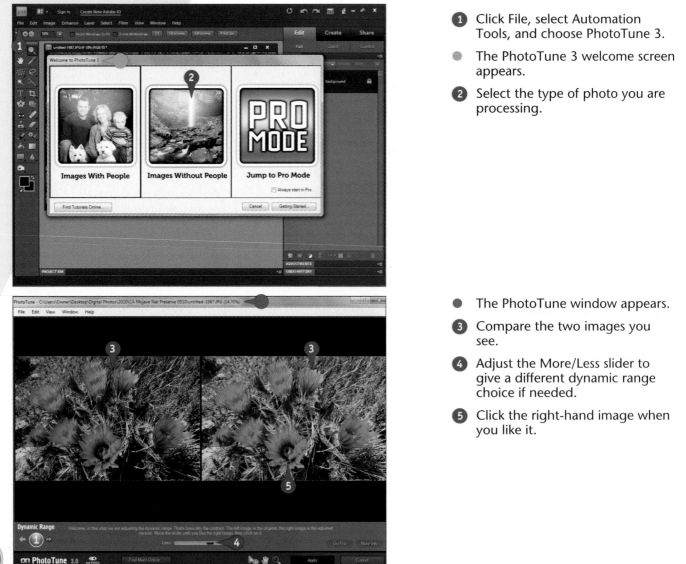

① Click File, select Automation Tools, and choose PhotoTune 3.

● The PhotoTune 3 welcome screen appears.

② Select the type of photo you are processing.

● The PhotoTune window appears.

③ Compare the two images you see.

④ Adjust the More/Less slider to give a different dynamic range choice if needed.

⑤ Click the right-hand image when you like it.

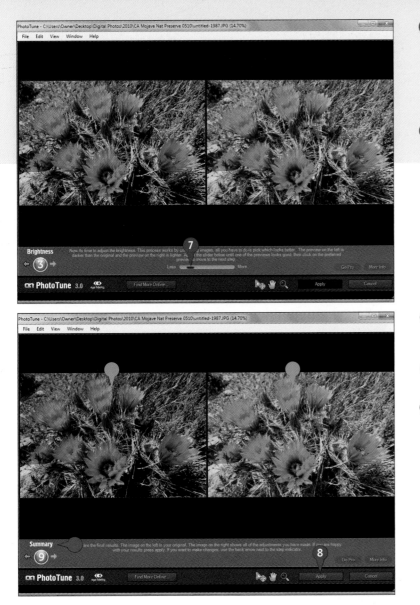

6 Keep clicking the better-looking image of the two.

Even if neither photo looks great, pick the better of the two.

7 Use the slider to increase or decrease the effect.

● When you have reached the last set of choices, you have arrived at the Summary panel.

● You will see a before-and-after of your image.

8 Click Apply to finish.

TIPS

Did You Know?

The Pro section of PhotoTune allows you to go deeper in your control over specific elements of change for your photo. This control is available at any time in PhotoTune by clicking the Go Pro button. The Pro section allows you to easily fine-tune any adjustments done by comparing two versions of your image.

More Options!

The People mode of PhotoTune is a unique application of PhotoTune's processing algorithms specifically geared toward making skin tones look better. In the SkinTune section of this mode, you click a skin tone, and then you get a set of comparison images designed to help you get the best skin tone and color from your subject.

Did You Know?

OnOne Photo Essentials is a collection of five different programs specifically chosen for Photoshop Elements. It includes a variation of PhotoTune called Make It Better, a selection program to remove a subject from a photo called Cut It Out, an enlarging program for poster-size enlargements of your photos called Enlarge It, and more.

Use Snap Art
FOR CREATIVE EFFECTS

Digital photography is great, but sometimes you want to get something from your images that goes a little bit beyond the typical photograph. You can do this in Photoshop Elements by using some of the filters, but that can take a lot of trial and error and does not always give satisfactory results without a lot of experimentation.

Alien Skin has a special plug-in called Snap Art 2. This plug-in takes your photograph and applies virtual paint strokes over it to create something that has the look of a painting or even a sketch. There are ten

basic looks from color pencil to comics to watercolor. Once you choose a look, the program offers you a lot of options to change how that look is applied to your photograph. You can adjust things like the colors used, the type of canvas, the lighting, and more.

The program builds the effect stroke by stroke so that it truly does look like the effect is hand-applied. You really do have to experiment with this program because it is very hard to predict how a given photograph will react to the changes Snap Art 2 makes to that image.

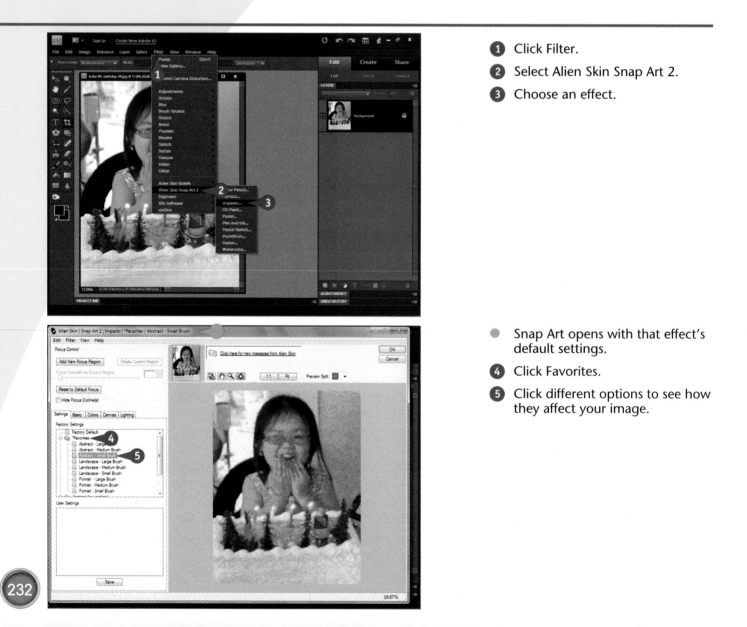

1 Click Filter.

2 Select Alien Skin Snap Art 2.

3 Choose an effect.

● Snap Art opens with that effect's default settings.

4 Click Favorites.

5 Click different options to see how they affect your image.

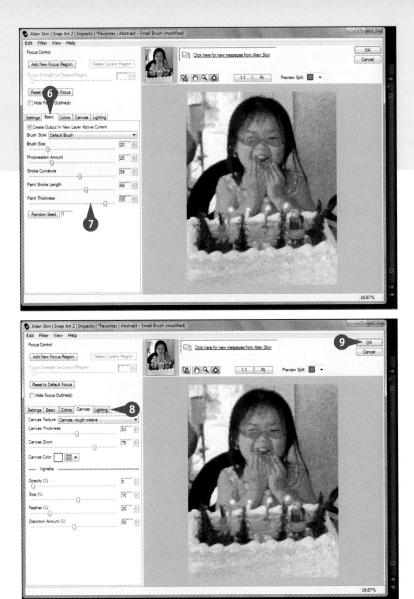

6 Click the Basic tab.

7 Try varying any of the controls, such as Stroke Curvature, Stroke Length, and Paint Thickness.

8 Click the Colors, Canvas, and Lighting tabs and play with the settings there.

9 Click OK.

TIPS

Did You Know?

One thing that makes it difficult to evaluate results of Snap Art is that the effects look very different depending on whether you are using the image small or large. If you are making a little postcard-sized image, then the effects must be stronger for them to be visible. For larger prints, you can often use more subtle tools such as shorter brushstrokes.

Did You Know?

Sometimes using "creative" effects like those from Snap Art 2 can be challenging because it is hard to decide where to go with the effects. Alien Skin's Web site, www.alienskin.com, includes both examples and case studies of photographs using Snap Art 2 so you can get some ideas of what might be possible with different sorts of subjects.

Check It Out!

If you really get into special effects, you might want to check out Alien Skin's Eye Candy plug-in. This is a unique plug-in that does everything from creating realistic texture even out of nothing except tone to generating realistic fire effects to making smoke, rust, and icicles.

Chapter 10

Get Photos out of Photoshop Elements

Once you have done all of your work on your pictures in Photoshop Elements, do not let them just sit in your computer. Get them out so that people can view your pictures, share your experiences, and learn about your passions.

The world of digital photography offers diverse ways to share pictures with others. There are online resources, including the Photoshop Elements Web site for users, Photoshop.com. Adobe really wants you to sign up for Photoshop.com, so they make it very easy

to do so. When you first open Photoshop Elements, you see an offer to sign up. Click Create Adobe ID to start.

Other ways of sharing include printing, of course, which is a very traditional and popular way to look at a photograph. Displaying your prints on the wall is a great way to share your experiences with others. You can even print groups of pictures and add special frame effects to them. Photoshop Elements makes it a lot of fun to be a photographer today!

Top 100

 # 97 Protect Your Photos with Online Backup . . . . 236 DIFFICULTY LEVEL

 # 98 Access Your Photos Anywhere Internet
Service Is Available . . . . 238 DIFFICULTY LEVEL

 # 99 Create Online Photo Albums . . . . 240 DIFFICULTY LEVEL

 # 100 Share Your Photos Online . . . . 242 DIFFICULTY LEVEL

 # 101 Print Your Photos . . . . 244 DIFFICULTY LEVEL

 # 102 Print a Group of Photos . . . . 248 DIFFICULTY LEVEL

 # 103 Add a Border Effect to Your Pictures . . . . 250 DIFFICULTY LEVEL

PROTECT YOUR PHOTOS
with online backup

Backing up your photos is very important. Although neither the 2GB available for the Basic Membership of Photoshop.com nor the 20GB for Plus can replace an accessory hard drive, this online backup can serve a very useful purpose. You can keep special archived images here separate from your home files. Hopefully, you never experience fire, floods, hurricanes, tornadoes, or any other disaster, but should any disaster happen, you will have the images backed up online.

You can certainly back up any of your photos at any time. This works best if you are shooting only JPEG

images. If you shoot RAW, your online backup fills in a hurry. You get the most from the Photoshop.com online backup by creating a special album for backup files and then saving finished images there as JPEGs. This is a fine use of JPEG: as an archival format to keep files small for storage.

Signing up for Photoshop.com is very easy to do. When you first open Photoshop Elements, click Create Adobe ID. This takes you to a wizard that helps you sign up for this Web service.

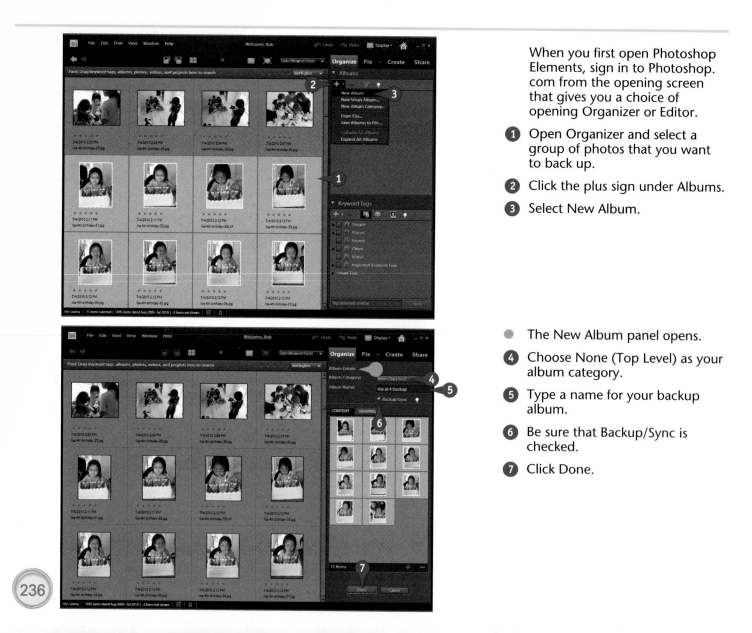

When you first open Photoshop Elements, sign in to Photoshop. com from the opening screen that gives you a choice of opening Organizer or Editor.

1. Open Organizer and select a group of photos that you want to back up.

2. Click the plus sign under Albums.

3. Select New Album.

• The New Album panel opens.

4. Choose None (Top Level) as your album category.

5. Type a name for your backup album.

6. Be sure that Backup/Sync is checked.

7. Click Done.

236

- A new album is created with the name that you gave it.

⑧ Double-click the album to open it.

The pictures in the album are shown.

- An icon appears at the lower right side of the photo that indicates the image is uploading for storage on Photoshop.com.

- A check in the icon means the photo has been uploaded.

⑨ Click the icon to the right of the album to share photos through Photoshop.com.

TIPS

Caution!

Never rely on only one form of backup, especially only one online. Even if you could get enough storage space online, you would always have to have online access to use that storage. Although online access is fairly reliable, it is never as reliably accessible as a hard drive plugged directly into your computer.

Try This!

JPEG files are excellent for archival backup because they let you reduce the size of your photos. Set Quality to 8 or higher in the JPEG Options dialog box. These should be files you have finished working on. Avoid reprocessing already-processed JPEG files. If you want to save an unprocessed file, you can use JPEG, and then save it at the highest Quality setting of 12.

More Options!

If you are connected to the Internet, Photoshop Elements continues to give you messages about things available on Photoshop.com and other offers. To change this, go to Preferences under the Edit menu in Windows or under the Photoshop Elements menu on a Mac and then Adobe Partner Services. You can select or deselect the options Adobe sends you from a whole series in the Check for Services section.

ACCESS YOUR PHOTOS
anywhere Internet service is available

You can access online storage anywhere that you have Internet access. If you travel a lot, Photoshop. com is a great way to access your photos from a distance. You can even create a special album just for travel in Photoshop Elements Organizer. Then you can move photos into that album as needed. Even if you do not have a laptop with you, you can access your photos using someone else's computer or even the guest computer at a hotel.

In addition, very small, compact computers are becoming very popular with travelers. These include the lightweight and popular iPad as well as the small

laptops often called "Web computers" or "netbooks." Designed for the ubiquitous Internet access that has become a part of the world today, iPads and Web computers have limited storage space built into the units. Because storage is restricted, you cannot store a lot of photos on them. Online photo storage makes great use of these computers.

Finally, many business travelers have no need to take their photos with them, but it is nice to access special images, such as those of family, friends, and events while on the road.

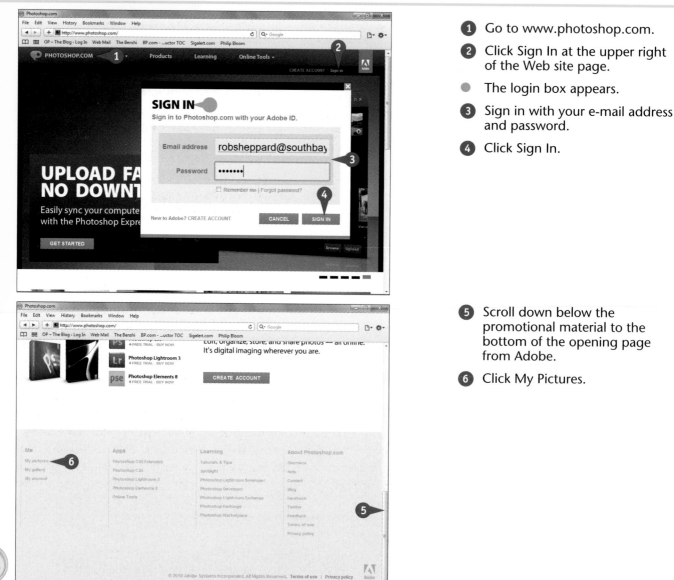

① Go to www.photoshop.com.

② Click Sign In at the upper right of the Web site page.

● The login box appears.

③ Sign in with your e-mail address and password.

④ Click Sign In.

⑤ Scroll down below the promotional material to the bottom of the opening page from Adobe.

⑥ Click My Pictures.

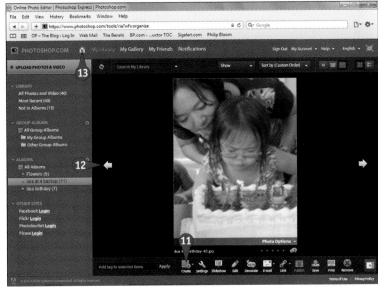

Your photos are now accessible for work. This can take some time depending on the speed of your Internet connection.

⑦ Click the sizing boxes to change the size of the thumbnails.

⑧ Position your cursor over a photo to access Photo Options for that photo.

⑨ Click the Photo Options down arrow to get a contextual menu of options.

⑩ Double-click a photo to work on it remotely.

The photo then appears as a single image.

⑪ Click any toolbar icon to work with your photo.

The toolbar is intuitive and lets you edit your photo, e-mail it, decorate it, print it, and so on.

⑫ Position your cursor over the photo to access Photo Options and to activate arrows to move you from one photo to another.

⑬ Click the Home icon to return to your complete library of photos at Photoshop.com.

TIPS

Did You Know?

If you find you are running out of room for your photos, you can always rent additional space. Click My Account and then Account Settings at the upper right of your Photoshop.com page. This opens an account summary. Click the Buy More button at the right of your storage slider.

Try This!

Photoshop.com is set up for sharing and makes it easy for you to do this. You can create a Friends List. This gives you immediate notification if anyone on this list updates galleries or adds images to her Photoshop.com account. You can set up your Friends List after browsing other public galleries, and you can interact with people who have photography you like.

Did You Know?

My Library, My Gallery, and My Friends are three buttons that give quick access to certain parts of Photoshop.com. My Library shows you all your images and lets you work on them, including moving or deleting them. My Gallery displays your photos in the gallery theme you choose; this is the gallery others see. My Friends lets you browse other photographers' public galleries.

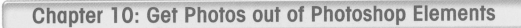

Create online PHOTO ALBUMS

Just as you did in the Organizer, you can create albums or special collections of your photos in your Photoshop.com library. When you upload images directly to Photoshop.com, they enter the library, which gives you only very basic organization. Albums not only let you group and find specific photos faster, but they also enable you to help friends and relatives find them. Albums have no effect on your photos on Photoshop.com other than to group them. Photos can go in more than one album, too, which gives you

great options for organizing them online. You can group photos by type, event, people, and so on.

Albums are a key part of your Photoshop.com image storage. You need albums in order to use many of the sharing features, such as galleries. One of the most important uses of albums in Photoshop.com is to create special collections that you can allow people to access directly. This can be a great way of sharing photos with friends and relatives. You can have an album open to everyone, open only to friends, or private.

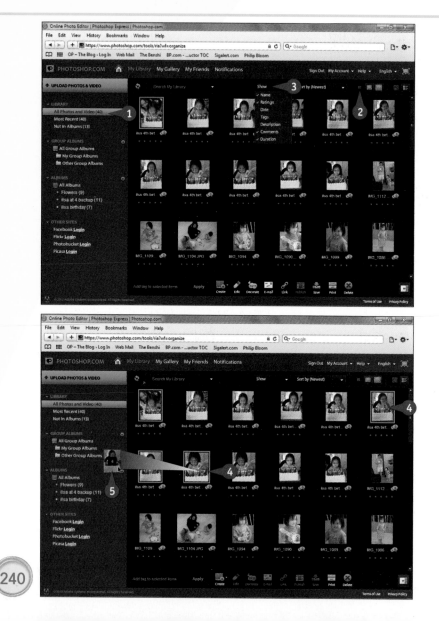

Note: To begin, open your Photoshop.com account and click My Library.

① Click All Photos and Video in your library to make them visible.

② Choose a size icon so the pictures are small and you can see many at once.

③ Click Show to access a menu that controls what information appears with your photos.

④ Press Ctrl/⌘ while you click several photos to make a selection of them.

⑤ Click and drag them onto the green plus (+) sign, which is the new album icon.

⑥ Release the images by releasing the mouse button.

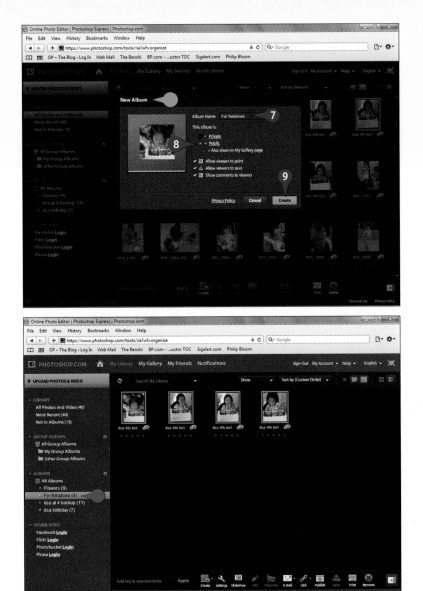

● A New Album window appears.

7 Type a name for the album.

8 Select an option for who is allowed to see this album online.

9 Click Create.

● Your album is created and now shows up in your library.

TIPS

Did You Know?
You can create an instant slide show of your photos when they are in an album. Once you open an album, you will find a Slideshow icon in the toolbar at the bottom of the screen; click that icon to create a slide show from that album. This creates a fun, 3-D, rotating slide show with an option panel on the right.

Try This!
You can also set up an album without selecting photos. While in the library, click the Create Album icon in the toolbar at the bottom of your screen, and then select New Album. This enables you to set up and name an album. You can then go through your library and drag photos onto the name of your new album to add photos to the album.

More Options!
You can upload an album directly when you create an album in the Organizer. Be sure that Backup/Synchronize is selected when the Album Details panel is open and you are setting up a new album. When you click Share, you get a series of options to choose as you prep your album for upload.

SHARE YOUR PHOTOS
online

One of the joys of photography is sharing photographs with others. On a most basic level, people like to see what others are doing, whether it is grandparents viewing photos of grandkids playing soccer or a businessperson in one geographic location showing how a retail store looks to an associate elsewhere. Plus, when big events occur, such as weddings, family reunions, and births, people love to see the visual record.

Everyone sees the world differently, and photography is a way of expressing those unique visions. Photoshop.com gives you the chance to share photos with not only friends and neighbors, but also people who share your love of photography. You have total control, too, of how people access your photos so you never have to worry about the wrong people seeing specific photos.

One of the nice things about the Photoshop.com online sharing site is that you can set up your albums to control who has access to them. You can make them totally public to show off your images to other photographers using Photoshop.com, or you can limit access to just people you have contacted via e-mail.

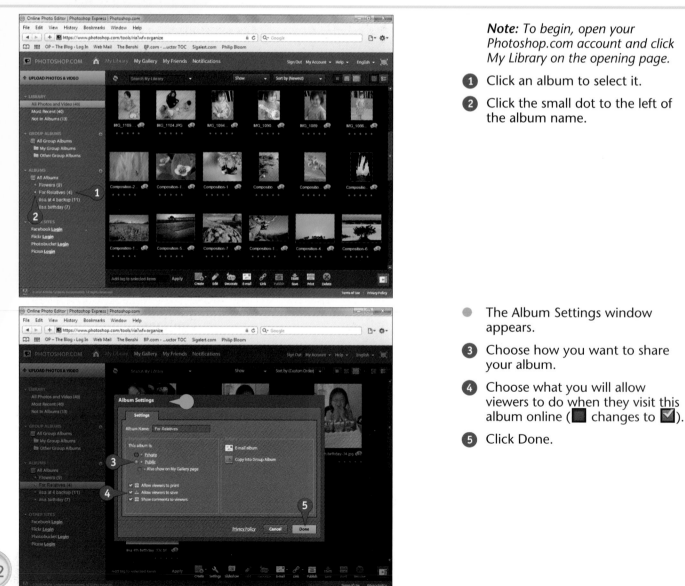

Note: To begin, open your Photoshop.com account and click My Library on the opening page.

1 Click an album to select it.

2 Click the small dot to the left of the album name.

● The Album Settings window appears.

3 Choose how you want to share your album.

4 Choose what you will allow viewers to do when they visit this album online (■ changes to ☑).

5 Click Done.

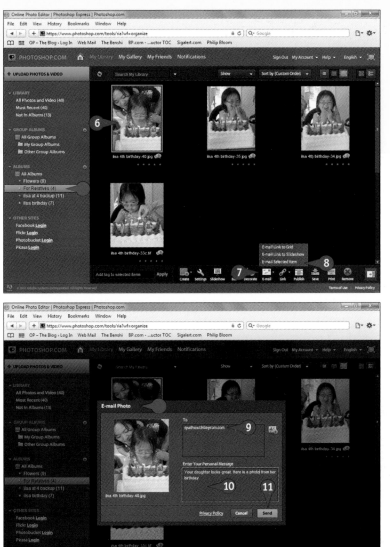

● The dot in front of your album changes color based on your sharing choice.

6 Click a photo.

7 Click the E-mail icon in the bottom toolbar.

8 Choose an e-mail option to e-mail friends or relatives a photo or a link to your photo or album.

● The E-mail dialog box appears.

9 Type the e-mail addresses of the people to whom you want to send a link to your photos.

10 Type a message to let recipients know about your album and that it is not spam.

11 Click Send.

TIPS

More Options!

You can personalize your gallery space with a photo of you as well as personal information. When you are in My Gallery, open your overall gallery section. You will find a place to add your personal photo, as well as information that appears when an album is permitted for public view, such as a personal tagline and gallery description.

Caution!

You might be tempted to return to previous pages within Photoshop. com by using the Back button on your Internet browser. Do not do it! That can take you off of Photoshop. com and you have to log in again. To move within Photoshop.com, only click links on your pages. You can navigate to library photos, galleries, albums, and more from right there.

Caution!

Be selective in the images you allow friends and relatives to access. They usually will not complain when confronted with a mass of photographs, but you can help them and your pictures by providing a selected group of photos. Link only to your best images in a special album in that will please your recipients as well as make them think you are a great photographer!

PRINT
your photos

With all the emphasis these days on seeing pictures on the Internet, on iPods and iPads, by e-mail, and other electronic media, one might think that the print is no longer important. That is definitely not the case. Inkjet printers are extremely popular, and paper and ink continue to be sold in large quantities.

And there is something more. The print has a real psychological aura to it. People love looking at prints, holding prints, sharing prints, putting them into frames and up on the wall, and so on. Prints are important. And photographers are making them bigger and bigger.

This book cannot make you a master printer, but the next four pages give you some ideas on how you can make better prints with your own inkjet printer. Photo-quality inkjet printers are available today at very reasonable prices all the way up to expensive pro-level printers. Be sure to pick a true photo-quality paper for your printing, too. The right paper can make a big difference in the final look of your prints. You can choose from a variety of surfaces from glossy to matte finish. Try them all to see which you like best.

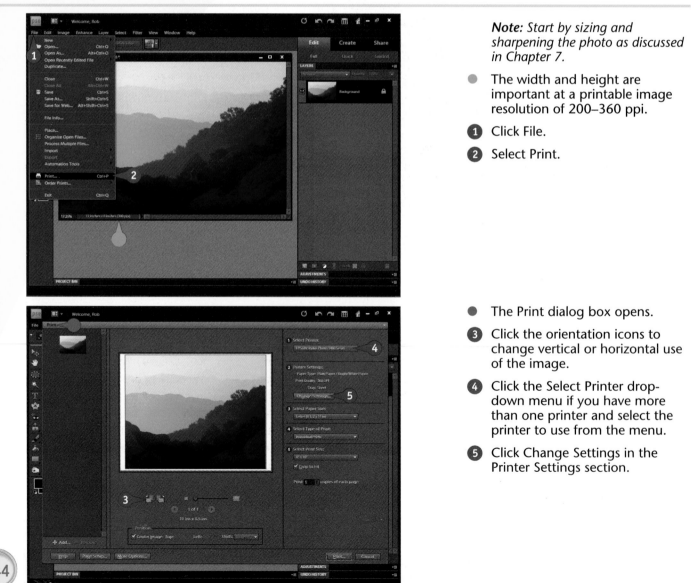

Note: Start by sizing and sharpening the photo as discussed in Chapter 7.

● The width and height are important at a printable image resolution of 200–360 ppi.

1 Click File.

2 Select Print.

● The Print dialog box opens.

3 Click the orientation icons to change vertical or horizontal use of the image.

4 Click the Select Printer drop-down menu if you have more than one printer and select the printer to use from the menu.

5 Click Change Settings in the Printer Settings section.

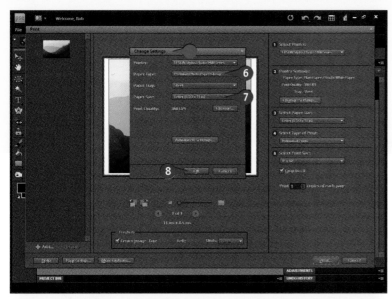

- The Change Settings dialog box appears.
- **6** Choose the correct paper type based on what you are using.
- **7** Choose the paper size that you are using.
- **8** Click OK.

- **9** Click the Select Print Size drop-down menu to set a size for the image on the paper.
- **10** Click More Options.
- The More Options dialog box opens.
- **11** Click Color Management.
- **12** Click the Color Handling drop-down menu to choose Printer Manages Colors or Photoshop Elements Manages Colors.

  Canon and Hewlett-Packard, as well as lower-priced Epson printers, often do well with Printer Manages Colors.

  Higher-end Epson printers usually do best with Photoshop Elements Manages Colors.
- **13** If you chose Printer Manages Colors in step 12, click Printer Preferences now.

TIPS

Important!
Calibrating your monitor is important. Monitor calibration is done using a special sensor that fits on your monitor screen and reads colors and tones from calibration software. A calibrated monitor gives you a predictable and consistent environment for working on images that will become prints.

Did You Know?
When the printer manages color, it takes the color information from Photoshop Elements and refines it based on the paper used and the color settings of the printer driver. When Photoshop Elements manages color, a very specific interpretation of color is sent to the printer based on paper profiles.

Did You Know?
Printer profiles are specific translations of color and tonality for printing based on testing specific papers with specific printers. They are also called *paper profiles*. A special image of colors is printed on paper, and then the colors are read and interpreted by colorimeters in order to define a profile.

PRINT
your photos

You often hear photographers say that their goal is to make a print that matches the monitor. Although it is important to have a calibrated monitor that gives predictable results when printing, your goal should be to make a good *print*. No one will care if it matches the monitor or not. Viewers care only about the print in front of them.

This is a different mindset than many digital photographers work with. It means that you have to take your print away from the monitor and really look at it as a print. Do you like the image that you see?

Does it have the appropriate brightness and balance of tonalities for the size of the print? Are there color casts that show up too strongly in a print but looked okay on the monitor? What you are looking for is a print that you can be proud to put up on the wall.

It can even help to take the print to the place where you plan to display it. Prints look different in different light. What surrounds the print also affects its look. A print that looks fine in one location may look too dark in another.

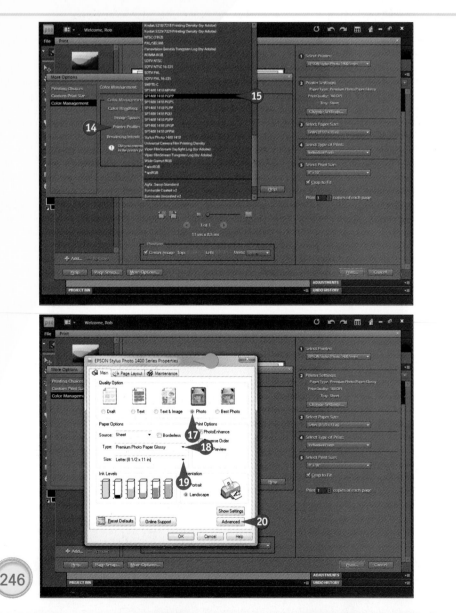

⑭ If you chose Photoshop Elements Manages Colors in step 12, click the Printer Profile drop-down menu.

A profile menu appears.

⑮ Select the profile that fits your printer and paper.

⑯ Click Printer Preferences, which is visible when the Printer Profile menu closes.

Important: Macs put the printer driver into the operating system, so you will not see Printer Preferences here. You set the same things when you get to the Print window that opens when you select Print on the Mac.

● The printer driver's properties dialog box appears.

Important: The driver interface varies depending on the printer model, but you must set the same things.

The properties dialog box sets most of the settings for you, but you want to confirm them and will need to work with an additional setting here.

⑰ Select the correct printing quality option (⊙ changes to ⊙).

⑱ Confirm the paper type.

⑲ Confirm the paper size.

⑳ Click Advanced.

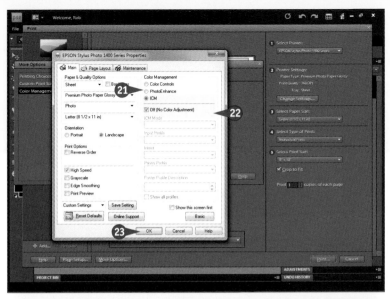

#101
CONTINUED

Important: The following settings appear in different places for various printer models and Macs or PCs, so you may have to look for them.

㉑ If you chose Printer Manages Colors in step 12, leave Color Controls selected in the Color Management section.

㉒ If you chose Photoshop Elements Manages Colors in step 12, select ICM and Off (No Color Adjustment), or Off (No Color Management) in some printer drivers, in the Color Management section.

㉓ Click OK.

㉔ Click OK to close the More Options dialog box.

㉕ Choose a number of prints to make.

㉖ Click Crop to Fit if you want the photo itself to fit a specific paper size (■ changes to ☑).

㉗ Click Print.

Important: On a Mac, you will now have to set the options noted in steps 17 to 22.

TIPS

Try This!
Photographers using traditional darkrooms almost always consider their first print a work print. They examine this print carefully to decide what else is needed to make the print better. Many photographers consider a work print a good idea for digital printing as well.

Did You Know?
Although you can use the Select Print Size drop-down menu to scale a picture fit a certain size of paper, use this sparingly. It works if you are making only a small change in size. For optimum quality, you need to size the picture with the specific resizing algorithms used inside Photoshop Elements itself.

Did You Know?
Printer resolution and image resolution are two different things. *Printer resolution* is set by the printer driver and affects how ink droplets are put on the paper. *Image resolution* is set by Photoshop Elements and is based on the pixels in the photograph. They deal with separate qualities for printing.

PRINT A GROUP
of photos

There are times when you want to print more than one photograph at once. Sometimes you simply want a number of pictures to represent a recent trip. Or you may want to print several photos on a single sheet of printing paper to make your printing more efficient. You print out a group all at once and cut out individual photos later. This can also make it easier to send a group of photos to someone.

This is very easy to do within the Organizer. In the Organizer, you see all your pictures from an album or a particular time and then choose the pictures that you want to print using the rating stars. It can be hard to select a variety of pictures throughout a large group of images. But you can click the individual pictures that you want to use and then give each one a rating, such as three stars. You then simply sort your images so those three-star pictures appear in the window. You can quickly process each one for optimum image quality and then select them all for printing.

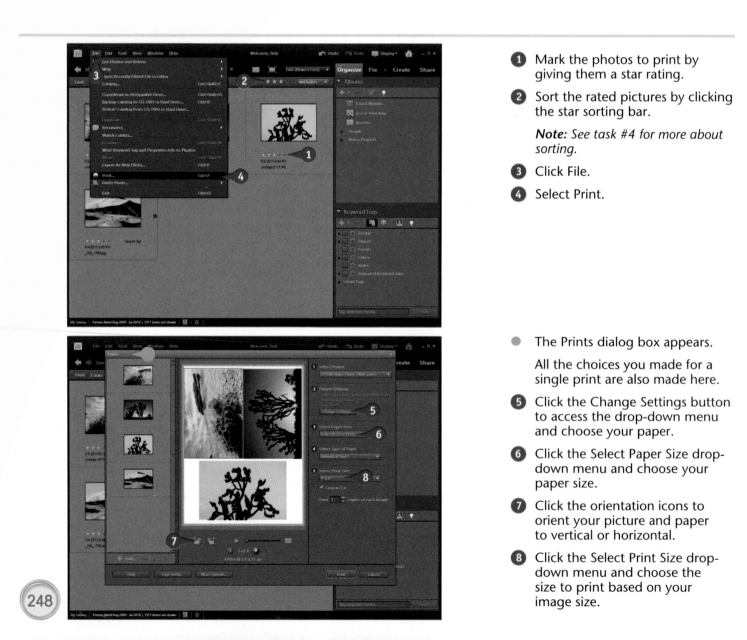

① Mark the photos to print by giving them a star rating.

② Sort the rated pictures by clicking the star sorting bar.

Note: See task #4 for more about sorting.

③ Click File.

④ Select Print.

● The Prints dialog box appears.

All the choices you made for a single print are also made here.

⑤ Click the Change Settings button to access the drop-down menu and choose your paper.

⑥ Click the Select Paper Size drop-down menu and choose your paper size.

⑦ Click the orientation icons to orient your picture and paper to vertical or horizontal.

⑧ Click the Select Print Size drop-down menu and choose the size to print based on your image size.

9 Click the Select Type of Print drop-down menu and choose Picture Package.

10 Click the Select a Layout drop-down menu and choose the layout that you want for your pictures.

● As soon as you select an option from Select a Layout, it appears in the center display.

  To have the printer manage colors, simply click Print.

11 Click More Options to print with Photoshop Elements managing colors.

● The More Options dialog box appears.

12 Click the Print Space drop-down menu and choose the paper profile for your paper and printer.

● Same as Source restores the default of having the printer manage colors.

13 Click OK for the More Options dialog box.

14 Click Print.

102

DIFFICULTY LEVEL

TIPS

Keyboard Trick!
Ctrl/⌘+P is the standard keyboard command for print. It enables you to print a picture whether you are in Editor or Organizer. Photoshop Elements for Windows recognizes if you are printing one or more images from Organizer and displays them accordingly in the Print screen.

Important!
Be careful about making big changes from the image you sized within Photoshop Elements to the size you are printing. Relatively small changes, such as the difference between 8×10 and 4×6, do not make much difference. But if you try to resize a large, high-megapixel camera image to 4×6 in this dialog box rather than in the Resize Image dialog box, you can lower image quality.

Did You Know?
When you print in Photoshop Elements, you have some additional options. For example, a popular choice is creating an iron-on transfer. To do a transfer, you need special paper and a flipped image. Instead of making you flip the original shot, a printing choice is available, called Flip Image in Iron-on Transfer, that does it for the print only. You can access this option in the More Options dialog box.

ADD A BORDER EFFECT
to your pictures

The edge of your photograph can be very important in a print. That is, after all, the place where the photograph connects with its surroundings. Borders can accentuate the photograph itself and keep the viewer's eye on the image.

You can apply some very interesting border effects to the edges of your picture in Photoshop Elements by using layers. What you do is limited only by your imagination. In this task, you will see how to apply a ragged-edged border very simply by having two layers. You can do similar effects using different colors and different brush types. By adding a layer,

you are essentially creating something that acts like a clear piece of plastic over your photograph. You can then paint or affect that plastic in any way without changing the original photograph.

Watch how edges interact with your photograph. One problem a lot of photographers run into is that they pick a color for a border that competes with the colors in the photograph. Another problem is that an edge color can be too similar to the colors in your photograph and pull visual energy from the image. Choose edges that complement the photograph.

① Click the New Layer icon at the bottom of the Layers panel.

● A blank layer appears over your image.

② Click the foreground color.

● The Color Picker appears.

③ Click the pure white at the top left of the color box.

④ Click OK.

⑤ Select the Paintbrush from the toolbox.

⑥ Right-click the photo for the Brushes panel.

⑦ Scroll down the brushes until you find an interesting shape that has some edges to it and click it to select it.

⑧ Click the two small arrows for a menu of other types of brushes.

⑨ Click the X to close the Brushes panel.

⑩ Choose a brush size big enough to create an interesting effect along the edge of your photograph.

⑪ Paint in a jagged way all around the edge of your photograph.

The photograph's border now has a torn-edge look.

TIPS

Try This!

If you do not like how your border is working, you can erase what you do not like with the Eraser tool and then paint over the problem. You can also add a layer mask to the layer. Then you can adjust what the border looks like by painting black into that layer mask to block the layer or white to allow that layer. See Chapter 5 for several tasks about layer masks.

More Options!

Because you are creating this effect on a layer separate from your photo, you can create some interesting effects by using the filters available from the Filter menu. There are all sorts of filters that do interesting things to a solid tone such as what you are painting around your photograph. You have to experiment.

Check It Out!

If you like interesting frame and edge effects, check out PhotoFrame from onOne Software (www.ononesoftware.com). This plug-in includes hundreds of frames that were developed by professional photographers but are now available for anyone to use. This plug-in works in Photoshop Elements.

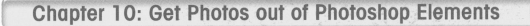

Index

A

Action Player, 45
Adams, Ansel
    darkroom work, 99
    edge darkening, 98
    enhancing photographs, 82
    toning images, 194
Add Noise dialog box, 165
Adjust Color Curves dialog box, 36, 50, 192
Adjust Color for Skin Tone control, 55
Adjust Color option, Enhance menu, 55
Adjust Layer Opacity button, Guided Edit panel, 45
Adjust Sharpness feature, 182–183
adjusting images
    applying adjustments to multiple photos, 78–79
    in black-and-white, 192–195
    bright highlights, 52–53
    color
        correcting to remove color casts, 54–55
        enhancing with Hue/Saturation, 56–57
    Color Curves feature, 50–51
    Crop tool
        straightening photos, 41
        tighter shots, 38–39
    dark shadows, 52–53
    Editor
        customizing interface, 32–33
        setting preferences, 34–35
    Guided Edit feature
        Crop Photo option, 42
        Enhance Colors option, 43
        special effects, 44–45
    Levels
        adjusting midtones, 48–49
        setting blacks and whites, 46–47
    opening pictures, 30–31
    Quick Edit, 58–59
    RAW photos
        adjusting midtones to modify tonalities, 68–69
        blacks and whites, 66–67
    resetting adjustments, 36
    reversing adjustments, 36
    Save As feature, 30–31
    Straighten tool, 40
    Undo History panel, 37
adjustment layers
    adding adjustments using black and white, 128–131
    Adjustment Layer icon, 107
    applying, 108–109
    balancing colors and tones, 134–135
    bringing out shadow detail, 136–137
    color
        correcting, 114–115
        enhancing, 116–117
    darkening highlight detail, 138–139
    fixing exposure problems with layer blending modes, 118–119
    flattening layers, 140–141
    layer masks
        combining two photos, 122–125
        combining with selections, 132–133
        overview, 120–121
    Levels adjustment layer
        blacks and whites, 110–111
        midtones, 112–113
    New Layer dialog box, 106
    overview, 104–105
Adjustments panel, 101
Adobe
    DNG file, 81
    white balance settings, 71
Adobe Partner Services, 237
AdobeRGB color space option, 35
advanced importing, 8–9
Advanced Options panel, 9
Album Details panel, 16
Album Settings window, 242
albums, 16–17, 241
Alien Skin Software
    Bokeh, 228–229
    Eye Candy, 233
    Snap Art 2, 232–233
Aligned option, Clone Stamp tool, 145
Allow Floating Documents in Full Edit Mode, Editor, 34
Also Delete Selected Item(s) option, Hard Disk check box, 13
altering reality, 157
Alt/Option button
    accessing tools, 199
    adjusting background, 169
    with black and white sliders, 46–47, 66–67, 111, 192
    Camera Raw, sharpening image, 75
    cloning out problems, 144
    with Layer mask icon, 137, 187
    removing selections, 93
Always Optimize for Printing option, Edit menu, 35
Amount slider
    Adjust Sharpness, 183
    Bokeh, 229
    Camera Raw, 74
    Quick Edit, 58
    Unsharp Mask, 180
Angle icon, Correct Camera Distortion window, 154
Aperture controls, Bokeh, 229
Apply Metadata section, Photo Downloader dialog box, 9
architectural photography
    perspective problems, 154
    selections and, 84
    sharpening photo, 181
artifacts, 146, 181
Auto Select Layer option, Move tool, 214–215
auto white balance, 54, 70
automated tools, 90–91
Automatic Download check box, Photo Downloader dialog box, 7
automatic exposure, 207
Automatic setting, Photomerge Exposure, 204

background
    adding for subject, 168–171
    out-of-focus, 158–159
backing up pictures, 26–27
Backup/Sync check box, Album Details panel, 16
balance, tone, 130
barrel distortion, 152
Basic Membership, Photoshop, 236
Bicubic Sharper option, Image Size dialog box, 175, 177
Bicubic Smoother option, Image Size dialog box, 175, 177
bit depth, 81
black and white
    adding adjustments, 128–131
    adjusting RAW photos, 66–67
    layer masks, 124–125
    Levels adjustment layer, 110–111
    removing adjustments, 126–127
    setting with Levels, 46–47
black blocking, 121
Blacks slider, Camera Raw, 66
blank skies, improving, 162–165
Blend slider, Color Efex Pro plug-in, 222
blending edges, 96–97
blending modes, 195
blocking effect, 127
Bokeh plug-in, 228–229
bracket keys, 125, 127
bright color, 160, 170
bright highlights, adjusting, 52–53
brightness, 66, 130
Brightness slider, 68, 99, 120, 193
Brightness/Contrast adjustment layer, 120, 133, 138
brushes
    adjusting, 125
    Content-Aware Spot Healing Brush, 149
    hard-edge, 97, 131, 150
    layer masks and, 131
    Selection Brush, 90
    Smart Brush, 100–101, 196–197
    soft-edge, 97, 131, 167
    Spot Healing Brush, 147, 150
burning in edges, 98

calibration, monitor, 245
Camera Raw software, 62. *See also* **RAW photos**
Change Settings button, Prints dialog box, 248
Change Settings dialog box, 245
Check All option, Photo Downloader dialog box, 8
checkerboard pattern, layer thumbnail, 167
circle selection, 87
clarity, 72–73
Clean Edges window, 210

Clear Crop option, Camera Raw, 65
Clone Stamp tool
    Aligned option, 145
    overview, 146
    using with Photomerge Scene Cleaner, 149
cloning
    versus Content-Aware spot healing, 151
    defined, 144
    general discussion, 144–147
cloning artifacts, 146
Cloudy white balance option, 114
Collage option, panoramic image, 210
color. *See also* **color casts**
    adding to blank sky, 164
    balancing with adjustment layers, 134–135
    boosting with Vibrance slider, 72
    effect of blacks, whites, and midtones, 69
    enhancing with adjustment layers, 116–117
    enhancing with Hue/Saturation, 56–57
    layer masks, 125
    removing distracting, 160–161
Color Auto button, 59
color casts
    correcting RAW photos to clean up, 70–71
    defined, 114
    removing, 54–55
Color Curves feature, 50–51
Color Efex Pro plug-in, 222–223
color noise, 76
color photo, converting to black-and-white, 190–191
Color Picker dialog box, 163, 170
Color Settings option, Edit menu, 35
Color slider, Camera Raw, 77
Colorize check box, Hue/Saturation dialog box, 85
comparing photos, 15
composition of photo, tightening up, 64
Confirm Deletion from Catalog dialog box, 13
Constrain Proportions box, Image Size dialog box, 175
Content box, albums, 16–17
Content-Aware Spot Healing Brush, 150–151
Contiguous check box, Magic Wand, 91, 94, 163
contracting selections, 92–93
Contrast control, Silver Efex Pro plug-in, 227
Contrast slider, Camera Raw, 68
control point, Nik Software, 220–221, 227
Convert to Black and White dialog box, 190
Correct Camera Distortion filter, 152
Correct Camera Distortion window, 153
Create Keyword Tag dialog box, Organizer, 19
Crop Photo option, Guided Edit feature, 42
Crop tool
    correcting distorted edges, 153, 155
    defined, 38–39
    versus Recompose tool, 156–157
    straightening photos, 41
cropping photos
    layers and, 113
    RAW files, 64–65
    for tighter shots, 38–39
Cut It Out program, onOne Software, 231
Cylindrical option, panoramic image, 210

Index

D

dark shadows, adjusting, 52–53
Darken Highlights slider, Shadows/Highlights dialog box, 53
dead space, removing, 156–157
depth-of-field effects, 228
deselecting selections, 85
destructive editing, 63
Detail slider, Camera Raw, 75
Detail tab, Camera Raw, 74
Dfine plug-in, Nik Software, 77, 224–225
digital camera, importing images from, 6–7
digital negative (DNG) file, 81
digital single lens reflex (dSLR) camera, 60, 152
Display button, Organizer, 15, 24
distracting colors, removing, 160–161
DNG (digital negative) file, 81
Done option, Camera Raw, 81
dSLR (digital single lens reflex) camera, 60, 152
Duplicate option, File menu, 195
dust spots, 147

E

edge darkening, 98–99
Edge Extension slider, 153
edges
    blending, 96–97
    blur and, 159
    distorted, 153, 155
    importance of, 131
    refining with layer mask, 171
    small areas of change and, 137
Edit icon, defined, 17
Edit Keyword Tag Icon dialog box, Organizer, 19
Editor
    customizing interface, 32–33
    moving pictures from Camera Raw, 80–81
    opening RAW files, 62
    setting preferences, 34–35
Effects panel, Editor interface, 32
Elements Organizer confirmation dialog box, 22
Elliptical Marquee tool, 86–87
e-mail
    sharing photos online, 243
    sizing photos for, 178–179
Enhance Colors option, Guided Edit feature, 43
Enlarge It program, onOne Software, 231
Eraser technique, 159
Eraser tool
    adjusting color in image, 201
    cloning and, 147
    modifying border effects, 251
    refining picture, 167
expanding selections, 92–93
exposure
    adjusting whites, 66
    bad, difficulty in correcting, 69

bright areas, 139
    fixing with layer blending modes, 118–119
Exposure (whites) slider, Camera Raw, 67
external hard drive, 26–27, 237
Eye Candy plug-in, Alien Skin, 233
Eye icon, Layers panel, 108
Eyedropper tool, 199

F

Face Recognition icon, Keyword Tags panel, 22
faces, 22–23, 181, 187
Feather Selection dialog box, 97, 166
feathering, 96–97, 133
Files Successfully Copied dialog box, Photo Downloader dialog box, 7
Fill Layer command, Edit menu, 129
Fill Layer dialog box, 129
fill layers, 107
Fill Light slider, Camera Raw, 66
Film Types section, Silver Efex Pro plug-in, 227
Filmstrip icon, 11
filters, 102, 251
Fix slider, Quick Edit, 58
flattening layers, 140–141
Flip Image in Iron-on Transfer option, Organizer, 249
focus
    creating with Gaussian blur, 166–167
    selective, 228
Folder Location view, Organizer, 24
Friends List, Photoshop, 239
full-screen mode, viewing photos, 10–11
Fun Edits, Guided Edit panel, 44

G

Gaussian Blur
    background, 171
    blurring edges, 137
    creating focus, 166–167
Gaussian Blur dialog box, 133, 159
glossy paper, 177
gradations, black-and-white image, 192
Gradient tool, 135, 165, 170–171
Graduated Neutral Density Filter, Color Efex Pro plug-in, 222
grayscale, 193
grouping images, 212–215
Guided Edit feature
    Crop Photo option, 42
    Enhance Colors option, 43
    special effects, 44–45

H

Hand tool
    adding new background, 169
    improving blank skies, 165
    Quick Edit, 59

hand-colored look, 198–201
Hard Disk check box, Confirm Deletion from Catalog dialog box, 13
hard drive, external, 26–27, 237
hard-edge brush
    feathering, 97
    layer masks, 131
    Spot Healing Brush, 150
Hide Task Pane, Organizer, 25
high dynamic range (HDR) photography, 203, 205
Highlight controls, Bokeh, 229
highlights
    adjusting with Recovery slider, 67
    bright, 52–53
    darkening detail, 138–139
histogram, 49, 111
History States button, Undo History panel, 35
Horizontal Perspective slider, Correct Camera
  Distortion window, 155
Hue slider
    Guided Edit panel, 43
    Hue/Saturation dialog box, 57
    Silver Efex Pro plug-in, 227
Hue/Saturation adjustment panel, 107, 109, 117
Hue/Saturation feature, 56–57

image resolution, 177, 247
Image Size dialog box, 174
Imagenomic Noiseware program, 77
imbalance problems, 134
importing images
    advanced importing, 8–9
    from digital camera or memory card, 6–7
inkjet printer, 176, 244
Interactive Layout option, panoramic image, 210
inverting selections, 94–95
iPad, 238
iron-on transfer, 249
ISO settings, 76, 224

JPEG file
    backup, 237
    defined, 63
    Editor, 30–31
    flattening layers, 140
    oversharpening, 187
    versus RAW, 60
    sharpening, 180
JPEG Options dialog box, 179

keywords, tagging images, 18–21

landscapes, 181, 187
Lasso tools
    adding and subtracting from selection, 93
    following picture elements, 88–89
layer blending modes, 118–119
layer mask
    changing between white and black, 161
    combining two photos, 122–125
    combining with selections, 132–133
    overview, 120–121
    refining edges, 171
layers. *See also* adjustment layers
    combining with effects into single layer, 141
    duplicating, 129
    sharpening photos, 184–185
Layers panel
    Adjustment Layer icon, 107
    Eye icon, 108
    moving layers, 105
    New Layer icon, 144, 162, 250
    Smart Brush and, 100–101
    Trash Can icon, 111
lens distortion, 152–153
lens flare, 146
Lensbaby system, 229
Levels
    adjusting midtones, 48–49
    setting blacks and whites, 46–47
Levels adjustment layer
    blacks and whites, 110–111
    midtones, 112–113
Levels dialog box
    black-and-white images, 192
    selections and, 97
Lighten Shadows slider, Shadows/Highlights dialog box, 52
local control features
    automated tools, 90–91
    blending edges by feathering, 96–97
    Lasso tools, 88–89
    Marquee tools, 86–87
        Elliptical Marquee tool, 87
        Rectangular Marquee tool, 86
    selections
        creating, 84–85
        expanding or contracting, 92–93
        inverting, 94–95
        using for traditional edge darkening, 98–99
    Smart Brush, 100–101
Loupe window, Dfine plug-in, 225
Lower Tonality slider, Color Efex Pro plug-in, 222
luminance noise, 76
Luminance slider, Camera Raw, 76

Mac Command key, 5, 37
Mac Photoshop Elements menu, 7

Index

Magic Wand tool
  Contiguous check box, 163
  improving blank skies, 162
  overview, 90
  selecting skies, 94
Magnetic Lasso tool, 88–89
magnification, Camera Raw, 63
Magnifier tool, 59
Make It Better program, onOne Photo Essentials, 231
manual exposure, 207
Manual setting, Photomerge Exposure, 204
Marquee tools, 86–87
  Elliptical Marquee tool, 87
  Rectangular Marquee tool, 86
Masking slider, Camera Raw, 75
Master drop-down menu, Hue/Saturation
  adjustment panel, 56–57, 117
matte finish paper, 177
megapixels, 75
memory card, importing images, 6–7
Merge and Make New Layer command, 185
merged-flattened layer, 159
merging photos
  for more detail, 204–205
  for panoramic image, 208–211
Method drop-down menu, Dfine plug-in, 225
Midtone Contrast slider, Shadows/Highlights dialog box, 53
midtones
  adjusting
      in black-and-white photos, 192
      with Color Curves feature, 50–51
      with levels, 48–49
      tonalities light or dark, 68–69
  Clarity slider, 72
  levels adjustment layer, 112–113
Midtones slider, Levels dialog box, 49, 50
monitor
  calibration, 245
  ppi, 179
monochrome, 109, 193
More Options dialog box, Organizer, 249
More/Less slider, PhotoTune plug-in, 230
motion blur effect, Bokeh, 229
Motion Blur tool, 183
Move tool, Auto Select Layer option, 214–215
moving layers, 105
moving pictures to Photoshop Elements, 80–81
Multiply exposure blending mode
  increasing effects, 129
  Opacity and, 118–119
muted color, background, 170
My Friends button, Photoshop.com, 239
My Gallery button, Photoshop.com, 239
My Library button, Photoshop.com, 239

naming layers, 107
netbooks, 238
neutral color, 71

New Album panel, Organizer, 236
New Layer dialog box, 106
New Layer icon, Layers panel, 144, 162, 250
New Smart Album dialog box, 17
Nik Software
  Color Efex Pro, 222–223
  Dfine, 77, 224–225
  Viveza 2, 220–221
noise
  Adjust Sharpness feature and, 182
  controlling in RAW photos, 76–77
  out-of-focus areas, 186
  Screen exposure mode and, 119
Noise Reduction controls, Camera Raw, 76
Noiseware program, Imagenomic, 77
nondestructive processing, 62–63

On First Save drop-down menu, Editor, 34
one-color photos, 109
onOne Software
  Photo Essentials, 231
  PhotoFrame plug-in, 251
  PhotoTune plug-in, 230
opacity
  defined, 115
  Eraser tool and, 167
  exposure blending modes and, 119
Open dialog box, Editor, 31
opening pictures, 30–31
Organizer
  Create Keyword Tag dialog box, 19
  Display button, 15, 24
  Edit Keyword Tag Icon dialog box, 19
  Folder Location view, 24
  Full-Screen icon, 10
  Hide Task Pane, 25
  interface, 24–25
  managing photos, 6
  More Options dialog box, 249
  New Album panel, 236
  opening RAW file, 62
  printing group of photos, 248
organizing photos for processing
  backing up pictures
      backup software, 27
      external hard drive, 26–27
  creating albums to group pictures, 16–17
  full-screen mode, 10–11
  importing images
      advanced importing, 8–9
      from digital camera or memory card, 6–7
  Organizer interface, 24–25
  sorting, 12–13
  stacking, 14–15
  tagging
      with face recognition, 22–23
      with keywords, 18–21
  workflow, 4–5

out-of-focus background, 158–159
overlapping images, 214
oversharpening, 185

panoramic image
    merging photos for, 208–211
    overview, 188
    photographing scene for, 206–207
paper profile, 245
parametric sliders, Color Curves, 50
Pencil tool, Photomerge Scene Cleaner, 149
People mode, PhotoTune plug-in, 231
People Recognition window, 23
personalizing photo gallery, 243
perspective control lenses, 155
Perspective option, panoramic image, 210
perspective problems, architecture, 154–155
Photo Downloader dialog box, 6–9
PhotoFrame plug-in, 251
Photographic Effects, Guided Edit panel, 44
photographing scenes
    for more exposure detail, 202–203
    for panoramic image, 206–207
Photomerge dialog box, 208
Photomerge Exposure feature, 204
Photomerge feature, 149
Photomerge Panorama feature, 209
Photomerge Scene Cleaner, 148–149
Photomerge Style Match feature, 216
Photoshop Document (PSD) file, 31, 109, 140, 172
photo-sizing controls, 174
Phototune plug-in, 230–231
pixels
    destructive editing, 63
    nondestructive processing, 62
    plug-ins and, 221
    working directly with, 102
pixels per inch (ppi), 177
playback toolbar, Organizer, 10
plug-ins. *See* **software plug-ins**
Plus Membership, Photoshop, 236
Polygonal Lasso tool, 88–89
portraits
    adjusting multiple photos, 78
    increased clarity and, 73
    sharpening, 181
ppi (pixels per inch), 177
Preferences dialog box, Editor, 34–35
presence, photograph, 72
preset effects, Silver Efex Pro, 226
Preview check box
    Camera Raw, 69
    Levels dialog box, 49
Preview window, Unsharp Mask dialog box, 181
Print Space drop-down menu, Organizer, 249
printer, inkjet, 176, 244
printer profile, 245
printer resolution, 177, 247

printing, sizing photos for, 176–177
Prints dialog box, Organizer, 248
Pro section, PhotoTune plug-in, 231
processing, organizing photos for
    backing up pictures
        backup software, 27
        external hard drive, 26–27
    creating albums to group pictures, 16–17
    importing images
        advanced importing, 8–9
        from digital camera or memory card, 6–7
    setting up workflow, 4–5
    sorting pictures, 12–13
    stacking images, 14–15
    tagging photos with face recognition, 22–23
    using keywords to tag images, 18–21
    viewing photos with full-screen mode, 10–11
Project Bin tab, Editor, 33
PSD (Photoshop Document) file, 31, 109, 140, 172

Quality slider, JPEG Options dialog box, 179
Quick Edit, 58–59
Quick Selection tool, 90

Radius slider
    Adjust Sharpness, 183
    Camera Raw, 75
    Gaussian Blur dialog box, 159
    Unsharp Mask, 181
RAW photos
    adjusting
        blacks and whites, 66–67
        midtones to make tonalities light or dark, 68–69
    applying adjustments to multiple photos, 78–79
    controlling noise, 76–77
    correcting color to clean up color casts, 70–71
    cropping photos to start processing, 64–65
    defined, 30
    moving picture to Photoshop Elements, 80–81
    nondestructive processing, 62–63
    sharpening, 74–75, 180
    using Clarity to intensify images, 72–73
    using Vibrance to intensify images, 72–73
Recompose tool, 156–157
Recovery slider, Camera Raw, 67
recropping, 65
Rectangular Marquee tool, 84, 86
Refine Edge dialog box
    adding new background, 169
    improving blank skies, 162
Refine Mask dialog box, 197
Remove Color Cast dialog box, 54–55
Remove Color option, Enhance menu, 193, 199

Index

Remove Distortion slider, Correct Camera Distortion window, 155
Remove drop-down menu, Adjust Sharpness, 183
removing
    color casts, 54–55
    dead space, 156–157
    distracting colors, 160–161
    people from scene, 148–149
    unwanted objects, 150–151
Reposition option, panoramic image, 210
Resample Image option, Image Size dialog box, 175, 177
Reset button, Guided Edit, 43
Reset Tool function, Gradient tool, 165
resetting
    adjustments, 36
    Camera Raw sliders, 73
resolution
    image sizing and, 176
    image versus printer, 177, 247
Resolution boxes, 38
reversing adjustments, 36
rotating images, 41
Rotation slider, Color Efex Pro plug-in, 223

Saturation slider
    brightening colors, 73
    Guided Edit panel, 43
    Hue/Saturation dialog box, 57
Saturation tool, 72
Save As feature, 30–31
Save Panel Locations option, Editor, 34
saving flattened layers, 141
scratch space, 35
Screen blending mode, 129
Screen exposure mode, 118–119
Select a Layout drop-down menu, Prints dialog box, 249
Select Paper Size drop-down menu, Prints dialog box, 248
Select Print Size drop-down menu, Prints dialog box, 247, 248
Select Type of Print drop-down menu, Prints dialog box, 249
Selection Brush, 90
selections
    circle, 87
    creating, 84–85
    expanding or contracting, 92–93
    inverting, 94–95
    square, 87
    using automated tools, 90–91
    using for traditional edge darkening, 98–99
selective focus, 228
sepia tone, 194
shadows, adjusting, 52–53, 136–137
Shadows/Highlights control, 52–53, 205
Sharpen slider, 59
sharpening photos
    Adjust Sharpness, 182–183
    with layers, 184–185
    RAW photos, 74–75, 180
    selectively, 186–187
    Unsharp Mask, 180–181

sharpness, 73
Shift key, moving photos with, 123
Show Bounding Box option, Move tool, 215
Show Crosshair in Brush Tip, Preferences dialog box, 35
Show Task Pane, Organizer, 25
Silver Efex Pro plug-in, 226–227
sizing photos
    for e-mail, 178–179
    for printing, 176–177
    workflow, 174–175
skies
    balance problems, 134
    blank, 162–165
skin texture, 73
SkinTune section, PhotoTune plug-in, 231
slide show, 241
Smart Brush, 100–101, 196–197
Smart Fix, Quick Edit, 58
Snap Art plug-in, 232–233
soft-edge brush, 97, 131, 167
software plug-ins
    Bokeh, 228–229
    Color Efex Pro, 222–223
    Dfine, 77, 224–225
    Eye Candy, 233
    PhotoFrame, 251
    PhotoTune, 230–231
    Silver Efex Pro, 226–227
    Snap Art, 232–233
    Viveza, 220–221
solid color layer, 104
solving photo problems
    adding new background for subject, 168–171
    cloning, 144–147
    Content-Aware Spot Healing, 150–151
    Gaussian blur, 166–167
    improving blank skies, 162–165
    lens distortion, 152–153
    out-of-focus background, 158–159
    perspective in building images, 154–155
    Photomerge Scene Cleaner, 148–149
    Recompose tool, 156–157
    removing distracting colors, 160–161
sorting pictures, 12–13
special effects, Guided Edit feature, 44–45
Spherical option, panoramic image, 210
Spot Healing Brush, 147, 150
square selection, 87
sRGB color space, JPEG files, 35
stacking images, 14–15
Straighten tool, 40
straightening photos, 40–41
Strength slider, Silver Efex Pro plug-in, 227
Structure control
    Silver Efex Pro plug-in, 227
    Viveza 2, 220
Style Bin, Photomerge Style Match panel, 216
Style Clarity slider, Photomerge Style Match panel, 217
Style Eraser tool, 217
Style Intensity slider, Photomerge Style Match panel, 217
Style Painter tool, 217
styles, transferring, 216–217

T

tagging photos
    with face recognition, 22–23
    with keywords, 18–21
Temperature slider, Camera Raw, 71
textures, background, 170
threshold screens
    defined, 111
    Unsharp Mask, 181
Thumbnail Size icons, Organizer, 24
TIFF file, 30–31, 140
TIFF Options dialog box, Editor, 31
tilting camera, 155
Tint slider, Camera Raw, 71
Tolerance setting, Magic Wand, 91
tonemapping, 205
tones
    balancing, 130
    balancing with adjustment layers, 134–135
    black-and-white image, 194–195
    midtones and, 68–69
transparency, 115
Trash Can icon, Layers panel, 111
tripod
    leveling, 207
    taking multiple exposures, 203

U

UnCheck All option, Photo Downloader dialog box, 8
underexposure, 77
Undo History panel
    correcting sky placement, 165
    Editor interface, 33–34
    flattened files, 141
    setting, 37
Unsharp Mask, 180–181
Upper Tonality slider, Color Efex Pro plug-in, 222
Use drop-down menu, Photomerge Panorama feature, 209

V

vertical panoramas, 207
Vertical Perspective slider, Correct Camera Distortion window, 154
Vertical Shift slider, Color Efex Pro plug-in, 223
vibrance, 72–73
View menu
    Organizer, 24
    positioning of photos on page, 215
viewing photos, full-screen mode, 10–11
views, Nik Software, 225
Vignette controls, Correct Camera Distortion window, 153
vignette effect, Bokeh, 229
Viveza plug-in, 220–221

W

warning icon, Camera Raw, 79
Web computers, 238
white balance control, 54
whites. *See* black and white
wideangle lens, 155
Windows Alt key, 5, 37
Windows Control key, 5, 37
work print, 247
workflow, 4–5

X

XMP file, 80–81

Z

Zoom tool
    adding new background, 169
    cloning out problems, 144
    feathering edges, 96
    improving blank skies, 165
    making selections, 92

Read Less–Learn More®

There's a Visual book
for every learning level...

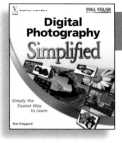

Simplified®

The place to start if you're new to computers. Full color.

- Computers
- Creating Web Pages
- Digital Photography
- Internet
- Mac OS
- Office
- Windows

Teach Yourself VISUALLY™

Get beginning to intermediate-level training in a variety of topics. Full color.

- Access
- Bridge
- Chess
- Computers
- Crocheting
- Digital Photography
- Dog training
- Dreamweaver
- Excel
- Flash
- Golf
- Guitar
- Handspinning
- HTML
- iLife
- iPhoto
- Jewelry Making & Beading
- Knitting
- Mac OS
- Office
- Photoshop
- Photoshop Elements
- Piano
- Poker
- PowerPoint
- Quilting
- Scrapbooking
- Sewing
- Windows
- Wireless Networking
- Word

Top 100 Simplified® Tips & Tricks

Tips and techniques to take your skills beyond the basics. Full color.

- Digital Photography
- eBay
- Excel
- Google
- Internet
- Mac OS
- Office
- Photoshop
- Photoshop Elements
- PowerPoint
- Windows

...all designed for visual learners—just like you!

Feb 14

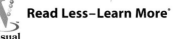

Read Less–Learn More®

Want more simplified tips and tricks?

Take a look at these

All designed for visual learners—just like you!

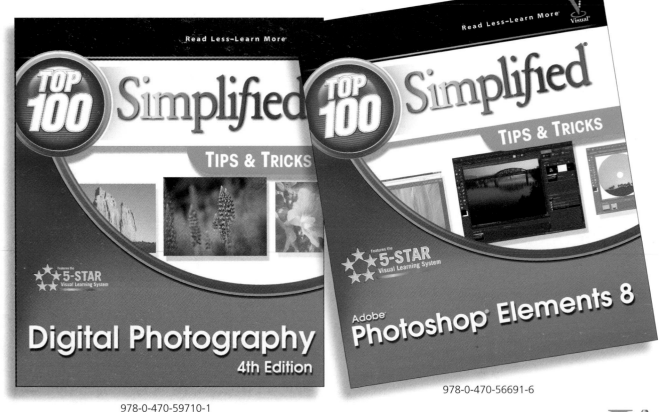

978-0-470-59710-1

978-0-470-56691-6

**For a complete listing of Top 100 Simplified® Tips & Tricks titles
and other Visual books, go to wiley.com/go/visual**

Wiley, the Wiley logo, the Visual logo, Read Less-Learn More, and Simplified are trademarks or registered trademarks of John Wiley & Sons, Inc. and/or its affiliates.
All other trademarks are the property of their respective owners.

Visual
An Imprint of ⊕**WILEY**
Now you know.